Motor vehicles are prominent among the flows of exports and imports for Canada, Germany, Japan, and the United States, and these trade flows are heavily influenced by the basic relative competitiveness of the production processes for automotive manufacturing. In this book the authors analyze in depth the factors that contributed to the comparative cost competitiveness of the four countries' auto industries over the period 1961–84, and disentangle the factors contributing to the Japanese cost and efficiency advantages. Their main contribution is to provide estimates of comparative costs of automobile production (both short-run and long-run) and the sources of these cost differences, based on the econometric cost-function methodology. An innovation is the careful treatment of capacity utilization, one of the most important sources of short-run cost and efficiency differences. This methodology is also used effectively in an analysis of the Canada–U.S. Auto Pact, a unique experiment in trade liberalization.

Costs and productivity
in automobile production

Costs and productivity
in automobile production

The challenge of Japanese efficiency

MELVYN A. FUSS
and
LEONARD WAVERMAN
University of Toronto

![Cambridge crest] **CAMBRIDGE**
UNIVERSITY PRESS

Published by the Press Syndicate of the University of Cambridge
The Pitt Building, Trumpington Street, Cambridge CB2 1RP
40 West 20th Street, New York, NY 10011–4211, USA
10 Stamford Road, Oakleigh, Victoria 3166, Australia

First published 1992

Printed in Canada

Library of Congress Cataloging-in-Publication Data
Fuss, Melvyn A.

Costs and productivity in automobile production : the challenge of
Japanese efficiency / by Melvyn A. Fuss and Leonard Waverman.

   p.   cm.

ISBN 0–521–34141–8

1. Automobile industry and trade – Canada. 2. Automobile industry
and trade – United States. 3. Automobile industry and trade – Japan.
4. Automobile industry and trade – Germany. 5. Automobile industry
and trade – Costs – Case studies. 6. Automobile industry and trade –
Labor productivity – Case studies. I. Waverman, Leonard.
II. Title.
HD9710.C22F87   1992
338.4′76292–dc20
                                           91–18785
                                                CIP

A catalog record for this book is available from the British Library.

ISBN 0–521–34141–8 hardback

To Susan and Hélène,
for their patience and understanding
despite much provocation

Contents

Preface

In recent years there has been heightened interest in the trading relationships among nations as trade liberalization interacts with the forming of trade blocks to create new realities. The strengthened integration of the European Economic Community in 1992, the Canada–U.S. Free Trade Agreement, and the proposed trilateral free trade agreement between Canada, the United States, and Mexico are examples of the changing world order.

Motor vehicles are prominent among the flow of exports and imports for many countries. In this book we compare the motor vehicle production sectors of four countries heavily involved in international trade: Canada, Germany, Japan, and the United States. The trade in automobile products among these nations as well as their exports to other countries are very much influenced by the basic relative competitiveness of their production processes for automobile manufacturing. We analyze in depth the factors that contributed to the comparative cost competitiveness of the four countries' auto industries over the period 1961–84.

We begin by evaluating previous estimates of intercountry cost and efficiency differences that use methodologies of plant inspection and comparison of company financial reports. We then proceed to our main contribution, which is to provide estimates of comparative costs of automobile production (both short-run and long-run), and the sources of these cost differences, based on the econometric cost-function methodology. We believe this methodology is superior to the methods used previously because it allows us to disentangle the factors contributing to cost and efficiency differences in a coherent and objective manner. In this volume there are two broad examples of applying the cost-function methodology: (1) exploration of the sources of the Japanese productivity "miracle" in automobile manufacturing (Chapters 6 and 7), and (2) analysis of the Canada–U.S. Auto Pact, a unique experiment in trade liberalization (Chapter 8). This methodology also facilitates the careful treatment of capacity utilization, one of the most important sources of short-run cost and efficiency differences.

The initial impetus for this volume came from a research project that we undertook for the Ontario Economic Council, a research arm of the Canadian provincial government. This project, completed in 1984, was the last one completed under the auspices of the Council before it was disbanded. The sponsorship of this project by the Ontario government explains to some extent the inclusion of Canada among the countries considered, as well as the space devoted to the Auto Pact. The motor vehicles sector is a major employer of the Ontario labor force and provides the bulk of Ontario's exports, primarily to the United States.

In subsequent research, the final year of the period considered was extended from 1980 to 1984 and the analysis was extensively revised and expanded. Although we are now somewhat beyond the mid-1980s, the lessons to be learned about international competition in automobile production from an in-depth study of the 1961–84 period are still relevant. In the final chapter of this volume, we provide some updating of our analysis to the beginning of the 1990s as a demonstration of that fact.

This study would not have been possible without the assistance and advice of Richard Knabl, Jeremy Rudin, and especially Stephen Murphy. We have also benefited from the typing skills of Claire Brenner, Carole Broadley, Sophia Knapik, and Brenda Rak. We are extremely grateful to the Donner Canadian Foundation, The National Science Foundation, the Ontario Economic Council, and the Social Sciences and Humanities Research Council of Canada for funding assistance during the course of bringing this volume to fruition.

CHAPTER 1

Introduction

One of the most important factors determining the health of any national economy is the level and pattern of international trade. For Canada, Germany, Japan, and the United States, motor vehicles are prominent among the flows of exports and imports. The trade flows in vehicles among these countries are heavily influenced by the relative competitiveness of the production processes for automotive manufacturing. International cost-of-production differentials are determined by differences in factor prices and, in the long run, by productivity differences. These differences can reflect true comparative advantage or can, to some extent, be contrived by government fiscal policies ("industrial policy" such as taxes and subsidies) and other policies affecting the exchange rate. The private sector may also distort measured comparative advantage through transfer pricing and other decisions internal to multinational firms.

Trade policy is often formulated in response to employment and price pressures caused by international cost differences; tariff barriers and quotas are obvious examples. The United States, Canada, and most European countries have placed import quotas on Japanese automobiles in response to the apparent cost disadvantage of domestic producers. The Canada–U.S. Auto Pact, which is a form of industrial policy, was designed to encourage North American producers to eliminate the Canadian productivity disadvantage through the rationalization of production facilities.

Trade and industrial policies can be thoughtfully analyzed only if knowledge is available about existing levels and sources of cost and productivity differentials. It is important to measure these differentials and to ascertain if they are due to variations among nations in factor prices (including exchange rates) or in technological conditions such as economies of scale, capacity utilization, or the rate of technical progress. The policies one would pursue depend on the relative importance of sources of the cost differential. In this study we attempt to shed some light on these issues by analyzing in detail the extent and sources of cost and productivity

1

differentials in motor vehicle production among producers in Canada, Germany, Japan, and the United States.

In 1980 and 1981, the four major American auto producers – General Motors (GM), Ford, Chrysler, and American Motors (Chrysler purchased American Motors in 1987) – lost vast sums of money as their sales in North American markets plummeted. Imports of foreign autos surged, reaching 27.9% of U.S. domestic sales (and 28.5% of Canadian domestic sales) in 1981. The U.S. government negotiated Voluntary Restraint Agreements (VRAs) with Japanese auto producers so as to allow these American firms time to reduce their cost and productivity disadvantages. The exact source of the American firms' disadvantages were unknown: Were they due to external events like the recession or the overvalued U.S. exchange rate, or to internal problems such as minimal productivity or lack of technical advances?

Most European countries place significant restrictions on the importation of Japanese automobiles. For example, quotas restrict Japanese automobiles to 3% of the French market; only 3,000 Japanese cars may be imported into Italy each year; and Japanese automobiles are restricted to 11% of the domestic U.K. car market (Cline 1983, p. 124).

The "productivity dilemma" in automobile production is not new to Canadians. Significant perceived productivity differentials between Canadian and U.S. automobile production in the 1950s resulted in the establishment in 1960 of the Bladen Royal Commission on the Auto Industry. That commission's 1961 report concluded that Canada suffered from "low scale" as well as a low number of cars produced per model, due to the small size of the domestic market. This small market size, combined with tariff protection, induced import competition as well as suboptimal entry into Canadian automobile production. The Bladen Plan was designed to encourage the rationalization of the Canadian automotive sector through duty remissions earned by exporting auto parts from Canada. In 1965 the Auto Pact was signed between Canada and the United States, eliminating duties and tariffs on finished vehicles and original equipment shipped by producers between the two countries if certain domestic-content provisions were met. The three major North American manufacturers (GM, Ford, Chrysler) have operated under the conditions of the Auto Pact since its inception.

Since the early 1980s, several Japanese auto producers have negotiated duty-remission schemes with the Canadian government in exchange for Canadian-content guarantees. These Canadian assembled cars might qualify for duty-free entry into the United States under the terms of the

Auto Pact. The recently signed Canada–U.S. Free Trade Agreement (FTA) grandfathers the existing Auto Pact while increasing protection against non–Auto Pact (i.e., Asian) producers. The Canadian auto industry under this protection has developed as an integrated part of North American production: few exports go to countries outside the United States, and the auto industry is now dominated by U.S. multinationals. In 1986, 100,000 autos were exported from the North American production facilities of U.S. multinationals; this number was 1% of North American capacity.

In the United States, the Federal Trade Commission (FTC) in 1984 approved a joint venture between GM and Toyota to produce a new subcompact automobile in California. This FTC decision explicitly argued that the joint venture would induce large U.S. productivity gains, and implicitly suggested that the Japanese cost advantage was the result not of lower Japanese factor prices but of superior Japanese productivity. Moreover, the FTC stated that Japan's productivity advantage was transferable to North America; that is, it was embodied in managers or technology and not simply in harder-working Japanese labor. Many observers felt that this joint venture would significantly affect the future structure of the world automobile industry by causing other large firms to plan competing joint ventures.[1]

The German auto industry in its infancy also relied on restrictions, such as tariffs and quotas, to prevent open access to foreign producers. After formation of the European Economic Community (EEC), Germany relied on the common EEC 10% tariff but not on other quantitative restrictions. By the mid-1960s, imports represented 20% of German domestic auto sales, a figure that would have goaded many other countries into implementing import controls. Germany, however, relied on its auto export performance to overwhelm auto imports. In 1986, 58.8% of German motor vehicle production was exported, while imports represented 46.3% of domestic German sales. In contrast to North America, Germany has developed a highly successful set of domestic auto producers who export around the globe, yet there has been scant analysis of the part played by high productivity in this successful export performance.

Like the German auto producers, Japanese auto producers have been driven by exports, which constituted 14.5% of domestic output in 1965, 57% in 1981, and 58.6% in 1986. Although Japanese tariffs on auto imports

---

[1] The FTC did examine the anticompetitive effects of the GM–Toyota joint venture, but concluded that certain safeguards added to the joint venture agreement would mitigate these effects.

are low (6.4%), imports have never been an important part of the Japanese market, totaling less than 1% of domestic sales in 1986. Intense domestic competition, an extraordinarily expensive domestic distribution system, a unique language, and – according to some observers – nontariff barriers have combined to make the Japanese market the most closed by far of the four countries under study. The Japanese auto industry is also the most successful in the world. It is instructive to remember that, in 1970, Japanese auto producers exported only 300,000 cars to North America and 48,000 to the EEC.

Analyses and policies in the automobile sector – trade restrictions, joint ventures, and government interventions generally (e.g., the U.S. government's 1981 bail-out of Chrysler) – have been pursued even though there is a lack of fundamental data on the real size and root causes of cost and productivity differentials among nations. Are the restrictions imposed against Japanese auto imports merely short-run policies designed to alleviate temporary aberrations between the demand for and supply of domestic automobiles? Or are the restrictions actually designed to prevent the Japanese from pursuing their competitive advantage in auto production? What are the sources of the Japanese advantage, and how has a nation that had no obvious advantage in 1970 grown to dominate automobile markets? Are the Canadian domestic-content rules and the Canada–U.S. Auto Pact also "temporary" tools (they have been in place for twenty-four years), or rather are they long-run solutions to managing the problems of a small industrial country?

Various noneconometric estimates have been made of the size of productivity differences between Japanese and North American automobile manufacturers. One of the latest (and probably the most quoted) studies, by Abernathy, Clark, and Kantrow (1983), suggests a production cost advantage for the Japanese of some $2,000 per vehicle – 30% of U.S. producers' costs. In addition, Abernathy et al. indicate that the Japanese automobile industry could produce an automobile with 40% lower total labor costs, 30% lower materials costs, and 25% lower capital costs than their American counterparts.[2] If these numbers are correct, protection against Japanese imports must be permanent unless there is a large realignment of exchange rates. But are the numbers correct, and if so are they static or changing? And if the numbers are correct, what are the sources of this enormous advantage?

---

[2] See Abernathy et al. (1983, Tables 5.1 and 5.4, pp. 61 and 63). These results are at odds with earlier work by Abernathy (1978), where Japanese firms are shown to have disadvantages in areas other than labor costs.

These are fundamental questions and fundamental problems, but rigorous analysis is needed to provide the crucial data: To what factors can we attribute the Japanese success in producing cars? This is the subject of our book; we use state-of-the-art statistical tools in attempting to disentangle the factors accounting for the Japanese cost advantage in automobile production.

1.1 Cost versus productivity advantage

One must carefully distinguish between the terms *cost advantage* and *productivity advantage*; these are not the same, although they are often represented as such in the public press. Producers in country A (or firm A in a country) may have lower total costs of production than producers in another country B (or another firm B in the same country). This cost differential need *not*, however, imply that producers in A are more efficient or make more productive use of inputs than producers in B. This issue is likely obvious to the reader, but an explanatory digression will assist in later discussions.

In Figure 1.1, two firms located in two different countries (or regions of one country) are shown. Both produce 100 cars annually using two factors of production (or "inputs"): labor and capital services. In country A, labor costs P_L are $1,000 per unit (man year) and capital services P_K cost $2,500 per unit, so the relative price of capital to labor is 5:2. One hundred cars are produced in country A using 10 units of labor (10 man years) and 10 units of capital for a total cost of $35,000, or an average (unit) production cost of $350 per car. In country B, capital is relatively cheaper and labor relatively more expensive than in A ($P_K/P_L = 4/2 < 5/2$), and both inputs are absolutely more expensive than in A (labor costs $1,500 per man year and capital $3,000 per unit).[3] The 100 cars produced in B cost $48,000 to produce (or $480 each) and use 8 units of labor and 12 units of capital. Producers in A then have a *cost advantage* over producers in B.

For each country, the factor-price line – the ratio of relative factor (input) prices – is drawn in Figure 1.1. For each country, an *isoquant* is drawn tangent to the factor price level at the input levels reflecting the different technical means of producing the output levels, 100 cars. In country A, for example, 100 cars would be produced with less capital and more labor than in country B. At the relative factor prices $P_K/P_L = 5/2$, E_A is the efficient way and E_B the inefficient way to produce 100 cars.

---

[3] We assume here that any exchange rate between A and B is at its true equilibrium level.

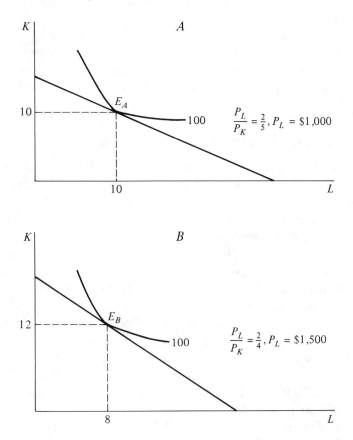

Figure 1.1. Hypothetical costs and productivity: country (firm) A and country (firm) B.

Does firm or country B have higher labor productivity than firm or country A? After all, 100 cars are produced in A with 10 units of labor while in B these same 100 cars require only 8 units of labor. The answer is obvious: Although B has higher labor productivity as conventionally measured, *B is not necessarily more productive (efficient) in using labor than A because relative factor prices differ between the two countries (firms)*. In Figure 1.1, assume that the same technology is used in the two countries so that the isoquants are exactly the same. In this case, A and B are equally "productive" in constructing cars; country A's greater use of labor simply reflects the lower price of labor relative to capital in country A as compared to country B.

From this example it is clear that one can test whether production in B is more or less efficient than in A (i.e., examine relative productivity or efficiency) only by removing factor-price differences between the two countries; that is, by examining *technical efficiency*. There is then a crucial distinction between differences in costs arising from technological versus factor-price differences in production; these differences are crucial for determining public policy.

One could complicate the analysis in Figure 1.1 by having, for example, a different technology in the two countries A and B. Assume that the technology in country A is superior in that, at equivalent factor prices, production in country A costs less than in country B because less of both labor and capital are needed to produce the same output. In this case, labor is more productive in country A, but – since technology differs between the two countries – one must determine the reasons for technological differences before condemning the managers in country B. For example, the technology in country A may be newer, known to country-B managers but uneconomic to install until existing capital depreciates further. Another reason for productivity differences might be that workers in country A work harder, so that managers in country B, if they migrated to country A, could produce as cheaply in country A as country A's managers. However, if country B's managers migrated to A they could not, simply by being from B, increase productivity in country A.

Another complication to the simple world depicted in Figure 1.1 would be to assume identical factor prices and technology in the two countries but have labor and capital as quasi-fixed factors, with excess productive capacity in country A but not in country B. By *quasi-fixed* we mean that labor and capital cannot be adjusted instantaneously by managers to whatever level they might wish. Capital is usually considered to be a quasi-fixed factor; it takes time to acquire new capital (buildings, dies, etc.) and existing capital may have little salvage value. Part of the labor input can also be a quasi-fixed factor; for example, overhead labor, which is not directly proportional to output changes. In addition, overhead and skilled labor may not be let go when output temporarily falls, owing to the difficulty of rehiring when conditions in the output market improve.

Now assume that although A and B each produce 100 cars, the quasi-fixed factors in B were designed to produce 150 cars; B then has a far lower utilization of its capacity than A. Simple arithmetic calculations would then show cost and productivity disadvantages to B, but these disadvantages would vanish were B's capacity utilization to increase. A careful analysis must then account for differences in capacity utilization.

These simple examples demonstrate the need to define productivity carefully and to examine differences in unit production costs to determine whether they are related to efficiency differences.

1.2   Concepts and measurement of productivity differentials

As indicated in Section 1.1, differentials in costs and productivity must be carefully defined and measured if the resulting values are used to "condemn" some countries or firms or to suggest necessary public policies. Before examining simple productivity measures in the automobile industry of the four countries in question, it is essential that we carefully define such terms as total factor productivity and labor productivity, and show how these terms are determined and measured.

We begin by examining the firm in country A from our earlier example. That firm used 10 units of labor and 10 units of capital to produce 100 cars. Labor productivity is then simply 100 cars/10 labor units, or 10 cars per man year (output divided by units of labor). *Total factor productivity* (TFP) is defined as the ratio of output to aggregate input (capital plus labor). But TFP is not 100 (output) divided by 200 (total units of labor and capital services), because units of labor cannot be added to units of capital.[4] To compute TFP we must choose a formula for aggregating labor and capital; for example, $X(L, K)$, where X is aggregate input. Then $\text{TFP} = Q/X$, where Q is output. A commonly used aggregation formula is the Tornqvist index (see Chapter 3):[5]

$$\log X_t - \log X_{t-1} = S_L(\log L_t - \log L_{t-1}) + S_K(\log K_t - \log K_{t-1}), \qquad (1.1)$$

where S_L and S_K are average cost shares (the shares of the costs of each factor in total costs) averaged over years t and $t-1$. Then the change in TFP can be calculated from:

$$\log \text{TFP}_t - \log \text{TFP}_{t-1} = (\log Q_t - \log Q_{t-1}) - (\log X_t - \log X_{t-1}). \qquad (1.2)$$

The usual practice is to index TFP so that, in the base year, $\text{TFP}_0 = Q_0 = X_0 = 1$.

Note the difference between TFP and labor productivity; the former examines all contributions to output from both labor and capital, whereas the latter attributes all changes in output to labor only. Hence, if the firm substituted capital for labor, TFP might not change but labor productivity would rise. This means that TFP is a superior measure of a firm's productivity performance.

Continuing with our example from country A, Table 1.1 lists hypothetical data on labor costs, capital costs, input levels, and output (cars

---

[4] If the 100 units of labor used were all different, then we could not calculate labor productivity by simply adding annual man years.

[5] The Tornqvist index aggregates inputs by weighting them by the input's share in total costs.

Table 1.1. *Hypothetical data on costs and quantities of auto production*

Year	Total labor costs (1)	Man years (2)	Units of capital (3)	Total capital costs (4)	Total costs (5)	Price of labor per man year (6)	Price of capital (per unit) (7)	Output (# of cars) (8)	Cost per car (9)
1977	$4,200	6	7.1	$15,975	$20,175	$700	$2,250	60	$336.25
1978	5,600	7	8	18,000	23,600	800	2,250	70	337.14
1979	7,200	8	8	20,000	27,200	900	2,500	80	340.00
1980	11,000	11	9.6	24,000	35,000	1,000	2,500	100	350.00
1981	10,000	10	10	25,000	35,000	1,000	2,500	100	350.00

Table 1.2. *Costs, productivity, and efficiency*

Year	Cost per car	Labor productivity	Total factor productivity	Cost efficiency
1977	1.00	1.00	1.00	1.00
1978	1.00	1.00	1.03	0.97
1979	1.01	1.00	1.14	0.88
1980	1.04	0.91	1.14	0.88
1981	1.04	1.00	1.14	0.88

produced) for a number of years. Cost per car, labor productivity, and total factor productivity (calculated from (1.1) and (1.2) and indexed so that $1977 = 1.00$) are given in Table 1.2.

In this example (Table 1.2), labor productivity was constant from 1977 to 1979, fell sharply in 1980, and then recovered to the previous level in 1981. Total factor productivity, which measures the real resource cost of producing a unit of output, increased from 1977 to 1979 and then remained constant. Another way of measuring this real resource cost is to compute an index of *cost efficiency* (CE), the unit cost change net of factor price changes. This index is computed as $(C/Q)/P$, where C/Q is average cost (C representing total cost) and P is an aggregate input price. The Tornqvist index of cost efficiency is computed as

$$\log \text{CE}_t - \log \text{CE}_{t-1} = [\log(C/Q)_t - \log(C/Q)_{t-1}] - [\log P_t - \log P_{t-1}],$$
(1.3)

where

$$\log P_t - \log P_{t-1} = S_L(\log P_{L,t} - \log P_{L,t-1}) + S_K(\log P_{K,t} - \log P_{K,t-1}).$$
(1.4)

As before, P_K, P_L are factor prices and S_K, S_L are average cost shares. The last column in Table 1.2 presents the index of cost efficiency corresponding to this example. Note that $\text{CE} = 1/\text{TFP}$, so that either measure can be used to determine the trend in real resource costs of producing output.[6]

From this example we see that nominal resource costs (nominal cost per car), real resource costs (TFP or CE), and labor productivity – all

---

[6] Strictly speaking, since both TFP and CE are approximations to continuous Divisia indices, they differ owing to third-order errors of approximation (Denny and Fuss 1980).

possible measures of production conditions – can have quite different trends and can suggest different problems and solutions.

While labor productivity was constant during 1977–9 ("poor" performance to some), TFP increased and CE decreased by 14% (remember that a decline in CE is favorable); nominal average cost rose 1%. Between 1979 and 1980, while labor productivity in this hypothetical world fell 9%, TFP (CE) remained constant. The difference in directions of these two measures is due to a substitution of labor for capital.

The moral is clear: Any story depends on the facts, yet the facts themselves tell no story unless *all* of the facts – in this case, including total factor productivity (cost efficiency) – are examined.

In this study we attempt to measure differences in unit production costs in the automobile industries of four countries. We attribute these differences to six possible causes: (1) factor prices (the cost of capital, labor, and materials); (2) economies of scale (the advantages, if any, of large-scale production); (3) technical progress (change in technology); (4) capacity utilization; (5) country-specific efficiency;[7] and (6) exchange-rate fluctuations. As we have demonstrated, it is important to distinguish the technological conditions of production (causes (2)–(5)) from price effects (causes (1) and (6)). We use this breakdown to determine the sources of intercountry *cost-efficiency differences* (CEDs): those efficiency differentials that remain when the effects of factor-price differences have been removed. (CED is the intercountry analog of the intertemporal CE measure introduced previously.)

We may now state the fundamental question: *If all four countries have the same factor prices, who would have a comparative advantage in automobile production?*

In Figure 1.2 we provide a graphic decomposition of some of these effects. We consider one country and two points in time (0 and 1). The cost curves C are considered to be functions of capacity output Q, factor prices P_L, P_K, and technical change T_1 for times 0 and 1:

$$C_0 = C(Q, P_{L0}, P_{K0}, T_{10}),$$
$$C_1 = C(Q, P_{L1}, P_{K1}, T_{11}). \tag{1.5}$$

Unit production costs in the two years are C_0/Q_0 and C_1/Q_1, labeled (respectively) CQ_0 and CQ_1.

Assume that, between time 0 and time 1, (i) both factor prices change and (ii) technical change occurs. An increase in the wage rate from P_{L0} to

---

[7] This term is used to capture all the efficiency effects not covered by the explicit inclusion of effects (2)–(4).

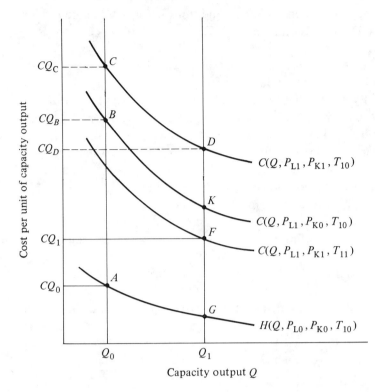

Figure 1.2. Decomposition of unit-cost change: one country, two points in time.

P_{L1} (everything else equal) increases unit costs from CQ_0 to CQ_B. The increase in the price of capital services increases unit production costs to CQ_C.

The improvement that lowers unit costs from CQ_C to CQ_1 is what we call the change in technical efficiency. This change could itself be decomposed (as we do econometrically) into its components: increases in scale (CQ_C to CQ_D); increases in capacity utilization (not shown); and technical change itself (CQ_D to CQ_1).

Note that this decomposition is not unique. We could just as easily move from A to G (scale economies) and then from G to K (the effect of the increase in the price of labor), and so on. Which decomposition is more correct? The answer clearly depends on how we weight the underlying sources; this is an index number problem. We have used the Tornqvist

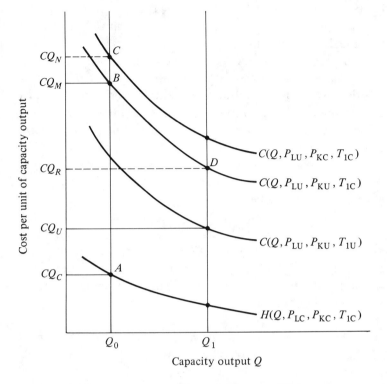

Figure 1.3. Decomposition of unit-cost differences: two countries, one point in time.

index, which is one of a set of nearly ideal aggregation indexes.[8] The Tornqvist index weights the logarithms of the relative change in variables by the geometric average of cost elasticities experienced at times 0 and 1.

In Figure 1.3 we decompose the average cost difference between two countries CQ_U and CQ_C at one point in time (the time subscript is suppressed for convenience). Again, the differences in unit costs between the two countries are decomposed into two major components. The distance from CQ_C to CQ_M represents the total difference in factor prices between the two countries (CQ_C to CQ_N representing the higher labor cost in U, CQ_N to CQ_M the higher capital cost in C). The component CQ_M to CQ_U is then the difference in technical efficiency between the two countries,

---

[8] More formally, it is an index in the class of superlative indexes that provides second-order approximations to an arbitrary aggregator function. See Diewert (1976).

with CQ_M to CQ_R representing scale differences and CQ_R to CQ_U the residual or *country-specific efficiency* differences (assuming capacity utilization to be equal for both countries).

Allocating intercountry productivity differentials to their underlying sources, as we attempt to do here, is important for public policy purposes. Consider another hypothetical case (summarized in Table 1.3). In this industry, country A's unit production cost is 20% less than that experienced in country B. Half of the sales of cars in country B are imports from country A. Four alternative explanations of these differentials could hold. In case 1, the source of the difference is the lower factor prices for labor and capital in country A as compared to country B, all other potential causes of cost differences being equal in the two countries. In case 2, country B has a 20% higher unit production cost because production in that country experiences scale diseconomies. In case 3, country A has a country-specific efficiency effect that lowers costs by 20% (but factor prices, scale, and capacity utilization are identical in the two countries). In case 4, country A's exchange rate is 20% below the fundamental exchange rate equilibrium[9] (all other conditions are equal between the two countries).

The government of country B is attempting to decide on the appropriate policy to increase domestic production and productivity. Four policies are on the menu: (1) rationalize the domestic industry so as to increase scale economies and thus lower unit costs; (2) require all producers in the domestic market to sell autos with at least 60% domestic content; (3) encourage country A's firms to engage in joint ventures with those in country B; and (4) lower interest rates.

Table 1.3 presents a matrix indicating the impact of each of the four possible policies on unit costs, depending on the source of the productivity differential. Policy 1, rationalizing the domestic industry in country B, will lower unit costs in B if suboptimal scale is the source of B's intercountry cost gap. Rationalization would, however, have no effect on unit costs in B if the underlying source of the differential were any one of the three other listed hypothetical factors.

Note the impact on unit costs of imposing domestic-content rules in B. If production in B suffers from diseconomies of scale, a domestic-content rule may tend to lower unit costs by increasing the scale of operations, but may also tend to raise costs in the world generally by shifting efficient

[9] The concept of the fundamental exchange rate equilibrium (called FEER) and its differences from actual exchange rates is important in the analysis that follows. FEER is closely related to purchasing power parity (see Williamson 1983, 1985).

Table 1.3. *Effect of policy on unit costs in both countries (first-order effects)*

Source of productivity differential	Policy in *B*			
	1 Rationalize domestic industry	2 Domestic-content rule	3 Encourage joint ventures	4 Lower interest rates
1. Higher labor costs in *B*	0	+	0	−
2. Suboptimal scale in *B*	−	−+?	−	0
3. Managerial or labor efficiency in *A*	0	+	−?	0
4. Currency in *B* overvalued	0	0	0	0

production away from *A*. If the new production in *B* is also of suboptimal scale, then no reductions in unit costs may occur. If the source of the 20% lower unit costs in *A* is due to country-specific factors (e.g., a more motivated work force) in *A*, then a domestic-content rule in *B* can only raise the total costs of producing cars. If the source of the underlying differential is a fundamentally misaligned currency, then shifting production from *A* to *B* under a domestic-content rule will raise the total cost (in a common currency) of producing cars in the short run, that is, until *B*'s currency is devalued.

A joint venture between a firm in *A* and a firm in *B* has no impact on unit costs in *B* unless the source of the differential is efficiency that is country-specific to *A* and embodied in a transferable asset (management or capital). No impact will occur if the efficiency advantage is embodied in *A*'s labor.

Finally, a policy of lowering interest rates to reestablish a lower equilibrium exchange rate has no direct impact on either country's unit costs (denominated in their own currencies), except where lowering interest rates in *B* lowers the cost of capital, thus lowering unit production costs. However, production costs in *B* denominated in country *A*'s currency will fall (subject to eventual balance-of-payments effects).

This hypothetical example highlights the importance for public policy purposes of carefully measuring the sources of intercountry cost differentials, and not just the differentials themselves.

1.3   Summary

Cost differences between producers in different countries can be due to a multitude of reasons – differences in factor prices or various differences in cost efficiency. The motor vehicle industries of the United States, Japan, Germany, and Canada are major employers and are of deep significance to their respective economies. The industries in each country have experienced very different growth patterns, and various forms of domestic policies have been used to assist producers. This study attempts to shed light on the differences in costs and cost efficiency in automobile production in the four countries, and thus to shed light on the effectiveness of such policies.

CHAPTER 2

International differences in output, productivity, and wages in the automobile industry: the 1950s to the mid-1980s

We begin with a brief overview of the automobile industries of the four countries under study. The purpose of this examination is to provide a context for analyzing productivity developments by examining production, imports, exports, changes in the uses of factors, and factor prices (Sections 2.1–2.3); to provide simple comparisons of productivity (Section 2.4), and to examine the productivity calculations made by others (Sections 2.5–2.8).

2.1 Imports, exports, and trade restraints

In Tables 2.1–2.4 we provide data on domestic production, imports, exports, and registration of automobiles in each of the four countries. Before discussing the production numbers, it is useful to examine the trade restraints operative in each country over the period 1961 to 1984. The U.S. auto industry did not have extensive protection against foreign suppliers until the 1981 Voluntary Restraint Agreements (VRA) were agreed to by the Japanese exporters. In 1970, the U.S. tariff was 4.5% on passenger cars and 8.5% on light trucks; no other trade restrictions existed. In 1973, just after the Kennedy Round of GATT (General Agreement on Tariffs and Trade), the tariff on passenger cars was cut to 3%. Despite the absence of substantial trade restrictions, imports were not significant in the United States until 1959, when they peaked at 9% of U.S. auto sales. Imports then fell until 1966, whereafter they rose again to 8% of U.S. sales. Part of this increase was due to the 1965 Auto Pact liberalizing trade between Canada and the United States. Most auto imports from Canada are made by U.S. multinationals from their own Canadian assembly plants. Auto imports into the United States doubled between 1960 and 1969; excluding cars from Canada, imports rose by 48% in those four years. In 1970 non-Canadian imports represented 9% of U.S. auto sales; Canadian imports represented 8% of sales. In 1969 imports into the United States from Germany exceeded imports from Canada.

17

Table 2.1. *Automobile production, imports, exports, and registrations: United States (thousands)*

Year	Domestic production	Imports				Exports		Registrations
		Total[a]	Canada	Germany[b]	Japan	Total	Canada	
1955	7,950	57	—	40	—	211	28	7,170
1960	6,703	444	—	208	1	117	27	6,577
1965	9,335	559	29	412	22	106	44	9,314
1966	8,604	913	166	575	50	178	114	9,008
1969	8,224	1,846	691	729	218	333	292	9,447
1970	6,550	2,013	693	757	233	285	246	8,388
1974	7,325	2,573	818	655	683	601	517	8,701
1975	6,716	2,075	734	374	712	640	551	8,262
1979	8,433	3,005	677	332	1,547	793	601	10,357
1980	6,376	3,248	594	336	1,819	617	510	8,761
1981	6,253	2,998	564	242	1,761	548	471	8,444
1982	5,073	3,067	703	257	1,696	379	334	7,754
1983	6,781	3,667	837	278	1,762	554	524	8,924
1984	7,773	4,880	1,073	335	1,949	616	590	10,118

Note: Data on imports into a country (e.g., the United States) are not necessarily identical to data on exports from the other country (e.g., Germany).
[a] Includes imports assembled in U.S. foreign trade zones. Excluding such imports for 1980 to 1984 leads to total imports of 3,116,448; 2,856,286; 2,928,407; 3,133,836; and 3,559,427 vehicles for 1980 to 1984 respectively.
[b] Includes Kombis (Kombinations-Kraftwagens), trucks, and buses.
Source: MVMA *World Motor Vehicle Data.*

Table 2.2. *Automobile production, imports, exports, and registrations: Japan (thousands)*

| Year | Domestic production (1) | Imports | | | Exports | | | |
		Total (2)	Germany (3)	U.S. (4)	Total (5)	EEC (6)	U.S. (7)	Canada (8)	Registrations
1955	20	5	n.a.[a]	0	0	n.a.	0	0	25
1960	165	4	n.a.	3	7	n.a.	1	0	145
1965	696	13	n.a.	3	101	n.a.	22	5	586
1966	878	15	n.a.	3	153	n.a.	50	3	740
1969	2,611	16	8	4	560	35	218	50	2,037
1970	3,179	19	10	5	726	48	233	65	2,379
1974	3,932	42	22	15	1,727	237	684	112	2,287
1975	4,568	45	22	16	1,827	374	712	73	2,738
1979	6,176	65	33	21	3,102	646	1,547	61	3,037
1980	7,038	46	27	11	3,947	763	1,819	158	2,854
1981	6,974	32	22	4	3,947	706	1,761	200	2,867
1982	6,882	35	28	3	3,770	641	1,692	153	3,038
1983	7,152	37	27	3	3,806	762	1,698	165	3,136
1984	7,073	44	35	2	3,981	790	1,852	176	3,096

Note: Starting in 1979, production and export statistics exclude "noncountable" knock-down (KD) sets.
[a] Not available.
Sources: Columns (1), (2), (4), (5), (7), and (8), MVMA *World Motor Vehicle Data;* columns (3) and (6), JAMA *Motor Vehicle Statistics of Japan.*

19

Table 2.3. *Automobile production, imports, exports, and registrations: Germany (thousands)*

Year	Domestic production[a]	Imports				Exports					Registrations
		Total	EEC	Japan	U.S.	Total	EEC	Japan	U.S.[b]	Canada	
1955	705	17	n.a.	0	0	320	n.a.	n.a.	40	6	394
1960	1,674	89	n.a.	0	1	781	n.a.	n.a.	208	37	914
1965	2,440	274	n.a.	0	4	1,259	n.a.	n.a.	412	39	1,382
1966	2,515	328	n.a.	0	3	1,352	n.a.	n.a.	575	28	1,375
1969	2,936	494	n.a.	0	2	1,667	n.a.	n.a.	730	31	1,687
1970	3,129	660	n.a.	0	3	1,706	n.a.	n.a.	757	36	1,931
1974	2,571	590	n.a.	20	2	1,541	816	n.a.	655	29	1,559
1975	2,687	769	n.a.	49	4	1,356	955	n.a.	374	28	1,956
1979	3,658	1,056	n.a.	176	24	1,881	1,491	n.a.	332	33	2,400
1980	3,239	1,027	n.a.	233	5	1,737	n.a.	n.a.	336	31	2,205
1981	3,281	947	n.a.	235	3	1,823	1,140	18	242	20	2,089
1982	3,488	837	n.a.	172	2	2,073	1,345	24	257	16	1,930
1983	3,562	1,072	658	260	1[c]	2,057	1,325	23	278	24	2,166
1984	3,504	1,109	638	308	1	2,101	1,267	30	367	27	2,139

[a] Excludes Kombis.
[b] Includes Kombis, trucks, and buses.
[c] United States and Canada.
Source: MVMA World Motor Vehicle Data.

Table 2.4. *Automobile production, imports, exports, and registrations: Canada (thousands)*

Year	Domestic production	Imports				Exports		Registrations
		Total	U.S.	Germany	Japan	Total	U.S.	
1955	375	49	27	6	0	12	0	382
1960	326	171	28	37	0	17	0	451
1965	707	136	46	39	5	78	46	687
1966	685	189	115	28	3	190	115	684
1969	1,026	458	291	31	50	715	676	756
1970	923	405	252	36	65	733	697	636
1974	1,167	665	495	29	112	840	810	901
1975	1,054	679	552	28	73	777	723	840
1979	988	707	589	33	60	650	590	998
1980	847	701	495	31	158	613	549	949[a]
1981	803	724	473	20	200	566	524	892
1982	808	542	334	16	153	704	684	727
1983	969	744	532	24	165	867	854	830
1984	1,022	863	601	27	176	1,103	1,086	915

[a] Incomplete.
Source: MVMA *World Motor Vehicle Data.*

In 1975, Japanese exports to the United States matched the Canadian imports of U.S. manufacturers, each representing 9% of U.S. auto sales. Between 1974 and 1975 imports from Germany into the United States plummeted. In 1979, total passenger car imports were 29% of U.S. car sales; non-Canadian imports, 22%. Japanese imports alone reached 21% of U.S. car sales in 1980; in that year all imports were 37% of U.S. car sales. In 1982, Japanese car sales (constrained by the VRA) represented 19.3% of U.S. car sales.

The U.S. auto industry, aside from exports to Canada under the Auto Pact, has never been oriented toward exporting. Total (non-Canadian) exports from the United States peaked in the early 1950s. The U.S. auto industry has also been a highly cyclical one, with production "booms" in 1965, 1978, and 1984 and production "busts" in 1970, 1975, and 1980–2 (see Section 2.2).

The Canadian auto industry, dominated by U.S. manufacturers, has had similar ups and downs. Prior to 1965, the Canadian auto industry was a typical example of an inefficient manufacturing sector, competing against imports with the aid of high trade barriers. The Canadian tariff was 17.5% and was combined with domestic-content rules. The Auto Pact signed between Canada and the United States was designed to rationalize Canadian production and increase trade flows between the two countries.[1] These facts are evident in Table 2.4. In 1960, Canada exported 17,000 cars, none to the United States, and imported 28,000 from the United States; in 1969, four years after the Auto Pact, Canadian exports to the United States were 676,000 passenger cars while 291,000 cars were imported from the United States. As can be seen from the table, trade with the United States is a major feature of the Canadian auto industry.

Canadian tariffs on autos have always been significantly higher than U.S. tariffs.[2] Imports into Canada from outside North America have been substantial even with tariff barriers and domestic content rules. In 1970, non-U.S. auto imports were 24% of car sales in Canada, but only 15% in 1975 and 12% in 1979. In 1980, however, these non-U.S. imports reached 22% of sales, with Japanese imports alone accounting for 17%. In 1981 and 1982, non-U.S. imports increased to 28% of domestic sales; Japanese vehicle sales represented 22% of the Canadian market, even with constraints on Japanese imports.

---

[1] Canada maintained domestic-content provisions, which are a continuing source of friction between Canada and the United States.

[2] In 1990, tariffs were 9.2% in Canada and 2.5% in the United States.

In its early period (1915 to 1940), German auto producers were assisted by a set of trade restrictions and tariffs, foreign exchange restrictions, and local-content requirements. The formation of the EEC broke down many of these trade barriers, and led to a common tariff (10% for many years) and the elimination of other trade restrictions in Germany against non-EEC producers (but not in France, Italy, or Great Britain).[3] In 1955, exports accounted for 45% of domestic production. Imports became significant in 1965 at 20% of domestic sales; in that same year exports were 4.6 times as great as imports, accounting for 52% of domestic production. Until 1975, exports to the United States exceeded all motor vehicle imports into Germany. In 1970, 55% of domestic production was exported; exports to the United States were 24% of domestic production. These trends altered in 1975, when domestic production was 14% below 1970 levels, exports to the United States were half of 1970 levels, and imports were 57% of export levels and 39% of domestic sales. By 1980, imports were nearly one-half of domestic sales, and exports had recovered to represent over half of domestic production. Imports fell in the 1980s, while exports continued to rise.

Japan's high tariffs (34–40% in the 1960s) dropped to 6.4% after the Kennedy Round of GATT. Despite the lack of explicit trade restrictions,[4] auto imports have never been a factor in the Japanese market. Exports, however, are clearly significant. In 1965, exports accounted for 14.5% of Japanese auto production; by 1970, 23%; and in 1981, 57% (nearly 4 million units). Exports to the United States were 16% of Japanese auto production in 1975 and 25% in 1979 through 1982. Exports to the EEC became significant in the mid-1970s, and in 1975 represented 8% of Japanese automobile production. In 1984, 4 million (of a total 7 million cars produced) were exported from Japan; North America absorbed 50% and the EEC 20% of these Japanese auto exports.

2.2   Production of motor vehicles in the four countries

The number of passenger cars produced in each country in each year from 1961 to 1984 is given in Table 2.5; trucks and buses are listed in Table 2.6. In 1961 the United States produced 5.5 million passenger cars,

---

[3] Germany does impose an annual road tax based on engine displacement, which works to the disadvantage of large (U.S.) cars.

[4] The Japanese impose an auto tax and an annual road tax that is based on engine displacement and wheelbase size.

Table 2.5. *Passenger car production (thousands)*

Year	U.S.	Canada	Japan[a]	Japan[b]	Germany[c]
1961	5,522	327	250		1,752
1962	6,943	428	269		1,945
1963	7,644	533	408		2,186
1964	7,745	559	580		2,370
1965	9,335	710	696		2,440
1966	8,604	696	878		2,515
1967	7,413	714	1,376		2,043
1968	8,849	900	2,056		2,535
1969	8,224	1,035	2,612		2,936
1970	6,550	937	3,179		3,129
1971	8,584	1,083	3,718		3,290
1972	8,828	1,147	4,022		3,166
1973	9,667	1,235	4,471		3,358
1974	7,325	1,185	3,932		2,571
1975	6,716	1,054	4,568		2,687
1976	8,498	1,146	5,028		3,301
1977	9,214	1,162	5,431		3,567
1978	9,177	1,143	5,976		3,626
1979	8,433	988	6,476	6,176	3,658
1980	6,376	847	7,350	7,038	3,239
1981	6,253	803	7,363	6,974	3,281
1982	5,073	808	7,344	6,882	3,488
1983	6,781	969	7,717	7,152	3,562
1984	7,773	1,022	7,754	7,073	3,504

[a] Includes noncountable KD sets.
[b] Excludes noncountable KD sets starting in 1979.
[c] Kombis classified as trucks.

2.37 times as many as the combined output of Canada, Japan, and Germany. Production in Germany in 1961 amounted to 1.75 million passenger cars, 32% of the volume of U.S. car output but 7 times Japanese output. In 1961, only 250,000 cars were produced in Japan, a mere 5% of the number produced in the United States.

In 1965, the year of the Canada–U.S. Auto Pact,[5] car production in the United States reached 9.3 million cars and had increased at a 14%

[5] In 1965, the governments of Canada and the United States allowed free trade for producers between the two countries in auto parts and finished cars, as long as domestic manufacturers met certain domestic-content provisions. This pact is analyzed in Chapter 8.

Table 2.6. *Truck and bus production (thousands)*

Year	U.S.	Canada	Japan[a]	Japan[b]	Germany[c]
1961	1,131	63	564		396
1962	1,254	80	722		411
1963	1,464	98	876		482
1964	1,562	109	1,123		539
1965	1,803	144	1,179		536
1966	1,792	200	1,409		535
1967	1,611	226	1,771		439
1968	1,972	276	2,030		572
1969	1,982	313	2,063		668
1970	1,734	251	2,110		713
1971	2,088	277	2,093		693
1972	2,483	317	2,272		650
1973	3,014	350	2,612		591
1974	2,747	376	2,620		529
1975	2,270	388	2,374		499
1976	3,000	500	2,814		567
1977	3,489	612	3,083		537
1978	3,723	675	3,293		561
1979	3,046	644	3,562	3,460	592
1980	1,634	528	4,132	4,005	639
1981	1,690	520	4,368	4,206	616
1982	1,912	469	4,003	3,850	575
1983	2,444	556	4,182	3,960	593
1984	3,166	808	4,624	4,392	541

[a] Includes noncountable KD sets.
[b] Excludes noncountable KD sets starting in 1979.
[c] Kombis classified as trucks.

annual rate from 1961 output levels. In 1965, auto production in Canada, Japan, and Germany totaled 3.85 million vehicles, or 41% of the U.S. output for that year (nearly the same ratio as in 1961). From 1961 to 1965, passenger car output had more than doubled in Canada, more than tripled in Japan, and increased by 39% in Germany.

The output level reached by U.S. passenger car producers in 1965 was not reached again until 1973; meanwhile, output continued to rise in the other three countries from 1965 to 1973. In 1970 (a very poor year for U.S. auto producers), U.S. passenger car production had fallen 30% from the 1965 level to 6.5 million vehicles. The combined auto output of Japan and Germany in 1970 nearly equalled that of the United States. Japanese car production increased at a 35% annual rate from 1965 to 1970, while German car production increased at only a 5% annual rate. Following passage of the Auto Pact, production in Canada from 1965 to 1970 increased at an annual rate of nearly 6%.

The year 1975 was another difficult one for North American car producers; production in Japan rose to 68% of U.S. output levels as the Japanese industry experienced a 7.5% annual rate of increase from 1970 to 1975. In 1977, a good year for U.S. auto producers, Japanese output was 59% of the U.S. output level. Japanese automobile output continued to climb while passenger car production continued to cycle and stagnate in the other three countries. In 1980, Japanese automobile producers fabricated more cars than did U.S. auto producers. In that year, with a severe recession for the world car industry outside Asia, the United States produced fewer cars than in 1962; Canada, fewer cars than in 1968; and Germany, the same number of cars as in 1971.

The year 1982 was the nadir of auto production in North America: The United States produced fewer passenger cars than in the 1950s; Canada, fewer than it had produced three years after the Auto Pact. In Japan, production in 1982 was at 1980 levels. In 1982 Germany produced 8% more automobiles than in 1980 (but still below the 1977 peak). By 1984, the increase in automobile demand in North America, combined with the VRAs, led to an increase in North American motor vehicle production of 55% over the trough of 1982. Production increased in Japan and Germany between 1982 and 1984 as well, but not to the same extent as in North America.

In this brief description of passenger car production, several highlights stand out. First, the Japanese auto industry experienced rapid and sustained growth, while the auto industry in the other three countries experienced substantial cyclical fluctuations and stagnant peak output levels. Productivity improvements are generally easier to achieve in quickly growing sectors than in stagnant sectors; for example, newer technology can be installed in growing sectors. Second, as pointed out in Chapter 1 (and as evidenced by Tables 2.5 and 2.6), capacity utilization must play an important role in both measured labor productivity and total factor productivity, as the presence of fixed and quasi-fixed factors will – in countries other than Japan – drag down measured productivity in years such as 1980 or 1982. Third, some explanation is in order for the Japanese "miracle" of rapid sustained increase in passenger car output and sales.

Table 2.7. *Motor vehicle industry sales revenue: nominal output (millions of Canadian dollars)*

Year	U.S.	Canada	Japan	Germany
1961	25,535	1,351	3,231	6,646
1962	34,337	1,741	3,911	7,813
1963	38,153	2,224	4,406	8,381
1964	41,730	2,505	5,530	9,496
1965	51,363	3,118	6,023	10,195
1966	50,587	3,318	7,040	10,721
1967	42,424	3,748	9,078	9,739
1968	51,742	4,694	11,505	11,188
1969	52,563	5,423	13,861	13,899
1970	42,254	4,801	16,083	17,333
1971	56,120	6,072	17,575	19,078
1972	60,657	6,949	22,180	21,434
1973	71,154	8,279	30,506	28,929
1974	62,713	9,267	31,979	27,270
1975	66,287	9,810	36,236	34,605
1976	89,583	11,373	41,434	39,948
1977	118,521	12,538	57,697	53,453
1978	142,231	15,102	89,696	71,519
1979	144,193	17,174	98,918	88,704
1980	111,178	15,286	110,992	91,642
1981	129,759	16,565	129,896	81,992
1982	126,752	17,740	120,421	n.a.
1983	169,058	23,848	132,288	n.a.
1984	214,716	30,402	151,195	n.a.

Note: Includes sales of cars, trucks, and buses.

In Tables 2.7 and 2.8 we compare sales revenues for all four automobile industries (nominal values in Table 2.7, real values in Table 2.8). Several caveats must be kept in mind for this and ensuing tables. First, the coverage of the term "motor vehicle industry" is not the same in all four countries; this point is discussed more fully in Chapter 4. Although the motor vehicle industry in all four countries includes motor vehicle parts, bodies, and assembly, in each country several components are classified as part of another industry. In the United States, foundries are excluded (they are included elsewhere); motorcycles are included in Japan and Germany.

Table 2.8. *Motor vehicle industry sales revenue: real output (millions of 1971 Canadian dollars)*

Year	U.S.	Canada	Japan	Germany
1961	32,967	1,555	n.a.	13,068
1962	41,333	1,994	n.a.	14,308
1963	45,501	2,517	n.a.	15,028
1964	49,118	2,825	n.a.	16,961
1965	59,991	3,504	n.a.	18,134
1966	58,657	3,685	n.a.	18,582
1967	48,506	4,093	10,475	16,779
1968	57,401	5,029	13,516	19,401
1969	57,219	5,731	16,450	23,330
1970	45,783	4,964	19,754	26,681
1971	59,420	6,072	21,609	27,092
1972	63,600	6,799	24,301	27,236
1973	72,933	7,916	29,133	29,123
1974	60,077	8,097	28,200	25,021
1975	54,178	7,882	30,054	26,621
1976	71,229	8,428	34,767	30,880
1977	81,496	8,454	40,543	33,969
1978	84,682	9,077	46,054	35,569
1979	77,219	9,559	51,392	37,587
1980	54,221	7,640	58,796	36,662
1981	53,795	7,386	63,800	38,137
1982	47,898	7,382	63,118	n.a.
1983	62,669	9,382	66,637	n.a.
1984	74,324	11,360	71,663	n.a.

Note: Includes sales of cars, trucks, and buses.

Second, Table 2.7 is given in nominal Canadian dollars, thus valuing all output in (say) Germany at the actual exchange rate between the deutsche mark and the Canadian dollar. As a result, "real" output changes can be swamped by exchange-rate movements. For example, the number of passenger cars and trucks produced in Germany in 1980 fell by 8.8% from 1979 levels, yet the sales revenue of German car and truck production denominated in Canadian dollars rose 3.3%. In order to eliminate this bias, Table 2.8 shows sales revenue in constant 1971 Canadian dollars.[6]

[6] See Chapter 4 for details of the construction of intercountry output-price deflators.

In 1961, the nominal sales revenue of the U.S. motor vehicles industry was $25 billion (Canadian), rising to $144 billion in 1979 and $215 billion in 1984. The value of the U.S. industry so defined was then 69% of the total industry value in all four countries in 1961, 41% of the total value in 1979, and 36% in 1981. This value share of the U.S. producers was greater than their share of the number of cars produced – U.S. producers manufacture more expensive (and larger and heavier) cars. In Section 2.6 we discuss the attempts of other researchers to compensate for these differences in output mix; in Chapters 4 and 5 we provide our own methodology of accounting for output mix.

In real terms (1971 Canadian dollars), the value of Japanese motor vehicle industry production exceeded that of the U.S. industry between 1980 and 1983. In 1967 the Japanese industry was one-fifth the size (real value of output) of the U.S. industry. By 1984, as the U.S. industry recovered, its real output was once again greater than that of the Japanese.

Table 2.9 presents the potential output of the motor vehicle industry in each country. *Potential output* is defined as actual real sales revenue divided by measured capacity utilization (capacity utilization data is given in Table 2.10).

Turning first to the data in Table 2.10, we see that capacity utilization in auto production was consistently high in Japan and high in Germany also (but with greater fluctuations than in Japan). Capacity utilization was both substantially lower and more variable in North America than in Japan and Germany. In 1982, the worst year in this period for the North American auto industry, capacity utilization in North America was barely 50%; in that same year Japanese auto producers were operating at 83% of potential capacity. In only one year (1973) since 1968 did capacity utilization in the United States exceed that in Japan (and then only marginally). The capacity utilization of the U.S. industry was close to that of the Japanese in 1969, 1971, and 1977.

In Table 2.9 we indicate the annual percentage changes in real potential output for each country. Changes in real potential output measure changes in the productive capacity of the industry. The largest changes in the industry's real potential output occurred in the United States in the period 1961-6; in Canada, from 1962 to 1967; in Japan,[7] from 1967 to 1973 and from 1975 to 1981; and in Germany, during the mid-1960s. Note that the most substantial increases in productive capacity in North America and in Japan occurred prior to 1977.

---

[7] We do not have data on Japanese real potential output prior to 1967.

Table 2.9. *Motor vehicle industry potential output (millions of 1971 Canadian dollars)*

Year	U.S.	% change	Canada	% change	Japan	% change	Germany	% change
1961	40,151		2,219		n.a.		15,468	
1962	48,027	19.6	2,798	26.1	n.a.		17,784	15.0
1963	51,518	7.3	3,328	18.9	n.a.		18,304	2.9
1964	59,863	16.2	4,069	22.3	n.a.		20,682	13.0
1965	64,998	8.6	4,706	15.7	n.a.		22,985	11.1
1966	68,423	5.3	5,271	12.0	n.a.		24,641	7.2
1967	66,540	−2.8	6,154	16.7	14,711		27,537	11.8
1968	67,535	1.5	6,817	10.8	14,940	1.6	26,466	−3.9
1969	71,379	5.7	7,017	2.9	18,713	25.3	27,377	3.4
1970	70,385	−1.4	7,403	5.5	22,535	20.4	29,927	9.3
1971	71,908	2.2	8,410	13.6	24,701	9.6	31,256	4.4
1972	75,654	5.2	8,964	6.6	27,883	12.9	32,881	5.2
1973	80,145	5.9	10,010	11.7	32,401	16.2	33,634	2.3
1974	83,823	4.6	10,692	6.8	33,800	4.3	34,176	1.6
1975	85,243	1.7	11,657	9.0	36,873	9.1	35,301	3.3
1976	88,570	3.9	11,328	−2.8	38,649	4.8	36,044	2.1
1977	94,228	6.4	11,154	−1.5	46,287	19.8	37,829	5.0
1978	100,521	6.7	12,294	10.2	50,710	9.6	40,102	6.0
1979	105,116	4.6	14,574	18.5	59,757	17.8	41,519	3.5
1980	99,909	−5.0	13,831	−5.1	66,550	11.4	44,115	6.3
1981	97,567	−2.3	13,890	0.4	72,939	9.6	46,453	5.3
1982	94,786	−2.9	14,387	3.6	75,953	4.1	n.a.	n.a.
1983	92,900	−2.0	15,421	7.2	80,160	5.5	n.a.	n.a.
1984	94,846	2.1	15,715	1.9	85,726	6.9	n.a.	n.a.

Note: Potential output is measured as real output (Table 2.8) divided by (unnormalized) capacity utilization (Table 2.10).

2.3　Employees and labor costs

Tables 2.11–2.17 provide information on the number of employees (total workers and production workers alone) and their compensation. In 1961, while the United States accounted for 74% of the four countries' total sales revenue, employment in the U.S. auto industry accounted for only 34% of the countries' combined employment in the auto industry. This discrepancy signals once again the more expensive mix of cars produced in the United States (or, perhaps, higher labor productivity). Employment in the U.S. auto industry increased by 353,000 employees (or 62%) between 1961 and 1978; employment fell by 210,000 between 1978 and 1980. The labor productivity improvement in the Japan industry is evident

Table 2.10. *Capacity utilization: passenger car production (%)*

Year	U.S.	Norm.[a]	Canada	Norm.	Japan	Norm.	Germany	Norm.
1961	82.1	93.8	73.2	83.7	n.a.	n.a.	84.5	96.5
1962	86.1	98.3	75.0	85.7	n.a.	n.a.	80.5	91.9
1963	88.3	100.9	78.9	90.1	n.a.	n.a.	82.1	93.8
1964	82.1	93.7	72.7	83.0	n.a.	n.a.	82.0	93.7
1965	92.3	105.4	78.8	90.0	n.a.	n.a.	78.9	90.1
1966	85.7	97.9	74.1	84.6	n.a.	n.a.	75.4	86.1
1967	72.9	83.3	68.0	77.8	n.a.	n.a.	60.9	69.1
1968	85.0	97.1	76 7	87.6	90.5	103.3	73.3	83.7
1969	80.1	91.6	81.3	92.8	83.9	100.4	85.2	97.3
1970	65.0	74.3	66.6	76.0	87.7	100.1	89.2	101.8
1971	82.6	94.4	75.1	85.8	87.5	99.9	86.7	99.0
1972	84.1	96.0	78.2	89.3	87.2	99.5	82.8	94.6
1973	91.0	103.9	82.5	94.2	89.9	102.7	86.6	98.9
1974	71.7	81.9	74.7	85.3	83.4	95.3	73.2	83.6
1975	63.6	72.6	66.6	76.1	81.5	93.1	75.4	86.1
1976	80.4	91.9	76.1	86.9	90.0	102.7	85.7	97.8
1977	86.5	98.8	79.1	90.4	87.6	100.0	89.8	102.6
1978	84.2	96.2	77.1	88.0	90.8	103.7	88.7	101.3
1979	73.5	83.9	67.7	77.3	86.0	98.2	90.5	103.4
1980	54.3	62.0	54.3	62.0	88.3	100.9	83.1	94.9
1981	55.1	63.0	53.3	60.9	87.5	99.9	82.1	93.8
1982	50.5	57.7	50.7	57.9	83.1	94.9	n.a.	n.a.
1983	67.5	77.0	62.9	71.9	83.1	94.9	n.a.	n.a.
1984	78.4	89.5	75.2	85.8	83.6	95.5	n.a.	n.a.

[a] Normalized to the average capacity utilization in Japan (87.6).

in Table 2.11: Between 1961 and 1980, employment doubled while output (number of cars produced) increased *29-fold*. Between 1961 and 1978, the number of employees in the German motor vehicle sector grew by 12%, with employment falling in the late 1960s and rising in the 1970s. In 1980, employment in Germany was only 16% above 1961 levels, while the number of vehicles produced was 85% greater.

The data on production employees (see Tables 2.11 and 2.12) shows that the United States in 1961 had 33.7% of the number of production workers in the four countries and 34% of the number of all automotive employees. In 1981, the United States employed 30.6% of the production workers but only 29.4% of all employees, suggesting a slightly higher ratio of nonproduction to production workers in the United States than

Table 2.11. *Number of automotive industry employees (total)*

Year	U.S.	Canada	Japan	Germany[a]
1961	571,700	49,395	310,127	743,509
1962	628,400	53,036	327,420	752,859
1963	643,800	61,297	366,039	753,177
1964	729,500	70,313	401,957	762,152
1965	827,600	79,846	416,495	761,200
1966	859,900	83,231	455,659	751,424
1967	739,400	82,772	501,152	708,190
1968	778,800	87,191	538,280	700,011
1969	817,300	93,586	560,725	762,487
1970	720,500	87,122	579,974	806,392
1971	775,900	98,183	576,818	826,514
1972	807,400	104,591	607,173	814,216
1973	888,400	116,872	634,447	831,107
1974	797,600	117,696	614,774	822,384
1975	699,000	105,583	601,156	759,059
1976	797,100	112,589	622,251	784,065
1977	876,400	116,861	629,402	808,098
1978	924,900	123,207	637,841	835,187
1979	892,100	123,382	651,342	854,907
1980	714,300	106,020	682,827	883,381
1981	695,600	106,394	700,078	862,618
1982	615,600	100,310	696,384	n.a.
1983	658,600	109,118	698,690	n.a.
1984	752,600	127,600	722,414	n.a.

[a] Includes the vehicle repair sector.

in the other three countries. In 1961, the highest ratio of nonproduction to production workers was in Canada (44%) and the lowest in Germany (20%), but German data include the repair sector.

The data on the number of employees is not a totally accurate picture of the labor input in each country's auto industry, because the hours worked per employee vary significantly from country to country. Table 2.14 provides data on hours worked per employee. The average Japanese employee in the auto industry in 1961 worked 22% more hours per year than the average U.S. employee, 27% more than the average Canadian employee, and 24% more than the average German employee in the auto

Table 2.12. *Number of automotive industry production employees*

Year	U.S.	Canada	Japan	Germany
1961	460,000	34,630	248,669	619,863
1962	514,600	38,236	257,430	625,475
1963	529,100	44,788	286,831	623,292
1964	600,400	52,259	314,860	625,330
1965	641,700	65,234	424,852	621,725
1966	716,400	62,183	348,786	608,729
1967	605,500	61,702	385,371	563,146
1968	641,700	65,234	424,852	560,800
1969	679,400	71,088	437,118	616,082
1970	580,400	63,908	443,969	652,694
1971	639,600	74,973	437,685	665,774
1972	669,100	80,256	460,671	650,860
1973	739,900	91,024	478,835	665,916
1974	652,100	91,624	460,606	652,915
1975	570,700	80,975	443,606	593,440
1976	661,800	87,206	456,661	622,704
1977	727,700	91,344	459,253	643,311
1978	766,500	96,762	462,747	664,441
1979	730,000	97,396	469,901	681,139
1980	561,000	81,056	489,902	696,678
1981	557,500	82,237	507,406	672,652
1982	485,400	76,717	504,664	n.a.
1983	529,600	85,790	506,310	n.a.
1984	612,800	102,054	523,732	n.a.

industry. By 1984, the average Japanese auto employee was working only 2.6% more hours per year than the average U.S. worker, only 10% more than the average Canadian, but 37% more than the average German auto employee (1981 data). Hours worked per year per employee are far lower in Germany than in the other three countries.

Labor unit costs are given in Table 2.15 and are calculated as total compensation (wages plus fringes) in Canadian dollars per hour. In 1961, labor compensation in the Japanese auto industry was $.38 per hour or *less than one-tenth of U.S. wage levels.* In 1984, Japanese nominal hourly compensation rates were 42% of U.S. levels, indicating a significant increase in the price of Japanese labor relative to the price of U.S. labor. Canadian

Table 2.13. *Total hours, all employees (millions of hours)*

Year	U.S.	Canada	Japan	Germany
1961	1,167	97	774	1,492
1962	1,342	111	785	1,468
1963	1,424	130	877	1,440
1964	1,583	145	969	1,466
1965	1,821	167	976	1,451
1966	1,814	167	1,085	1,412
1967	1,488	165	1,205	1,253
1968	1,694	179	1,254	1,310
1969	1,663	188	1,306	1,435
1970	1,430	168	1,340	1,534
1971	1,564	192	1,308	1,505
1972	1,674	211	1,366	1,441
1973	1,866	237	1,433	1,462
1974	1,580	229	1,308	1,352
1975	1,349	203	1,221	1,302
1976	1,629	218	1,314	1,358
1977	1,836	234	1,349	1,377
1978	1,904	239	1,356	1,389
1979	1,786	227	1,412	1,420
1980	1,372	192	1,513	1,415
1981	1,338	198	1,540	1,382
1982	1,171	179	1,499	n.a.
1983	1,351	212	1,515	n.a.
1984	1,628	258	1,604	n.a.

labor compensation rates, which were at 75% of U.S. levels in 1961, fell to 68% of U.S. levels in 1984. As we will see in the ensuing chapters (primarily Chapter 8), this result is more a function of exchange-rate movements than of relative wage increases for U.S. as compared to Canadian labor. German labor costs in 1961 were less than one-third of U.S. labor costs, just over half of U.S. labor costs in 1972, and nearly equal to U.S. costs in 1981. This shows a significant rise in the price of German labor relative to U.S. and Canadian labor. Table 2.16 provides information for each country on the ratio of nonwage compensation (fringe payments and benefits) to the wage rate. The U.S. and German industries have far higher nonwage payments than do Canadian and Japanese firms.

Table 2.14. *Hours worked per year per employee*

Year	U.S.	Canada	Japan	Germany
1961	2,042	1,970	2,495	2,007
1962	2,135	2,096	2,399	1,950
1963	2,211	2,124	2,395	1,912
1964	2,170	2,061	2,410	1,924
1965	2,200	2,088	2,344	1,906
1966	2,110	2,006	2,381	1,879
1967	2,012	1,995	2,404	1,769
1968	2,175	2,058	2,330	1,871
1969	2,034	2,006	2,329	1,882
1970	1,985	1,930	2,310	1,902
1971	2,015	1,953	2,268	1,821
1972	2,073	2,014	2,250	1,770
1973	2,101	2,026	2,258	1,759
1974	1,981	1,946	2,128	1,644
1975	1,930	1,927	2,030	1,717
1976	2,043	1,936	2,112	1,732
1977	2,095	2,003	2,143	1,704
1978	2,059	1,937	2,125	1,663
1979	2,002	1,837	2,167	1,661
1980	1,920	1,808	2,216	1,602
1981	1,923	1,857	2,200	1,602
1982	1,902	1,785	2,153	n.a.
1983	2,052	1,946	2,168	n.a.
1984	2,163	2,019	2,220	n.a.

In 1977, hourly labor costs in Germany significantly exceeded those in Canada for the first time. By 1981, German labor costs were 38% above those in Canada. Over the period 1961 to 1984, hourly labor costs (in Canadian dollars) rose 571% in the United States, 505% in Canada, 1,725% in Germany (to 1981), and 2,813% in Japan!

Table 2.17 provides information on total labor costs as a percentage of total output (value of shipments) for the motor vehicle industry. In 1961, labor compensation amounted to 19% of total output in North America, 25.3% in Germany, and only 9.2% in Japan. Labor compensation as a percentage of total output (LCO) was 26.6% in the United States in 1980 (its peak), 35.1% in Germany, 16.7% in Canada, and 11.6% in Japan. In

Table 2.15. *Labor costs: wages plus fringe benefits (Canadian $/hour)*

Year	U.S.	Canada	Japan	Germany
1961	3.92	2.95	0.38	1.12
1962	4.29	2.99	0.47	1.34
1963	4.47	3.10	0.52	1.42
1964	4.75	3.26	0.57	1.53
1965	5.00	3.51	0.65	1.74
1966	5.32	3.69	0.70	1.89
1967	5.63	3.83	0.76	1.99
1968	5.89	4.28	0.91	2.03
1969	6.35	4.58	1.12	2.37
1970	6.65	5.08	1.25	2.57
1971	7.30	5.45	1.45	3.39
1972	7.68	5.75	1.86	4.14
1973	8.31	6.17	2.54	5.80
1974	9.20	7.10	3.10	6.47
1975	10.90	7.97	3.87	8.03
1976	11.41	9.10	4.09	8.10
1977	13.55	9.86	5.27	11.12
1978	16.15	11.00	8.21	13.95
1979	18.21	12.10	8.63	19.22
1980	22.02	13.43	8.51	22.72
1981	23.45	14.82	9.62	20.44
1982	25.11	16.33	9.54	n.a.
1983	25.03	16.60	10.50	n.a.
1984	26.29	17.84	11.07	n.a.

1984, LCO as a percentage of shipments fell to 20% in the United States, remained at 12% in Japan, and rose to 14% in Canada. What accounts for these differences, and why did LCO rise substantially in the United States and fall significantly in Canada?

The first reason for these LCO differences is that wage rates are relatively high in Germany but relatively low in Japan. Second, German auto producers make more expensive cars that include more labor content. Third, as discussed earlier, there are data problems concerning what is classified as being in the industry. For example, the definition of the motor vehicle industry in Germany includes the repair sector, a labor-intensive sector not included in industry data for the other three countries. The second phenomenon (relative changes in the United States and Canada)

Table 2.16. *Ratio of total compensation to wages*

Year	U.S.	Canada	Japan	Germany
1961	1.23	1.11	1.12	1.43
1962	1.25	1.11	1.12	1.43
1963	1.24	1.11	1.12	1.44
1964	1.25	1.11	1.12	1.43
1965	1.27	1.11	1.12	1.44
1966	1.30	1.13	1.12	1.45
1967	1.29	1.13	1.13	1.44
1968	1.29	1.14	1.13	1.44
1969	1.31	1.14	1.13	1.44
1970	1.34	1.15	1.13	1.48
1971	1.37	1.15	1.13	1.52
1972	1.37	1.15	1.13	1.56
1973	1.38	1.15	1.13	1.59
1974	1.42	1.17	1.13	1.63
1975	1.47	1.18	1.13	1.66
1976	1.45	1.18	1.14	1.71
1977	1.46	1.18	1.15	1.74
1978	1.49	1.19	1.18	1.76
1979	1.51	1.19	1.19	1.80
1980	1.63	1.19	1.16	1.83
1981	1.54	1.19	1.15	1.87
1982	1.55	1.19	1.17	1.89
1983	1.50	1.17	1.18	1.91
1984	1.49	1.19	1.16	1.92

is due to the rationalization of the Canadian industry in the years following the Auto Pact. This rationalization was characterized by increased use of semifinished materials in Canadian auto production.

2.4   Simple measures of productivity

Tables 2.18 and 2.19 show various measures of output per employee for use in making simple comparisons of productivity. (In Section 2.6 we provide more of these simple measures, based on the work of other researchers.) We emphasize the rudimentary nature of these comparisons, insofar as no accounting has been made of the differences in each country's outputs, relative factor prices, technology, use of other inputs (capital, materials), or capacity utilization.

Table 2.17. *Labor compensation as percentage of total value of shipments*

Year	U.S.	Canada	Japan	Germany[a]
1961	17.9	21.5	9.2	25.3
1962	16.7	19.2	9.3	25.2
1963	16.7	18.5	10.4	24.3
1964	18.1	19.2	10.0	23.7
1965	17.8	19.0	10.6	24.7
1966	19.2	18.8	10.7	24.9
1967	19.7	16.9	10.1	25.6
1968	19.3	16.5	10.0	23.8
1969	20.0	16.0	10.5	24.4
1970	22.4	17.9	10.4	22.8
1971	20.3	17.2	10.8	26.9
1972	21.4	17.6	11.5	27.8
1973	21.9	17.9	12.0	29.3
1974	23.1	17.8	12.8	32.1
1975	22.0	16.5	13.1	30.2
1976	20.9	16.8	13.0	27.5
1977	21.1	16.7	12.4	28.7
1978	21.6	16.1	12.4	27.1
1979	22.4	16.0	12.3	30.8
1980	26.6	16.7	11.6	35.1
1981	24.1	16.7	11.4	34.5
1982	23.1	15.5	11.9	n.a.
1983	20.1	14.2	12.0	n.a.
1984	20.0	14.0	11.8	n.a.

[a] Figures for Germany show compensation as percentage of total value of production and include vehicle repair sector.

Table 2.18 presents data on nominal output per employee. In 1961, output per worker in the United States was 63% greater than in Canada, 4 times that of Japanese workers and 5 times that of German workers. In 1970, nominal output per U.S. auto employee was only 6% above that of Canadian workers, more than twice that of Japanese workers, and 2.7 times that of workers in the German motor vehicle sector. In 1974, U.S. and Canadian nominal output per employee were equal, 50% above that of Japanese workers and 2.4 times that of German workers. In 1984, nominal output per U.S. auto worker was 20% above that of Canadian

Table 2.18. *Nominal output per employee*
(Canadian $/employee)

Year	U.S.	Canada	Japan	Germany[a]
1961	44,666	27,357	10,418	8,939
1962	54,642	32,824	11,945	10,378
1963	59,262	36,279	12,037	11,128
1964	57,202	35,620	13,758	12,459
1965	62,063	39,051	14,461	13,393
1966	58,828	39,863	15,450	14,268
1967	57,376	45,276	18,114	13,752
1968	66,438	53,839	21,373	15,983
1969	64,312	57,945	24,720	18,229
1970	58,644	55,103	27,730	21,495
1971	72,329	61,840	30,468	23,082
1972	75,126	66,440	36,529	26,325
1973	80,092	70,834	48,083	34,808
1974	78,627	78,736	52,017	33,160
1975	94,831	92,908	60,277	45,589
1976	112,386	101,014	66,587	50,950
1977	135,236	107,291	91,668	66,147
1978	153,779	122,577	140,624	85,632
1979	161,633	139,192	151,868	103,759
1980	155,646	144,182	162,548	103,740
1981	186,542	155,694	185,545	95,050
1982	205,899	176,850	172,923	n.a.
1983	256,692	218,553	189,337	n.a.
1984	285,298	238,247	209,291	n.a.

[a] Figures for Germany include the motor vehicle repair
sector.

workers, 36% above that of Japanese workers, and still double that of
German workers (1981 data).

This data seems to indicate that U.S. auto workers have provided the
most productive labor of the four countries examined, even in the depths
of the 1980–2 recession – an erroneous supposition. Nominal output per
employee is an unreliable indicator of relative efficiency, for various reasons. First, simple comparisons between Germany and the other three
countries must be dismissed because German data includes employees in
the motor vehicle repair industry. Second, such comparisons are affected
by differences in vertical integration, and may also be explained by the

Table 2.19. *Real output per employee (1971 Canadian $/employee)*

Year	U.S.	Canada	Japan	Germany
1961	57,665	44,929	n.a.	17,576
1962	65,774	52,758	n.a.	19,005
1963	70,675	54,291	n.a.	19,953
1964	67,331	57,867	n.a.	22,254
1965	72,488	58,944	n.a.	23,833
1966	68,213	63,333	n.a.	24,729
1967	65,602	74,344	20,901	23,693
1968	73,704	78,179	25,109	27,715
1969	70,010	74,978	29,336	37,336
1970	63,542	84,968	34,060	33,087
1971	76,582	85,651	37,462	32,779
1972	78,771	85,705	40,022	33,451
1973	82,094	85,652	45,918	35,041
1974	75,321	90,842	45,869	30,425
1975	77,507	110,408	49,993	35,071
1976	89,359	100,615	55,872	39,384
1977	92,989	95,444	64,415	42,036
1978	91,557	99,783	72,202	42,588
1979	86,558	118,120	78,902	43,966
1980	75,907	130,455	86,106	41,502
1981	77,537	130,553	91,133	44,211
1982	79,480	143,430	90,637	n.a.
1983	92,454	141,323	95,373	n.a.
1984	91,586	123,148	99,198	n.a.

differences described previously (factor prices, etc.). It is not nominal output per employee but rather levels and changes in total factor productivity that demonstrate relative efficiency. For example, the data in Table 2.18 suggests that workers in the Canadian motor vehicle industry are much more efficient than Japanese workers, a conclusion at sharp variance with reality (see Perry 1982).

In Table 2.19 we present a similar comparison, but one that uses real output (1971 Canadian dollars) per employee. The large increases in output per employee seen in nominal terms (Table 2.18) are not evident here, particularly for the United States. This data, moreover, wrongly indicates that Canadian workers were the most productive of all countries since 1969, producing nearly 25% more real output per employee in 1984 than the Japanese! Such naive comparisons ignore the amount of capital per

Table 2.20. *Price of materials (Canada
1971 = 100.0)*

Year	U.S.	Canada	Japan	Germany
1961	84.2	82.7	n.a.	81.6
1962	87.7	82.6	n.a.	86.5
1963	85.7	83.9	n.a.	88.1
1964	88.7	84.8	n.a.	88.8
1965	90.7	85.7	n.a.	90.0
1966	92.6	87.6	n.a.	91.5
1967	95.1	89.6	77.2	90.1
1968	97.8	92.6	75.8	89.2
1969	100.9	94.7	77.7	93.4
1970	101.9	98.0	79.0	102.9
1971	103.7	100.0	78.2	108.1
1972	106.0	101.3	88.4	117.9
1973	111.9	107.2	113.9	150.3
1974	127.2	117.2	137.8	171.2
1975	153.2	132.6	143.7	196.3
1976	158.5	145.8	146.8	193.0
1977	182.9	159.4	184.3	230.0
1978	211.9	178.2	255.2	290.0
1979	241.2	193.0	255.9	342.0
1980	265.3	217.6	275.3	364.2
1981	294.0	240.0	294.2	309.4
1982	311.0	256.7	267.9	n.a.
1983	317.4	262.3	281.7	n.a.
1984	343.5	280.7	297.5	n.a.

worker, the degree of vertical integration, or (conversely) the amount of materials used, and so yield calculations that are mathematically correct but hardly realistic.

2.5   Materials and capital

So far we have concentrated on labor. Tables 2.20 and 2.21 present data on the price of materials and capital services in the four countries. In 1971, materials used in automobile production were 3.7% more expensive in the United States than in Canada, 8% more expensive in Germany than in Canada, and 22% cheaper in Japan than in Canada. Materials used are largely semifinished components, as well as materials such as steel; the lower Japanese materials costs likely reflect the lower costs in

Table 2.21. *Price of capital services*

Year	U.S.	Canada	Japan	Germany
1961	0.56	0.38	n.a.	0.23
1962	0.66	0.39	n.a.	0.25
1963	0.72	0.40	n.a.	0.27
1964	0.76	0.41	n.a.	0.28
1965	0.82	0.43	n.a.	0.29
1966	0.81	0.48	n.a.	0.30
1967	0.73	0.53	0.44	0.30
1968	0.74	0.58	0.49	0.31
1969	0.62	0.63	0.51	0.33
1970	0.56	0.71	0.49	0.38
1971	0.60	0.76	0.47	0.41
1972	0.66	0.66	0.60	0.45
1973	0.64	0.69	0.59	0.56
1974	0.52	0.72	0.51	0.62
1975	0.61	0.92	0.62	0.73
1976	0.73	1.09	0.67	0.87
1977	0.90	1.15	0.74	1.05
1978	1.16	1.19	1.05	1.33
1979	1.39	1.32	1.18	1.75
1980	1.61	1.54	1.25	1.98
1981	1.69	1.94	1.35	1.87
1982	1.76	1.83	1.26	n.a.
1983	1.82	1.81	1.35	n.a.
1984	1.94	2.13	1.45	n.a.

Note: Figures in this table are computed as user costs of capital services. See Chapter 4 for details of computation.

Japan of constructing these semifinished components rather than a lower cost in Japan of raw materials per se.

In 1981, materials were 22% more expensive in the United States and Japan than in Canada, and 29% more expensive in Germany than in Canada. To what do we attribute this Canadian advantage in materials costs? The "advantage" is explained by the devaluation of the Canadian dollar against the U.S. dollar, the yen, and the deutsche mark. If we set the 1971 Canadian dollar at 100 relative to the U.S. dollar, yen, and deutsche mark, then in 1980 the Canadian dollar was at 86 relative to the U.S. dollar, 56 relative to the yen, and 45 relative to the deutsche mark (see Tables 2.22 and 2.23 for exchange rates).

Table 2.22. *Actual exchange rates*

Year	U.S. / Can.$	Yen / Can.$	Mark / Can.$	Yen / U.S.$	Yen / Mark	Mark / U.S.$
1961	0.987	355	3.967	360	90	4.018
1962	0.935	337	3.740	360	90	4.000
1963	0.927	334	3.694	360	90	3.986
1964	0.927	334	3.684	360	91	3.975
1965	0.928	334	3.705	360	90	3.994
1966	0.929	336	3.712	362	91	3.999
1967	0.927	336	3.694	362	91	3.986
1968	0.929	335	3.707	360	90	3.992
1969	0.929	333	3.645	358	91	3.925
1970	0.958	343	3.493	358	98	3.647
1971	0.990	344	3.448	347	100	3.482
1972	1.009	306	3.218	303	95	3.189
1973	1.000	271	2.673	271	101	2.673
1974	1.022	298	2.646	292	113	2.588
1975	0.983	292	2.419	297	121	2.460
1976	1.014	301	2.554	296	118	2.518
1977	0.941	251	2.185	267	115	2.322
1978	0.876	182	1.760	208	104	2.009
1979	0.854	186	1.565	218	119	1.833
1980	0.855	193	1.555	225	124	1.818
1981	0.834	183	1.879	220	98	2.252
1982	0.810	201	1.965	248	102	2.424
1983	0.812	193	2.070	237	93	2.551
1984	0.772	183	2.193	237	84	2.840

The index of prices for capital services is given in Table 2.21.[8] Capital service prices in Japan were lower than those in the United States throughout the period 1961–84. Canadian capital service prices were considerably lower than U.S. prices in the early 1960s, but have generally exceeded U.S. prices since 1970. Capital costs in Germany were low relative to the other three countries until 1974; in 1978 capital costs in Germany exceeded those in Canada.

Tables 2.22 and 2.23 present data on exchange rates. Actual exchange rates as well as Fundamental Equilibrium Exchange Rates (FEER) are shown. The latter are derived from Williamson (1985) and represent fundamental purchasing power parity. The differences between actual rates

[8] See Chapter 4 for the construction of this variable.

Table 2.23. *Fundamental Equilibrium Exchange Rates (FEER)*

Year	U.S. Can.$	Yen Can.$	Mark Can.$	Yen U.S.$	Yen Mark	Mark U.S.$
1977	0.93	219	1.942	236	113	2.088
1978	0.90	195	1.850	217	106	2.056
1979	0.88	186	1.720	210	107	1.954
1980	0.89	189	1.638	212	115	1.840
1981	0.88	183	1.611	207	113	1.831
1982	0.86	177		205		
1983	0.84	169		201		
1984	0.82	160		195		

and FEER are substantial, and these differences play an important part in explaining what has occurred in the motor vehicle industries of these four countries.

2.6   International differences in productivity and wages in the automobile industry: the 1950s to the 1980s

2.6.1   *The 1950s and 1960s*

In the previous section we developed simple aggregate productivity measures for motor vehicle production in the four countries. We concluded that these simple measures were misleading. In this section we examine attempts by other researchers to measure productivity in the automobile industry.

It is clear that the Japanese advantage in the production of automobiles and other manufactured goods is a relatively new phenomenon. Some twenty or thirty years ago, manufacturing productivity in Japan was lower than in most Western industrialized countries.

Bain (1966) examined, among other industries, the average size (in terms of number of employees) of the twenty largest plants in the motor vehicles and parts industries in each of seven countries – United Kingdom, France, Japan, Italy, Canada, India, and Sweden – relative to the United States.[9]

---

[9] The average size of the 20 largest plants in the United States was considered as the base, and the average size of the 20 largest plants in the other countries was computed relative to that base.

Table 2.24. *Summary of automobile industry unit-cost comparisons index, 1974 (U.S. cost=1.000)*

Country	Unit cost			
	Labor	Other value added	Inputs from other sectors	Weighted average
Japan	0.423	1.000	1.089	0.832
Germany	0.812	1.000	1.288	1.093

Source: Toder et al. (1978).

Automotive plants in the United Kingdom were, on average, 48% of the size of U.S. plants, and Japanese and Canadian auto plants were much smaller – only 17–18% of the U.S. average size. For all thirty-four industries examined, the average size of the twenty largest Japanese manufacturing plants was 34% of comparable U.S. plants; because Japanese automotive plants were only 18% the size of comparable U.S. plants, Japan's automobile industry in the 1950s was a particularly small-scale one. Thus, most Japanese manufacturing (and the Japanese motor vehicles industry in particular) faced large scale and productivity disadvantages when compared to U.S. manufacturing in the mid- to late 1950s.

With respect to Canada, for all thirty-four industries the average plant size was 28% of those in the United States. Hence for Canada as well, the automobile industry was small-scale.

2.6.2 The 1970s and 1980s

In the 1970s, as Japanese auto producers expanded, a number of studies examined the labor and total factor productivity differences among U.S., Canadian, German, and Japanese automotive industries. In contrast with studies of the previous decade, these studies showed large advantages of Japanese producers.

Tables 2.24 and 2.25 present (respectively) comparisons of total unit cost and unit labor cost for 1974, based on a study by Toder, Cordell, and Burton (1978). That study indicated that the Japanese automotive industry in 1974 had a 17% lower unit production cost than did U.S. automobile producers.[10] Based on this analysis, Toder et al. concluded

[10] As detailed later (Chapter 7), we calculate that in 1974 the Japanese automobile industry had a unit cost advantage of 13%, reasonably close to Toder's estimate. Our detailed

Table 2.25. *Summary of relative unit-labor cost computations, 1974*

Country	Local compensation per hour (U.S.\$)	U.S. compensation per hour (U.S.\$)	Relative hourly compensation	Relative productivity index	Relative labor cost[a]
Japan	3.10	8.34	0.372	0.880	0.423
Germany	6.70	8.34	0.803	0.989	0.812

[a] Relative labor cost = (relative hourly compensation)/(relative productivity index).
Source: Toder et al. (1978).

that the U.S. automotive industry was in severe difficulty, facing a Japanese comparative advantage. For 1974 Toder et al. also estimated that German auto producers had a 9% unit cost disadvantage compared to U.S. auto producers, resulting from the combination of a German unit labor cost advantage (lower labor compensation but similar productivity) and a large U.S. unit-cost disadvantage in capital and materials.[11]

Table 2.26 summarizes a major automotive industry study (Abernathy, Harbour, and Henn 1981) of the amount and source of unit cost differences between the United States and Japan. Abernathy et al. concluded that in 1979 Japanese auto makers had a near $1600 total landed cost advantage over U.S. producers. This advantage was due mainly to labor cost differences, since the authors concluded that the Japanese auto producers had a disadvantage for other inputs. Using a plant-by-plant comparison, Abernathy et al. estimated that in 1979 the Japanese automotive industry required 80.3 man hours to produce a vehicle, while the U.S. industry required some 144 hours to produce a similar vehicle.

In a study by Perry (1982) these 1979 estimates were adjusted to a 1980 basis, arriving at a one-year 33% increase in output per man day in Japan compared to a 1.5% increase in the United States. A 33% measured increase in labor productivity in one year is probably erroneous, as indeed are any comparisons of labor productivity between the United States and Japan in 1980. In that year, the Japanese automotive industry utilized over 88% of potential capacity while the U.S. industry operated at only 54% of capacity. This enormous difference in capacity utilization suggests that measured labor productivity in 1980 reflects short-run disequilibria more than any fundamental differences in efficiency between the two countries' automotive industries. Perry arrived at estimates of unit production costs for 1981 by assuming no change in labor productivity between 1980 and 1981. Again, these measures are unlikely to reflect real long-run efficiency differentials.

Perry applied these statistics to determine the advantage of the Japanese automotive manufacturers as compared to Canadian producers, assuming that: (1) producing a car required 53 man hours in Japan (80.3 hours calculated by Abernathy et al. (1981) for Japan in 1979, adjusted downward by the 33% assumed improvement for Japan in 1980); and (2) Canadian production was as inefficient as U.S. production, requiring

results substantiate two important assumptions made by Toder: that in 1974 (1) producers in Japan and the United States were approximately equally efficient, and (2) producers in the two countries had equal costs of capital services.

[11] Our estimate of the German disadvantage in 1974 is 4% (see Chapter 7).

Table 2.26. *Comparative costs and labor productivity in selected U.S. and Japanese automobile companies*

	Ford	GM	Toyo Kogyo	Nissan
Labor productivity[a]				
Employee hours per small car	84	83	53	51
Costs per small car ($)				
Labor	1,848	1,826	620	593
Purchased components[b] and material	3,650	3,405	2,858	2,858
Other manufacturing costs[c]	650	730	350	350
Nonmanufacturing costs[d]	350	325	1,100	1,200
Total	6,498	6,286	4,928	5,001

Note: Nonmanufacturing costs include the costs of ocean freight (for Japanese producers), as well as selling and administrative expenses. Other manufacturing costs include costs of warranty, capital costs, energy costs, and miscellaneous items like insurance.

[a] U.S. figures were based on 1979 annual reports on number of domestic workers, multiplied by average hours worked per person; total hours worked were divided by domestic production. Figures for GM were adjusted for higher vertical integration (value-added/sales = 0.54) by multiplying total hours by 0.4/0.54. Hours per car size were estimated using 1974 data (corrected to 1979 costs) on relative costs of different sized cars (see Toder et al. 1978); product-mix statistics were used to derive hours per car.

[b] U.S. figures reflect data from company reports adjusted for vertical integration (see previous note) and corrected for product mix (index 1.00 = small, 1.35 = medium, 1.71 = large). Figures for Japan are from Anderson (1981); 1978 data for Nissan was valued at exchange rate of 220 yen = $1 U.S.

[c] Includes energy costs, depreciation, warranty costs, and miscellaneous costs. Energy costs in the United States were assumed to be $150 per car. For Nissan, data was obtained from Anderson (1981) and Harbour (1980).

[d] Includes shipping, marketing, and distribution. Japanese figures reflect the assertion that "most Wall Street analysts and industry executives cite a figure of $400 for the costs added to a Japanese car by ocean freight and U.S. tariffs" (AHH 1981, p. 139).

Source: Abernathy, Harbour, and Henn (1981).

142 man hours to produce a vehicle identical to that produced in Japan. Assuming that Canadian content represented 60% of the Canadian vehicle (a value that is actually too low), Perry used a weighted average of Canadian and U.S. labor rates to arrive at his estimate of labor productivity differences between Japan and Canada. From these comparisons

he made both policy recommendations and forecasts, stating that either wages in the Canadian automotive industry would have to fall some 67% relative to wages in Japan, or that imports would rise to some 50% of Canadian automobile sales. Such forecasts and policy recommendations are almost certainly unwarranted, given the very rough, short-run, and economically suspect measurement techniques used by Perry.

2.6.3 *Abernathy, Harbour, and Henn (1981) and Abernathy, Clark, and Kantrow (1983)*

In 1981 Abernathy, Harbour, and Henn (AHH) estimated total costs from company financial statements. They estimated real labor costs by actually observing auto production and assembly, counting the labor hours required to produce a small car in the United States and Japan.

Consider first the computation of real labor costs. Because cars made in Japan were smaller than those made in the United States, the total "actual" observed labor hours of the U.S. automotive producers were reduced 15% by AHH to account for this difference in size. This correction is arbitrary and unsubstantiated. Similarly, materials costs for production in the United States were arbitrarily reduced by 40% to render the U.S. data comparable to the output mix of Japanese automotive producers. These are unlikely to be accurate means of accounting for different outputs, output mix, and size of cars in the two countries. Producers also differ in their degrees of vertical integration, which obviously affects the measured hours required to produce a car in an assembly plant. The adjustments made by AHH for vertical integration are also arbitrary. For example, General Motors' costs were lowered to reflect the difference between its ratio of value-added : sales and the average value-added : sales ratio for all other firms (because GM's degree of vertical integration is higher than other producers). It is not obvious that this type of correction is adequate to account for differences in vertical integration. Finally, the reported labor costs for Japanese producers were increased by an arbitrary 15% (to make the results "conservative," the authors claim).

The Federal Trade Commission (FTC) report (1984) on the GM–Toyota joint venture in Fremont, California, suggested that the AHH unit-cost estimates (based on company annual reports of financial data) were severely overstated for the U.S. firms. The FTC claimed that certain errors were made in using data from these annual reports; for example, AHH included all production costs for auto producers – including those for

Table 2.27. *Cost comparisons, adjusted to 1979 and actual product mix*

Cost	Ford	GM
Labor[a]	$1,887	$1,879
Materials	4,748	4,654
Other manufacturing costs and nonmanufacturing costs (Abernathy 1978)	630	691
	$7,265	$7,224

[a] The 1979 unit labor cost was calculated by adjusting ACK's estimate for 1981 by the FTC's (1984, p. 804) estimates of wage rates for 1979 and 1981 ($13.68 and $17.55, respectively). *Source:* Abernathy, Clark, and Kantrow (1983).

replacement parts and interarea sales – in the numerator (total costs), while the denominator contained only the output of cars produced in the United States. The result is an overstatement of the unit costs of production in the United States.

In 1983 Abernathy, Clark, and Kantrow (ACK) extended the earlier AHH analysis of automobile industries in the United States and Japan. The ACK study concluded that, for 1981 also, the Japanese cost advantage was on the order of $1,500. Most of the ACK analysis used numbers calculated for 1979 and extrapolated to 1981. The authors used 1979 data "because 1979 was the most recent year during which the U.S. producers enjoyed levels of capacity utilization comparable to those of the Japanese" (ACK 1983, p. 62).

This 1983 study is subject to many of the same criticisms as the 1981 AHH study; for example, U.S. unit production costs appear to be overstated, as the following simple exercise shows. Table 2.27 presents the 1979 operating costs per automobile for Ford and GM for the actual mix of automobiles produced, as estimated by ACK; these costs were $7,265 and $7,224, respectively. At the average wholesale price in 1979 of approximately $6,000 per car, Ford and GM would have had operating losses of about $1,200 per car; this result is not inconsistent with the facts. In 1979 Ford and GM reported per-share earnings of $9.75 and $10.04, respectively (FTC 1984, p. 187). Clearly, the methodology used by Abernathy

and his co-researchers yields costs per automobile for American manufacturers in 1979 that are too high.

2.6.4 *The Federal Trade Commission (1984) analysis*

In 1984, the Federal Trade Commission also estimated a Japanese cost
advantage in auto production of $1,500–$2,000, this time for 1983, based
primarily on its Bureau of Economics staff research (FTC 1984, Appendix B). The FTC criticized the AHH approach and findings, but its own
analysis is also subject to criticism. The FTC estimated 1980 relative costs
by using data from the Annual Survey of Manufacturers for the United
States and from Japanese auto company reports. This raw data was then
adjusted for output mix by using relative vehicle weights. Freight, tariffs,
and exchange values were then added. The FTC's 1983 estimates were
obtained by projecting a 1980 estimate to December 1983, adjusting only
the relative exchange rates between the two periods (1980: $1 U.S. = 212
yen; 1983: $1 U.S. = 240 yen). This simplistic approach cannot provide a
reasonable estimate of 1983 unit-cost differentials. As we have shown, one
important reason is that the U.S. automobile industry was operating at
50–60% of capacity in 1980, whereas capacity utilization had increased
to approximately 80% in 1983. Japanese auto producers utilized approximately 90% of capacity during the entire 1980–3 period. The relative
increase in capacity utilization for American firms would by itself narrow
the Japanese cost advantage.

The FTC also calculated the Japanese cost advantage for 1979 and
1980; this calculated advantage is reproduced as Table 2.28. The FTC's
differentiating between "strict" and "liberal" weights is an attempt to adjust the output mix in the two countries to reflect the relative weight of
the cars produced: Strict weights adjust unit costs for the actual weight
differences in production; liberal weights assume that Japanese and American cars of the same category (subcompacts and compacts) were comparable in the eyes of consumers, even though the Japanese cars weighed
less (FTC 1984, p. 793). The liberal weighting scheme results in a larger
Japanese cost advantage.

It is important to note that, according to the FTC analysis, in 1979
only Toyota (strict and liberal weights) and Honda (liberal weights) had
a landed cost advantage over U.S. producers. Even these estimated advantages are low compared with the AHH estimates for the same year.
The FTC's estimates for 1980 show a substantial widening of the Japanese

Table 2.28. *Comparative Japanese and U.S. costs,*
1979–80 (212 yen = $1 U.S.)

Company	Strict weights		Liberal weights	
	1979	1980	1979	1980
Unit costs ($)				
Toyota	5,504	5,776	4,882	5,122
Datsun	6,632	6,912	5,756	5,953
Honda	6,934	6,903	5,625	5,596
U.S. average	5,743	6,893	5,743	6,893
Cost difference				
Toyota	−239	−1,117	−861	−1,771
Datsun	+889	+19	+13	−940
Honda	+1,119	+10	−118	−1,297

Source: FTC (1984), table B, p. 796.

advantage, particularly when using liberal weights. The FTC (1984, p. 800) attributes this widening to three effects:

(1) depreciation of the yen,
(2) recession in the U.S. auto industry (underutilization of capacity), and
(3) relative increase in U.S. labor costs due to increased relative wage rates and declining relative labor productivity.

The depreciation of the yen and an increased relative wage-rate differential are not, however, efficiency-related effects. Capacity utilization and labor productivity differentials are efficiency related, but accrue from different sources: The efficiency disadvantage due to differential capacity utilization rates is a short-term effect caused mainly by final product design differences, whereas unit-cost increases resulting from underutilization of production capacity stem from the existence of quasi-fixed factors. The 1980 cost increases for U.S. manufacturers are attributable to insufficient consumer demand for the American product, which in turn was a consequence of the recession and of the fact that U.S. producers were not designing automobiles favored by consumers. The cost increases due to economic recession are reversible, independent of Japanese competition, as evidenced by the U.S. auto industry's 1983–4 recovery. We contend that the design problems of U.S. producers should not be conflated with production-cost problems.

The supposed increase in Japan's labor productivity advantage from 1979 to 1980 is also due primarily to capacity utilization effects. Recall that overhead labor is a quasi-fixed factor of production. Labor productivity in the U.S. automobile industry fell by 6.4% in 1979–80 while Japan's labor productivity increased by 3.5% (FTC 1984, pp. 801, 802).[12] If there were no long-run labor productivity changes in U.S. auto production in 1979–80, then the 6.4% decrease in measured labor productivity can be attributed to underutilization of capacity. If the FTC's 3.5% estimate is in fact a long-run Japanese efficiency improvement; if wages did not increase in Japan from 1979 to 1980; and if the average car cost $5,000 to produce in Japan, where labor costs are 30% of total costs; then labor productivity improvements increased Japan's long-run cost advantage by only $53 between 1979 and 1980. This number is far below the FTC's estimated change in the Japanese cost advantage between those two years.

2.6.5   *Summary*

The studies examined in this section all place the Japanese cost advantage at $1,500–$2,000, so it appears that they are in general agreement. But this is not the case; the studies are mutually contradictory in their details, so the apparently common bottom line is accidental. Our discussion indicates that these studies sometimes relied on erroneous data and sometimes included short-run dislocations as part of productivity differentials.

There is then a great confusion concerning three issues. First, what is the cost differential between Japanese and U.S. auto producers? Second, what are productivity differentials (i.e., differences in efficiency) as opposed to price differentials (e.g., differences or changes in relative wage rates or changes in the yen/dollar ratio)? Third, what are short-run dislocations as opposed to long-run movements? Clearly, public policy must be designed differently to deal with price effects as opposed to productivity differentials, and short-run disruptions as opposed to long-run competitive advantage.

We now turn to our own analysis of the possible sources of the Japanese cost advantage – remembering that differences in costs reflect not only differences in both input prices and input use (productivity), but short-run and long-run effects as well.

---

[12] Compare this to Perry's 33% estimated improvement in labor productivity between these two years.

2.7   Possible sources of the Japanese cost advantage in automobile production

We present, in general terms, twelve possible sources of the Japanese cost advantage. The first eight follow from our discussions in Chapter 1; the other four have been discussed generally in the literature. The possible sources of cost differences include:

  (1)   lower per-unit cost of labor,
  (2)   more efficient use of labor,
  (3)   lower per-unit material cost,
  (4)   more efficient use of materials,
  (5)   lower per-unit cost of capital services,
  (6)   more efficient use of capital,
  (7)   greater use of existing capacity,
  (8)   undervalued currency,
  (9)   more favorable tax treatment,
 (10)   higher economies of scale in producing small automobiles,
 (11)   higher tariff and ocean transportation costs, and
 (12)   higher selling and administrative costs.

(1) *Lower per-unit cost of labor:*   Japanese manufacturers clearly have a wage rate cost advantage. However, authors disagree as to the price of labor in Japan and the United States; Table 2.29 displays various estimates. Compensation estimated by the FTC probably does not include all fringe benefits. Abernathy, Clark, and Kantrow (1983) considered all fringe benefits, including subsidization of housing in Japan; they obtained 1981 hourly wage rates of $20.00 for the United States and $11.28 for Japan, a difference of $8.72 per hour. The exchange rate used by ACK was $1 U.S. = 220 yen. In contrast, the FTC's estimated labor costs were $17.55 and $7.74, respectively; our data (Table 2.15) shows labor costs of $23.45 and $9.62, respectively. Japanese wage rates as a percentage of U.S. wage rates, based on our estimates in Table 2.15, are presented in column (5) of Table 2.29. The differences in relative wage rates are not large; the larger absolute levels in our data are likely due to the Bureau of Labor Statistics including all fringe benefits and other compensation in their estimates.

(2) *More efficient use of labor:*   The studies analyzed in Section 2.6 used "relative labor productivity" or "relative labor input" per car to measure

Table 2.29. *Hourly compensation in motor vehicles and equipment industry*

Year	FTC estimates			Our estimates
	U.S. ($/hr) (2)	Japan ($/hr) (3)	Japan as % of U.S. (4)	Japan as % of U.S. (5)
1967	4.58	0.69	15	13
1970	5.65	1.14	20	19
1973	7.51	2.54	34	31
1976	10.27	4.02	39	39
1977	11.45	4.82	42	39
1978	12.67	6.85	54	51
1979	13.68	6.90	50	47
1980	16.31	6.89	42	39
1981	17.55	7.74	44	41

Sources: Columns (2)–(4), FTC (1984, p. 804), listing Bureau of Labor Statistics (BLS) unpublished data; column (5) from Table 2.15, including fringe payments from BLS unpublished statistics.

relative labor efficiency. As we have emphasized, these are not the same thing!

Relative labor efficiency should be measured as the labor input per unit output, when all other factors affecting input use are held constant across the comparison. These factors, as we have shown, include input prices, capacity utilization, output mix, and the degree of vertical integration. Most studies attempt (with varying degrees of success) to control for the output mix by concentrating on small cars. Both AHH and ACK use an arbitrary scaling factor to adjust for vertical integration. Capacity utilization is a particularly crucial issue for 1980, 1981, and 1982 comparisons, because U.S. capacity was substantially underutilized during those years. Capacity utilization problems are mitigated in most of these studies by concentrating data for 1979, when capacity underutilization was not a severe problem in the U.S. auto industry.

Estimates of labor input required to manufacture a small car are not very consistent, as Table 2.30 shows. All of these estimates suggest that the Japanese have a substantial labor productivity advantage. However,

Table 2.30. *Estimated manufacturing time (hours)*

Source	U.S.	Japan
AHH (1981)	74.3	38.6
ACK (1983)	83.5	52
ACK (1983) revised[a]	65.7	41

[a] Revised by Fuss and Waverman so that ACK's estimates of U.S. costs in 1979 correspond to the actual costs in 1979. See Section 2.9.

there is no way to verify the results since they tend to be based on "personal impressions" and "discussions with industry personnel" (FTC 1984, pp. 770, 773). It is very difficult to subject estimates that are based on impressions and confidential data to scrutiny and verification; this makes such estimates unreliable.

(3)–(6) *Input costs (other than labor):* None of the studies of the Japanese cost advantage separate the costs of materials and capital into their two components: differences in unit costs and differences in technical efficiencies. There is some nonquantitative evidence that the Japanese automotive industry is more efficient in materials usage ("just-in-time" supply system) and operates smaller plants than its North American counterpart. By ACK's estimate, in 1981 Japanese auto producers had a per-vehicle advantage of $600–$800 in materials costs and $300–$400 in capital costs when compared to U.S. auto producers. These measured advantages are, however, based on relatively flimsy data.

(7) *Greater use of existing capacity:* All the relative cost estimates are computed for the period 1979–81, when the Japanese enjoyed a capacity utilization advantage; this advantage was especially pronounced in 1980 and 1981. Estimated capacity utilization rates are given in Table 2.31.

Ignoring capacity utilization effects while using 1980 and 1981 data will greatly overstate the current Japanese cost advantage, since U.S. producers are now operating at much higher levels of capacity utilization. Cost comparisons based on 1979 data suffer less from this defect; these include the FTC (1984) 1979 comparisons and ACK (1983), but not the FTC 1980 comparison. Recall that even though underutilization of capacity

Table 2.31. *Capacity utilization rates (%)*

Year	Japan	U.S.
1979	0.98	0.84
1980	1.01	0.62
1981	1.00	0.63
1982	0.95	0.58
1983	0.95	0.77
1984	0.96	0.90

Note: Constructed by the authors. These rates have been normalized so that the average utilization rate for Japan during 1969–80 is 1.00.

does increase per-unit cost, we argue that this does not imply a Japanese efficiency advantage that should be considered in an evaluation of the long-run Japanese cost advantage.

(8) *Undervalued currency:* Cost differences are influenced to a large extent by exchange rates. Many observers argue that the U.S. (and Canadian) currency were for a number of years substantially overvalued relative to European and Japanese currencies. The large and rapid relative decline of the U.S. and Canadian currencies vis-à-vis Japan and Europe (except Britain) since September 1984 may add credence to this overvaluation argument. If the Japanese currency was undervalued in some years, then part of the measured cost difference can be attributed to the undervalued yen. Williamson (1983) has estimated a Japanese–U.S. FEER for 1983 based on the doctrine of purchasing power parity (for the data, see Table 2.23). Table 2.32 provides an example of the effect of an undervalued yen on cost comparisons. From this table, it can be seen that if there were no net advantages to Japanese automobile producers other than a fundamentally undervalued currency, in December 1983 they would have incurred per-unit production costs $854 lower than if the yen/dollar ratio had been at its fundamental equilibrium level.

(9) *Favorable tax treatment:* Ford and Chrysler have argued that the different tax systems in the United States and Japan give the Japanese auto producers a cost advantage. The Japanese government relies on an

Table 2.32. *Effects of undervalued yen*

Year	Exchange rate (yen/dollar)	Equilibrium exchange rate[a] (yen/dollar)	Cost advantage attributed to undervalued yen[b]
1979	218	210	$190
1980	226	212	330
1981	220	207	314
1983[c]	240	205	854

[a] Calculated using Williamson's FEER for 1983 and relative U.S.-Japan inflation rates as measured by the Wholesale Price Index.
[b] Assuming that Japanese car production cost is $5,000 (U.S.) at actual exchange rate, and that no costs are denominated in U.S. dollars. According to industry sources, about 15% of Japanese material costs are denominated in U.S. dollars; that complication is ignored here, but not in our econometric analysis (see Chapter 7).
[c] December.

auto sales tax to raise revenue, but this tax of 17.5% on small cars is rebated for exported cars. The U.S. government, on the other hand, relies more on income and employment (social security) taxes, which have the effect of raising input prices. To the extent this is true, a portion of any tax advantage is already captured in higher U.S. relative input prices that are part of the Japanese cost advantage. It is not a separate effect, but could in principle be disentangled from input-price effects.

(10) *Scale economies:*   Scale economies would help explain cost differentials if U.S. producers were not at minimum efficient scale while Japanese producers were. This is unlikely, as we discuss in detail in our empirical findings (see Chapter 5).

(11) *Tariff and ocean transportation:*   The U.S. tariff on imports of passenger cars from Japan was 2.9% in 1980. This tariff, combined with ocean transportation costs, added about $400–$450 to Japanese costs, according to most studies. Tariff and ocean transportation charges are thus costs that Japanese (but not U.S.) firms must bear on sales in the U.S. market.

(12) *Selling and administrative costs:*   Most studies estimate that Japanese producers have higher per-unit selling and administrative costs than

do U.S. producers (see ACK 1983, pp. 61–2). The reasons are not well documented, but may be due to economies of scale in advertising and the fact that some labor costs (such as housing subsidies) may be buried in administrative expenses.

As the preceding brief discussion of these twelve cost elements suggests, the case for substantial Japanese cost and productivity advantages over U.S. producers is not well established. In addition, the disentanglement of price versus technical efficiency elements, as well as short-run aberrations versus longer-run equilibrium levels, is often missing.

Despite our reservations about studies of U.S.–Japan cost and productivity comparisons based on data found in company annual reports, in Section 2.9 we provide a set of such estimates. Our methodology is to combine the most sensible features of the studies just discussed with data collected for our econometric analysis. For the reasons enumerated previously, we do not expect our results to be very accurate; however, they should provide a basis for evaluating the reasonableness of the econometric results presented in Chapter 7.

2.8 Estimates of the Japanese cost advantage based on company annual reports

We believe that the most conceptually consistent previous study of the Japanese cost advantage is ACK (1983). However, as noted earlier, the major problem with their estimates is the double counting of data in the calculation of U.S. costs. In the calculations that follow, we have corrected for this problem by forcing the total Ford and GM costs for an average-size automobile to equal $6,118 in 1979, which is our revision of the FTC (1984) unit-cost estimates for an average U.S. car produced in 1979.

The FTC estimated 1979 average U.S. unit production cost to be $5,743, excluding equity costs. We estimated equity costs as follows: ACK (1983, p. 63) gave the book value of equity for Ford and GM. Hunker (1983) estimated the percentage of financial capital in equity for GM, Ford, and Chrysler. Assuming that all non-GM production can be characterized by the level of financial capital per car for Ford, and assuming a 15% cost of equity capital, we arrive at an average per-car U.S. equity cost of $375 in 1979. We can obtain ACK's implied Ford and GM unit production cost for average-size cars in 1979 by reversing the procedures described by ACK (1983, Appendix B), who calculated small-car unit costs in 1981

Table 2.33. *Comparative costs and labor productivity in selected U.S. and Japanese automobile companies, 1979 (small cars only)*

	Ford	GM	Toyo Kogyo	Nissan
Labor productivity				
Employee hours per small car	67[a]	67[a]	46[b]	43[b]
Costs per small car ($)				
Labor[c]	1,220	1,220	397	371
Purchased materials	2,752	2,600	2,719	2,719
Other manufacturing and nonmanufacturing costs	669	698	876	959
Equity costs	326	242	79	157
Total	4,967	4,760	4,071	4,206

Note: Exchange rate used is 218 yen = $1 U.S.
[a] Calculated by dividing labor costs by an estimate of unit labor costs from our data base.
[b] These numbers differ from the entries in ACK, because we adjusted their estimates to reflect Japanese production of some cars that were not small.
[c] Calculated by multiplying the employee hours per car by an estimate of unit labor costs from our data base.

from 1979 data on costs for average-size cars. The implied 1979 unit costs (including equity costs) are $7,672 and $7,523 for Ford and GM respectively; our revision of the FTC's 1979 unit production cost estimate ($6,118) is 80% and 81% of these values. We therefore multiplied ACK's implied 1979 estimates for each cost category for Ford and GM by 0.80 and 0.81, respectively. Table 2.33 contains our version (for 1979) of Table 5.2 of ACK (1983, p. 61).

We calculated 1981 cost estimates for Ford and GM by taking these revised 1979 estimates and adjusting the individual components to 1981. For the price of labor, we referred to our data base (see Chapter 4). For the cost of materials and other manufacturing and nonmanufacturing costs, we applied the rate of increase of the materials price index, 1979–81, taken from our data base. The same procedure was applied to equity costs, referring to our data on the user cost of capital. Finally, we reduced unit cost 1% per year for the United States and 4% per year for Japan, reflecting our econometric estimates of cost efficiency gains over the period

Table 2.34. *Comparative costs and labor productivity in selected U.S. and Japanese automobile companies, 1981 (small cars only)*

	Ford	GM	Toyo Kogyo	Nissan
Labor productivity				
Employee hours per small car	65.7	65.7	42.4	39.6
Costs per small car ($)				
Labor	1,540	1,540	408	382
Purchased materials	3,288	3,107	2,880	2,880
Other manufacturing and nonmanufacturing costs	799	834	929	1,017
Equity costs	388	349	84	165
Total	6,015	5,830	4,300	4,444

Note: Exchange rate used is 218 yen = $1 U.S.

1979–81. Table 2.34 contains our 1981 estimates of U.S. and Japanese production costs.

From Table 2.33, the estimated Japanese production cost advantage in 1979 ranges from a high of $896 (Ford–Toyo Kogyo) to a low of $554 (GM–Nissan). Using ACK's estimate of $400 for tariff and transportation costs, the U.S. landed cost disadvantage is in the range ($496, $154). By contrast, ACK's implied 1979 estimate is in the range ($1,159, $886). From Table 2.34, the estimated Japanese cost advantage in 1981 ranges from a high of $1,715 to a lower of $1,386, implying a U.S. landed cost disadvantage in the range ($1,315, $986); ACK's estimate for the 1981 cost disadvantage is in the range ($1,570, $1,285).[13]

These results indicate that ACK's implied 1979 estimates of the Japanese cost advantage are overstated. However, their 1981 estimates are fairly close to both the estimates we have calculated here and the econometric estimates presented in Chapter 7. This convergence of results for 1981 occurs because, although ACK start from too high an advantage in 1979, they underestimate the Japanese relative improvement over the period 1979–81 in both the factor-price and efficiency dimensions.

---

[13] Our estimate of the production cost advantage is in the range (40%, 31%); ACK's is (44%, 37%). The econometric estimate for motor vehicles is 31%.

Table 2.35. *Decomposition of 1981 Japanese production cost advantage, Ford–Toyo Kogyo*

Cost advantage (to Toyo Kogyo)	$1,715
Labor productivity effect (computed at average wage)	392
Wage effect (computed at average hours)	715
Purchased materials	227
Other manufacturing costs and nonmanufacturing costs	−187
Equity costs	298
Undervalued yen	270

We can decompose our estimate of the 1981 Japanese production cost advantage to arrive at an estimate of labor productivity differences. In Table 2.35 we disaggregate the highest cost differential (Ford–Toyo Kogyo) given in Table 2.34. The calculations yielding the cost differentials for purchased materials, other manufacturing and nonmanufacturing costs, and equity costs are transparent: these are simply the differences between the separate values for each component as given in Table 2.34, adjusted to a (FEER) yen : dollar ratio of 207 : 1 rather than the actual ratio of 220 : 1. The exchange rate effect is computed as the difference between total cost ($1,715) and the sum of the cost categories valued at $1 U.S. = 207 yen. To derive the labor productivity and wage effect components separately, we make the following calculation. The difference between the total wage bills $(P_L \cdot L)$ in Japan and the United States, at the actual yen : dollar ratio, can be decomposed as follows:

$$(P_L \cdot L) = \tfrac{1}{2}(P_{LU} + P_{LJ}) \cdot (L_U - L_J) + \tfrac{1}{2}(L_U + L_J) \cdot (P_{LU} - P_{LJ}), \qquad (2.1)$$

$$\underbrace{\phantom{(P_L \cdot L) = \tfrac{1}{2}(P_{LU} + P_{LJ}) \cdot (L_U - L_J)}}_{\text{[labor productivity advantage]}} \quad \underbrace{\phantom{+ \tfrac{1}{2}(L_U + L_J) \cdot (P_{LU} - P_{LJ})}}_{\text{[wage rate advantage]}}$$

where

P_{LU} = wage rate in the United States;
P_{LJ} = wage rate in Japan;
L_U = labor hours per car in the United States;
L_J = labor hours per car in Japan.

We have assumed for Ford and Toyo Kogyo that:

$P_{LU} = \$23.45;$
$P_{LJ} = \$9.62;$
$L_U = 65.7;$
$L_J = 42.4.$

Substituting these values into equation (2.1) results in estimates of $385 for Toyo Kogyo's labor productivity advantage and $748 for their wage rate advantage over Ford's U.S. production.

To estimate the labor productivity advantage at FEER, we make the following calculation:

$$\tfrac{1}{2}(\$23.45 + [220/207 \cdot \$9.62]) \cdot (65.7 - 42.4) = \$392. \qquad (2.2)$$

A similar calculation yields the wage rate advantage at FEER.

The decomposition reveals wide variations in advantages for certain aspects of production. In 1981, the United States had an advantage in other manufacturing and nonmanufacturing costs; the Japanese advantages were in labor productivity, wages, equity costs, purchased materials, and the existence of an undervalued yen.

We stated at the beginning of this section that these estimates would be suspect, based as they are on a number of arbitrary assumptions. In the next chapter we turn to a different methodology for decomposing cost advantages: the use of an econometrically estimated cost function.

CHAPTER 3

The cost-function approach to the analysis of cost and total factor productivity differences

3.1 Introduction

As noted in Chapter 1, previous studies of international differences in cost and productivity for the automobile industry have in essence been accounting studies, and have not employed rigorous analytical methods.[1] In this chapter we set out the theoretical basis for the analytical framework we will employ throughout the rest of our study. This framework is composed of an econometric cost function and the decomposition of cost and productivity proposed by Denny and Fuss (1983).

This methodology permits us to overcome two major shortcomings of previous studies: the inability to disentangle factor price effects from efficiency effects, and the inability to account correctly for short-run disequilibrium. The major source of disequilibrium that we are concerned with is due to variations in capacity utilization; these variations affect both unit costs and total factor productivity. Accounting for capacity utilization effects is particularly crucial in the automobile industry, an industry characterized by quasi-fixed factors (capital and part of labor) and product-specific manufacturing facilities. Hence swings in consumer tastes among different products can lead to variations in capacity utilization that may greatly affect measured unit cost and productivity. In fact, the empirical results presented in Chapter 6 indicate that long-run total factor productivity growth during the period 1970–84 would have been overestimated by 22% in the United States and 20% in Canada if capacity utilization effects had not been accounted for.

---

[1] In 1986 Fuss and Waverman (1990) were the first to apply the cost-function technique to a study of U.S.–Japan motor vehicle cost and productivity differences. Since then, Conrad (1987) and Aizcorbe, Winston, and Friedlaender (1987) have produced cost function studies. However, these two 1987 studies ignore the issue of short-run disequilibrium. We have not referenced Aizcorbe et al. in the text because it is difficult to compare their study with ours, since they claim there was no technical progress in Japanese vehicle production during the period 1958–83. We estimate technical progress for the period 1968–84 to be about 3% per annum, a significant difference.

There are two possible approaches to this problem. First, a variable cost function with exogenous quasi-fixed factors could be specified, and capacity utilization rates determined endogenously. An example of such an approach is Berndt and Fuss (1986). Second, capacity utilization, rather than the quasi-fixed factors, could be treated as exogenous; in this case the demands for quasi-fixed factors are determined endogenously.[2] An example of this second approach is Cowing, Small, and Stevenson (1981).

Although we intend to pursue the first approach in subsequent research, in this study we adopt the second approach. This second approach is likely to be successful when plants are designed, ex ante, to produce a normal flow of output that can be measured with relative ease.[3] Specifying capacity utilization (rather than the levels of quasi-fixed factors) as exogenous has two advantages. First, the identity of the quasi-fixed factors need not be determined a priori. Second, the analysis can proceed without the assumption that quasi-fixed factors are fixed in the short run.[4]

3.2   Cost comparisons: a decomposition analysis

From the previous discussion, it is clear that we should model the motor vehicle industry as producing a flow of output utilizing quasi-fixed capital and labor inputs, and variable material inputs. In addition, firms in the industry will usually be in short-run rather than long-run equilibrium.

Suppose the firm is in short-run equilibrium, minimizing the cost of variable factors of production that are subject to the levels of the quasi-fixed factors and output. The firm's variable cost function is given by $VC(v_{it}, q_{it}, x_{it}, T_{it})$, where v_{it} is the vector of factor prices of variable factors at time t in country i, q_{it} is actual output, x_{it} is a vector of quasi-fixed inputs, and T_{it} is an index of technical change.

---

[2] Of course, neither quasi-fixed factors nor utilization rates are truly exogenous to the firm's decision process. What is meant by "exogenous" in this context is that the observed variables are not in long-run equilibrium; that is, the levels of quasi-fixed factors are not necessarily chosen to equate the marginal rate of factor substitution with the current ratio of factor prices, and the rate of actual output flow is not necessarily equal to the designed (or normal) rate of flow.

[3] The major components of the production process – vehicle assembly and the manufacture of engines, transmissions, and transaxles – satisfy this requirement. See Miller and Bereiter (1985) for a discussion of the case of assembly.

[4] The main disadvantage of the approach taken in this chapter is that the only disequilibrium feature that can be captured is the deviation of actual from designed output. But this is by far the most important source of disequilibrium in the automobile industry. Disequilibrium due to fluctuations in factor prices can be captured by the variable cost-function model.

At this point the usual way to proceed is to combine the variable cost function with the variable factor demand functions, $-\nabla_v VC = \mathbf{z}$ (where $\mathbf{z}$ is a vector of variable inputs), in a joint estimation of the cost function parameters. However, since we have only a single variable input (materials), this strategy cannot be followed. The variable cost function alone could be estimated, but a degrees-of-freedom limitation precludes this option.[5] The way out of this impasse is to recognize that the capacity utilization (CU) rate effectively tracks the short-run disequilibrium, owing to the quasi-fixed nature of the capital and labor inputs. In addition, it is possible to measure the CU rate because capacity output is a well-defined concept in this industry. We now proceed to show how a capacity utilization model, which contains the essence of the short-run equilibrium model and which is derived from the variable cost function, can be developed and implemented empirically. We begin with the expression for total short-run cost,

$$C_{it}(\mathbf{v}_{it}, \mathbf{u}_{it}, q_{it}, \mathbf{x}_{it}, T_{it}) = VC + \mathbf{u}_{it} \cdot \mathbf{x}_{it}, \tag{3.1}$$

where $\mathbf{u}_{it}$ is a vector of the ex ante prices of the quasi-fixed factors. The firm is in long-run equilibrium when C_{it} in (3.1) is minimized with respect to the choice of the quasi-fixed factors $\mathbf{x}_{it}$, that is, when

$$-\nabla_x VC(\mathbf{v}_{it}, q_{it}, \mathbf{x}_{it}, T_{it}) = \mathbf{u}_{it}. \tag{3.2}$$

Following Berndt and Morrison (1981) and Berndt and Fuss (1986), capacity output Q_{it} is defined as the level of q_{it} that solves (3.2) for a given vector of quasi-fixed inputs:

$$-\nabla_x VC(\mathbf{v}_{it}, Q_{it}, \mathbf{x}_{it}, T_{it}) \equiv \mathbf{u}_{it}. \tag{3.3}$$

That is, capacity output should be thought of as the flow of output per unit time that is viewed as "normal" by the firm, in the sense that if the output flow is sustained over time then the firm has no incentive in the long run to adjust the level of its quasi-fixed factors. Normal capacity utilization then occurs when actual and designed (normal) output flows per unit time are equal. Hence it is natural to index capacity utilization to unity when the actual output flow is at its normal rate.

Solving (3.3) for the vector $\mathbf{x}_{it}$ yields

$$\mathbf{x}_{it} = \mathbf{x}_{it}(\mathbf{v}_{it}, \mathbf{u}_{it}, Q_{it}, T_{it}), \tag{3.4}$$

---

[5] If perfect competition is assumed, an additional equation based on the ex post residual return to both quasi-fixed factors can be added (Morrison 1988). Perfectly competitive behavior is not a reasonable assumption for the motor vehicle industry.

the vector of long-run equilibrium demands for the quasi-fixed factors. Define

$$T_{1it} = \frac{q_{it}}{Q_{it}} \qquad (3.5)$$

as the capacity utilization rate. It is also convenient from the point of view of compact notation to rename the technology index T_{it} as T_{2it}.

Substituting (3.4) and (3.5) in (3.1) to eliminate x_{it} and q_{it}, and defining $w_{it} = (v_{it}, u_{it})$ and $T_{it} = (T_{1it}, T_{2it})$,[6] we arrive at the short-run total cost function

$$C_{it} = G_{it}(w_{it}, Q_{it}, T_{it}), \qquad (3.6)$$

which incorporates the effects of quasi-fixed factors of production. Because the firm is in long-run equilibrium when $q_{it} = Q_{it}$ or $T_{1it} = 1$ (from 3.3), the long-run equilibrium cost function can be written as $G_{it}(w_{it}, Q_{it}, T_{2it})$.

Suppose the cost function (3.6) is approximated by a translog cost function (a quadratic function in the logarithms of w_{it}, Q_{it}, and T_{it}) in which the zero- and first-order parameters differ across countries but the second-order parameters are the same for each country. In that case the translog cost function will be of the form

$$\log C_{it} = G(\log w_{it}, \log Q_{it}, \log T_{it}, D), \qquad (3.7)$$

where G is a quadratic function and D is a vector of country-specific dummy variables: $D_{ji} = 1$ if $j = i$ and $D_{ji} = 0$ otherwise. We can decompose the translog cost function to compare both intertemporal and interspatial cost differences and their sources.

3.2.1 Intertemporal cost and productivity differences

Following Denny and Fuss (1983), we can apply the quadratic lemma to (3.7) for the ith country and time periods 1 and 0 to obtain

$$\Delta \log C = \log C_{i1} - \log C_{i0}$$

$$= \frac{1}{2} \left[\frac{\partial G}{\partial D} \bigg|_{D=D_{ii}} + \frac{\partial G}{\partial D} \bigg|_{D=D_{ii}} \right] \cdot [D_{ii} - D_{ii}]$$

---

[6] T_{it} is a vector of technological characteristics of the production process. The use of this characteristics approach was proposed by McFadden (1978) and has been applied to telecommunications (Denny, Fuss, and May 1981; Denny, Fuss, and Waverman 1981), trucking (Spady and Friedlaender 1978; Kim 1984), and U.S. automobile production (Friedlaender, Winston, and Wang 1983).

$$+\frac{1}{2}\sum_k\left[\frac{\partial G}{\partial\log w_k}\bigg|_{w_k=w_{ki1}}+\frac{\partial G}{\partial\log w_k}\bigg|_{w_k=w_{ki0}}\right]\cdot[\log w_{ki1}-\log w_{ki0}]$$

$$+\frac{1}{2}\left[\frac{\partial G}{\partial\log Q}\bigg|_{Q=Q_{i1}}+\frac{\partial G}{\partial\log Q}\bigg|_{Q=Q_{i0}}\right]\cdot[\log Q_{i1}-\log Q_{i0}]$$

$$+\frac{1}{2}\sum_l\left[\frac{\partial G}{\partial\log T_l}\bigg|_{T=T_{li1}}+\frac{\partial G}{\partial\log T_l}\bigg|_{T=T_{li0}}\right]\cdot[\log T_{li1}-\log T_{li0}].$$

$$(3.8)$$

Assuming price-taking behavior in factor markets and utilizing Shephard's lemma, (3.8) can be written as

$$\Delta\log C=\frac{1}{2}\sum_k[S_{ki1}+S_{ki0}][\log w_{ki1}-\log w_{ki0}]$$

$$+\frac{1}{2}[ECQ_{i1}+ECQ_{i0}][\log Q_{i1}-\log Q_{i0}]$$

$$+\frac{1}{2}\sum_l[ECT_{li1}+ECT_{li0}][\log T_{li1}-\log T_{li0}]$$

$$+\theta_{ii},\qquad(3.9)$$

where

$$\theta_{ii}=\frac{1}{2}\left[\frac{\partial G}{\partial D}\bigg|_{D=D_{ii}}+\frac{\partial G}{\partial D}\bigg|_{D=D_{ii}}\right]\cdot[D_{ii}-D_{ii}]=0\qquad(3.10)$$

and

ECQ = elasticity of cost with respect to capacity output,
ECT_l = elasticity of cost with respect to the lth technological characteristic.

If we subtract $(\log q_{i1}-\log q_{i0})$ from both sides of equation (3.10), and recall that $q_{it}=Q_{it}\cdot T_{1it}$ $(t=0,1)$, then (3.10) provides a decomposition of the actual average cost increase between periods 1 and 0 for country i:

$$\Delta\log\left(\frac{C}{q}\right)=\frac{1}{2}\sum_k[S_{ki1}+S_{ki0}][\log w_{ki1}-\log w_{ki0}]$$

$$+\frac{1}{2}[ECQ_{i1}+ECQ_{i0}-2][\log Q_{i1}-\log Q_{i0}]$$

$$+\frac{1}{2}[ECT_{1i1}+ECT_{1i0}-2][\log T_{1i1}-\log T_{1i0}]$$

$$+\frac{1}{2}\sum_{l\neq1}[ECT_{li1}+ECT_{li0}][\log T_{li1}-\log T_{li0}].\qquad(3.11)$$

If the time period is one year, equation (3.11) is just the formula for the decomposition of yearly proportionate changes in average cost.

The translog (Tornqvist) index of the growth in cost efficiency or total factor productivity (see Appendix 3.A for the explanation of the equality of Total Factor Productivity and Cost Efficiency Growth) between periods 0 and 1 for country i is obtained from (3.11) by subtracting the factor-price effects from both sides of the equation and multiplying the result by -1:

$$\log \text{TFP}_{i1} - \log \text{TFP}_{i0} = -(\log \text{CE}_{i1} - \log \text{CE}_{i0})$$

$$= -\left[\Delta \log\left(\frac{C}{q}\right) - \frac{1}{2} \sum_k [S_{ki1} + S_{ki0}] \right.$$

$$\left. \cdot [\log w_{ki1} - \log w_{ki0}] \right] \qquad (3.12)$$

and

$$\Delta \log \text{TFP}_i = \log \text{TFP}_{i1} - \log \text{TFP}_{i0}$$

$$= \frac{1}{2} [\text{ECQ}_{i1} + \text{ECQ}_{i0} - 2][\log Q_{i1} - \log Q_{i0}]$$

$$- \frac{1}{2} [\text{ECT}_{1i1} + \text{ECT}_{1i0} - 2][\log T_{1i1} - \log T_{1i0}]$$

$$- \frac{1}{2} \sum_{l \neq 1} [\text{ECT}_{li1} + \text{ECT}_{li0}][\log T_{li1} - \log T_{li0}]. \qquad (3.13)$$

Equations (3.11), (3.12), and (3.13) provide the formulas for decomposing into their various sources the average (unit) cost differences and total factor productivity differences over time within a specific country.

Consider equation (3.11). The left-hand side is the average cost difference, which is due to differences in factor prices (the first row on the right-hand side), the effects of scale economies (the second row), and the effects of capacity utilization (the third row) and other technological conditions (the fourth row). Now consider equation (3.12). The average cost efficiency (total factor productivity) difference between two points in time is equal to the difference between average unit costs and the sum of the differences in factor prices multiplied by the average factor shares. Finally, consider equation (3.13). Total factor productivity growth over time within a country is due to output growth in the presence of scale economies (the first row) and changes in technological conditions (the second and third rows).

3.2.2   *Interspatial cost differences*

Analogous to the intertemporal unit cost analysis is that of interspatial (i.e., between countries) cost differences at a given time. In this case the decomposition of actual average cost difference (in a common currency) between countries i and o can be obtained by applying the quadratic lemma to (3.7) for countries i and o at time t (suppressed for convenience):

$$\Delta \log\left(\frac{C}{q}\right) = \frac{1}{2}\sum_k (S_{ki} + S_{ko}) \cdot (\log w_{ki} - \log w_{ko})$$

$$+ \frac{1}{2}(ECQ_i + ECQ_o - 2) \cdot (\log Q_i - \log Q_o)$$

$$+ \frac{1}{2}(ECT_{1i} + ECT_{1o} - 2) \cdot (\log T_{1i} - \log T_{1o})$$

$$+ \frac{1}{2}\sum_{l \neq 1}(ECT_{li} + ECT_{lo}) \cdot (\log T_{li} - \log T_{lo})$$

$$+ \theta_{io}, \tag{3.14}$$

where

$$\theta_{io} = \frac{1}{2}\sum_j \left(\frac{\partial G}{\partial D_{ji}} + \frac{\partial G}{\partial D_{jo}}\right) \cdot (D_{ji} - D_{jo}),$$

with $D_{ii} = D_{oo} = 1$; $D_{ji} = D_{jo} = 0$ when $j \neq i$, $j \neq o$.

Following Denny and Fuss (1980), the index of cost efficiency difference between countries i and o at any time is given by

$$CED_{i,o} = -\left\{\Delta \log\left(\frac{C}{q}\right) - \frac{1}{2}\sum_k [S_{ki} + S_{ko}][\log w_{ki} - \log w_{ko}]\right\}. \tag{3.15}$$

The expression for CED in equation (3.15) is just the dual formulation of the translog index of interspatial productivity difference introduced by Jorgenson and Nishimizu (1978).

Rearranging equation (3.15), we obtain an alternative equation for $\Delta \log(C/q)$:

$$\Delta \log\left(\frac{C}{q}\right) = \frac{1}{2}\sum_k [S_{ki} + S_{ko}] \cdot [\log w_{ki} - \log w_{ko}] - CED_{i,o}. \tag{3.16}$$

Combining (3.15) and (3.16), we obtain an expression for CED in terms of efficiency sources:

$$CED_{i,o} = -\frac{1}{2}[ECQ_i + ECQ_o - 2] \cdot \Delta \log Q$$

$$- \frac{1}{2}(ECT_{1i} + ECT_{1o} - 2) \cdot (\log T_{1i} - \log T_{1o})$$

$$- \frac{1}{2}\sum_{l \neq 1}(ECT_{li} + ECT_{lo}) \cdot (\log T_{li} - \log T_{lo})$$

$$- \theta_{io}. \tag{3.17}$$

The interpretations of equations (3.14), (3.15), and (3.17) parallel those of equations (3.11), (3.12), and (3.13).

Consider equation (3.14). The left-hand side is the average cost difference between two countries at a point in time. This difference is due to differences in factor prices (the first row on the right-hand side), the effects of scale economies (the second row), the effects of capacity utilization differences (the third row), the effects of other technological characteristics (the fourth row), and θ_{io} (the fifth row). The term θ_{io} measures any systematic cost difference between the two countries not accounted for by factor prices, scale, and technology; this term is called the *country-specific efficiency effect,* and is presumably a combination of managerial and environmental effects.

Now consider equation (3.15). The average cost difference between the two countries is due to differences in factor prices (the first term) and differences in cost efficiency (the second term). Finally, consider equation (3.17). The cost efficiency difference between two countries is due to scale effects (the first row), capacity utilization (the second row), other technological effects (the third row), and country-specific efficiency differences (the third row).

3.3   Incorporating capacity utilization effects into the cost function: an application of the Viner–Wong envelope theorem

Equation (3.3) is just the envelope theorem in ex ante price, shadow-price space. An alternative version of this theorem is the Viner–Wong envelope result between long-run and short-run marginal costs (Viner 1952):[7] $\mathrm{LRMC}_{it} = \mathrm{SRMC}_{it}$, $q_{it} = Q_{it}$. An expanded form of the envelope result can be written as

$$\mathrm{SRMC}_{it} = \mathrm{LRMC}_{it}, \quad \text{if } q_{it} = Q_{it};$$

$$\mathrm{SRMC}_{it} < \mathrm{LRMC}_{it}, \quad \text{if } q_{it} < Q_{it}; \qquad (3.18)$$

$$\mathrm{SRMC}_{it} > \mathrm{LRMC}_{it}, \quad \text{if } q_{it} > Q_{it}.$$

---

[7] The link between these two versions of the envelope theorem has been made by Fuss (1987), who developed the equation

$$\mathrm{LRMC} = \mathrm{SRMC} + \sum_{j} \frac{\partial x_j}{\partial q} \cdot \left(\frac{\partial \mathrm{VC}}{\partial x_j} + u_j \right),$$

where $\mathrm{LRMC} =$ long-run marginal cost and $\mathrm{SRMC} =$ short-run marginal cost. This equation is analyzed in detail in Berndt and Fuss (1989).

Relationship (3.18) is satisfied if the cost–normal output and cost–capacity utilization elasticities satisfy the following:

$$ECT_{1it} = ECQ_{it}, \quad \text{normal capacity utilization} \qquad (q_{it} = Q_{it}),$$

$$ECT_{1it} < ECQ_{it}, \quad \text{below-normal capacity utilization} \quad (q_{it} < Q_{it}), \qquad (3.19)$$

$$ECT_{1it} > ECQ_{it}, \quad \text{above-normal capacity utilization} \quad (q_{it} > Q_{it}),$$

where ECT_{1it} is the cost–capacity utilization elasticity and ECQ_{it} is the cost–capacity output elasticity.

The relationship (3.19) is obvious for the case of long-run constant returns to scale, once it is recognized that ECT_{1it} is just the output elasticity of the short-run average cost curve[8] and ECQ_{it} is the output elasticity of the long-run curve (equal to unity). For the case of increasing returns to scale, consider Figure 3.1. At the normal capacity utilization rate (output level $0A$), short-run marginal cost equals long-run marginal cost and short-run average cost (SRAC) equals long-run average cost (LRAC). Because

$$ECQ_{it} = \frac{LRMC_{it}}{LRAC_{it}} \quad \text{and} \quad ECT_{1it} = \frac{SRMC_{it}}{SRAC_{it}},$$

we have

$$ECQ_{it} = ECT_{1it}.$$

Now suppose output is expanded to $0B$. If output expansion occurs with designed (normal) output Q constant, movement is along the SRAC curve (actual output q increasing) and capacity utilization is above normal. If output expansion occurs with capacity utilization T_{1it} constant at the normal rate, then the movement is along the LRAC curve (as Q increases). From Figure 3.1 it can be seen that, for output expansion beyond $0A$, SRAC is falling less rapidly than LRAC; thus

$$\frac{\partial SRAC_{it}}{\partial Q_{it}} > \frac{\partial LRAC_{it}}{\partial Q_{it}}, \qquad (3.20)$$

[8] Note that

$$\begin{aligned}
ECT_1 &= \frac{\partial \log C}{\partial \log T_1} = \frac{\partial \log C}{\partial \log(q/Q)|_{Q \text{ constant}}} \\
&= \frac{(q/Q)}{C} \cdot \frac{\partial C}{\partial (q/Q)|_{Q \text{ constant}}} \\
&= \frac{(q/Q)}{C} \cdot Q \cdot \frac{\partial C}{\partial q} = \frac{q}{C} \cdot \frac{\partial C}{\partial q} \\
&= \frac{\partial \log C}{\partial \log q}\bigg|_{Q \text{ constant}}
\end{aligned}$$

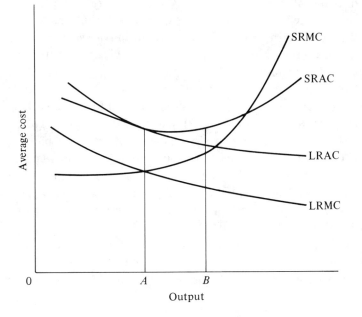

Figure 3.1. The envelope theorem and capacity utilization.

where

$$\frac{\partial \mathrm{SRAC}_{it}}{\partial Q_{it}}, \frac{\partial \mathrm{LRAC}_{it}}{\partial Q_{it}} < 0.$$

Inequality (3.20) can be manipulated into the form[9]

$$(\mathrm{ECT}_{1it} - 1) > \frac{\mathrm{SRTC}_{it}}{\mathrm{LRTC}_{it}} \cdot (\mathrm{ECQ}_{it} - 1), \qquad (3.21)$$

where SRTC_{it} and LRTC_{it} are short- and long-run total costs, respectively. Since $\mathrm{SRTC}_{it} > \mathrm{LRTC}_{it}$ it follows that $\mathrm{ECT}_{1it} > \mathrm{ECQ}_{it}$.

Similarly, for output contraction below $0A$, we have $\partial \mathrm{SRAC}/\partial Q < \partial \mathrm{LRAC}/\partial Q$, which implies that $\mathrm{ECT}_{1it} < \mathrm{ECQ}_{it}$. Hence relationship (3.19)

[9] For example,

$$\frac{\partial \mathrm{SRAC}}{\partial Q} = \frac{\partial (C/q)}{\partial q} = \frac{\partial [C/(q/Q)]}{\partial [q/Q]}$$

$$= \frac{\partial (C/T_1)}{\partial T_1}$$

$$= \mathrm{SRTC}^{-1}[\mathrm{ECT}_1 - 1].$$

has been demonstrated for the case of increasing returns to scale. An analogous argument exists for the case of decreasing returns to scale.

Output increases that affect costs can occur in two ways. Existing capacity can be utilized more intensively, or capacity can be increased with utilization held constant. In this setting, the envelope consistency conditions (3.19) impose constraints on the parameters of the cost function (3.6). In order to specify these constraints, we must first specify the parametric form of the cost function (3.7) that is to be estimated. The exogenous variables are specified as follows: Factor prices $\mathbf{w}_{it}$ include capital (w_{1it}), materials (w_{2it}), and labor (w_{3it}); output Q_{it} represents capacity output per plant; technological conditions $\mathbf{T}_{it}$ include capacity utilization rate (T_{1it}), index of the stock of R & D (T_{2it}), and output mix (T_{3it}). A detailed explanation of the calculation of these variables is contained in Chapter 4.

We have chosen to estimate a translog cost function with zero- and first-order terms that differ across countries and second-order terms that are common across countries. This function can be written out for the ith country at time t as

$$\log C_{it} = G(\log \mathbf{w}_{it}, \log Q_{it}, \log \mathbf{T}_{it}, \mathbf{D})$$

$$= \alpha_o + \alpha_{oi} D_i + \sum_k (\alpha_k + \alpha_{ki} D_{ii}) \log w_{kit}$$

$$+ (\beta_1 + \beta_{1i} D_{ii}) \log Q_{it} + \sum_l (\theta_l + \theta_{li} D_{ii}) \log T_{lit}$$

$$+ \frac{1}{2} \left[\sum_k \delta_{kk} (\log w_{kit})^2 + \mu_{11} (\log Q_{it})^2 + \sum_l \phi_{ll} (\log T_{lit})^2 \right]$$

$$+ \sum_k \sum_m \delta_{km} \log w_{kit} \log w_{mit}$$
$$\scriptstyle k\ m \atop k<m$$

$$+ \sum_l \sum_p \phi_{lp} \log T_{lit} \log T_{pit} + \sum_k \lambda_{k1} \log w_{kit} \log Q_{it}$$
$$\scriptstyle l\ p \atop l<p$$

$$+ \sum_k \sum_l \Lambda_{kl} \log w_{kit} \log T_{lit} + \sum_l \tau_{1l} \log Q_{it} \log T_{lit}, \quad (3.22)$$

where C_{it} is cost of production per plant. The dummy variable $D_{ii} = 0$, $i =$ Canada, because Canada is chosen as the reference country.

In order to develop the parameter constraints implied by the envelope theorem, recall that the capacity utilization rate was indexed so that it equals unity at the normal utilization rate. *When capacity utilization is at the normal rate,* the elasticities can be written as

$$ECT_{1it} = \theta_1 + \sum_i \theta_{1i} D_{ii} + \sum_{l \neq 1} \phi_{1l} \log T_{lit} + \sum_k \Lambda_{k1} \log w_{kit} + \tau_{11} \log Q_{it}, \quad (3.23)$$

$$ECQ_{1it} = \beta_1 + \sum_i \beta_{1i} D_{ii} + \mu_{11} \log Q_{it} + \sum_k \lambda_{k1} \log w_{kit} + \sum_{l \neq 1} \tau_{1l} \log T_{lit},$$
$$(3.24)$$

since $\log T_{1it} = 0$.

For the left-hand sides of (3.23) and (3.24) to be equal for all values of the exogenous variables, the following parameter constraints must be imposed:

$$\theta_1 = \beta_1, \qquad \theta_{1i} = \beta_{1i},$$

$$\phi_{1l} = \tau_{1l} \quad (l \neq 1), \qquad\qquad\qquad (3.25)$$

$$\Lambda_{k1} = \lambda_{k1}, \qquad \tau_{11} = \mu_{11}.$$

When the equalities (3.25) are imposed,

$$ECT_{1it} - ECQ_{it} = (\phi_{11} - \tau_{11}) \log T_{1it}.$$

Hence for the envelope inequalities in (3.19) to hold, it must be the case that $\phi_{11} > \tau_{11}$.

Normally the cost share equations, which form a part of the system of equations used to estimate the parameters of the cost function, are obtained by applying Shephard's Lemma to the cost function. In the present case, we must be careful because Shephard's Lemma is an equilibrium concept and thus is applicable only to equation (3.22) when $T_{1it} = 1$. Denote equilibrium cost ($T_{1it} = 1$) by C_{it}^* and the equilibrium share by S_{kit}^*. Then Shephard's Lemma implies that

$$\frac{\partial \log C_{it}^*}{\partial \log w_{kit}} = S_{kit}^*$$

or

$$S_{kit}^* = \alpha_k + \alpha_{ki} D_{ii} + \delta_{kk} \log w_{kit} + \sum_{m \neq k} \delta_{km} \log w_{mit}$$

$$+ \lambda_{kl} \log Q_{it} + \sum_{l \neq 1} \Lambda_{kl} \log T_{lit} \quad (k = 1, \dots, K). \quad (3.26)$$

The parameters of (3.26) must satisfy the usual adding-up and symmetry constraints

$$\sum_k \alpha_k = 1, \qquad \sum_k \alpha_{ki} = 0, \qquad \sum_m \delta_{mk} = 0, \qquad \delta_{mk} = \delta_{km},$$
$$(3.27)$$
$$\sum_k \lambda_{k1} = 0, \qquad \sum_k \alpha_{ki} = 0, \qquad \phi_{lp} = \phi_{pl}, \qquad \sum_k \Lambda_{kl} = 0 \quad (l \neq 1).$$

We now proceed to link the unobserved equilibrium share S_{kit}^* to the observed actual share S_{kit} by using the capacity utilization rate. It is convenient to assume that the disequilibrium process with respect to cost shares can be modeled as

$$S_{kit} = S_{kit}^* + \Lambda_{k1} \log T_{1it}, \tag{3.28}$$

which implies[10]

$$S_{kit} = \alpha_k + \alpha_{ki} D_{ii} + \delta_{kk} \log w_{kit} + \sum_{m \neq k} \delta_{km} \log w_{mit}$$

$$+ \lambda_{k1} \log Q_{it} + \sum_l \Lambda_{kl} \log T_{lit} \quad (k = 1, \ldots, K). \tag{3.29}$$

Because $\sum_k S_{kit} = \sum_k S_{kit}^* = 1$, there exists the following adding-up constraint that must be satisfied:

$$\sum_k \Lambda_{k1} = 0. \tag{3.30}$$

One final conceptual problem must still be addressed. Imposition of the envelope consistency constraints (3.19) unfortunately renders the second-order translog function less flexible than desired.[11] Because

$$\frac{\partial S_{kit}}{\partial \log T_{1it}} = \Lambda_{k1} = \lambda_{k1} = \frac{\partial S_{kit}}{\partial \log Q_{it}}, \tag{3.31}$$

factor-cost shares change to the same extent when output increases, independent of whether the output increase is due to increased capacity utilization or increased capacity. Since capital is the most quasi-fixed input, the capital-cost share should decline when capacity utilization increases relative to when capacity increases. To permit this possibility, third-order terms must be added to the cost function. A parsimonious, sufficiently flexible specification is obtained by adding terms of the form

$$\frac{1}{6} \sum_k \sum_{i=1}^1 \sum_{j=1}^1 \rho_{kij} \log w_k \log T_i \log T_j = \frac{1}{2} \sum_k \rho_{k11} \log w_k (\log T_1)^2 \tag{3.32}$$

to the cost function. As a result of (3.32), a term of the form

$$\frac{1}{2} \rho_{k11} (\log T_1)^2 \tag{3.33}$$

is added to the kth cost share equation.[12]

---

[10] Note that the equation $(\partial \log C_{it})/(\partial \log w_{kit}) = S_{kit}$ is not an application of Shephard's Lemma, but rather results from the assumed structure of the disequilibrium process.

[11] This problem is similar to the one encountered when separability restrictions are imposed on the translog functional form (Denny and Fuss 1977).

[12] This specification is still not sufficiently flexible to deal with the case of overutilization of capacity, since when $T_1 > 1$ an increase in T_1 will lead to an increase in the cost share

Finally, the condition required for the envelope inequalities in (3.19) to hold becomes

$$\phi_{11} + \sum_k \rho_{k11} \log w_k > \tau_{11}. \tag{3.34}$$

3.4   Production characteristics obtained from the cost function

From the cost function developed in Section 3.3, the following production statistics can be derived: factor substitution, scale economies, and technological characteristics.

3.4.1   *Factor substitution*

The own-factor price elasticity of demand (outputs held constant) is given by

$$E_{kk} = \frac{1}{S_k} [\delta_{kk} - S_k + S_k^2]. \tag{3.35}$$

The Allen–Uzawa elasticity of substitution is given by

$$\sum_{km} = \frac{1}{S_k S_m} [\delta_{km} + S_k S_m]. \tag{3.36}$$

3.4.2   *Scale economies*

The scale elasticity is given by

$$SE_i = (ECQ_i)^{-1}, \tag{3.37}$$

where

$$ECQ_i = \frac{\partial \log C_i}{\partial \log Q_i} = \beta_1 + \beta_{1i} D_{ii} + \mu_{11} \log Q_i$$

$$+ \sum_k \lambda_k \log w_{ki} + \sum_l \tau_{l1} \log T_{li}. \tag{3.38}$$

of capital, which is counterintuitive. One possible solution is to replace the coefficients with $\rho_{k11} \cdot SV$ where SV, a switch variable, equals +1 when $T_1 \leq 1$ and equals −1 when $T_1 > 1$. This solution was adopted for the empirical application contained in this study.

The addition of (3.32) to the cost function can be interpreted as specifying that the deviation of the observed cost shares from the long-run equilibrium cost shares is a quadratic function of the capacity utilization rate, since $S_{kit} = S_{kit}^* + \Lambda_{k1} \log T_{1it} + 0.5\rho_{k11}(\log T_{1it})^2$. It can be shown that the CU model implies that the deviation of actual average cost from equilibrium average cost is also a quadratic function of T_1.

3.4.3   *Technological characteristics*

The elasticity of cost with respect to the technological characteristics T_l can be expressed as

$$ECT_{li} = \frac{\partial \log C_i}{\partial \log T_{li}} = \theta_l + \theta_{li} D_{ii} + \sum_p \phi_{1p} \log T_{1i} + \sum_k \Lambda_{k1} \log w_{ki} + \tau_{11} \log Q_i.$$

$$(3.39)$$

3.5   Alterations to the decomposition formula

The addition of (3.32) to the cost function implies that the allocation formulas of Section 3.2 must also be altered. By applying the theoretical framework developed by Denny and Fuss (1983), it can be shown that an interaction term of the form

$$-\frac{1}{3} \sum_k \rho_{k11} [\log w_{ki} - \log w_{ko}] \cdot [\log T_{1i} - \log T_{1o}]^2 \qquad (3.40)$$

must be added to the right-hand side of the decomposition formula (3.14) for the interspatial comparison, with an analogous interaction term added for the intertemporal analysis. Equation (3.14) then becomes

$$\Delta \log\left(\frac{C}{q}\right) = \frac{1}{2} \sum_k (S_{ki} + S_{ko}) \cdot (\log w_{ki} - \log w_{ko})$$

$$+ \frac{1}{2}(ECQ_i + ECQ_o - 2) \cdot (\log Q_i - \log Q_o)$$

$$+ \frac{1}{2}(ECT_{1i} + ECT_{1o} - 2) \cdot (\log T_{1i} - \log T_{1o})$$

$$+ \frac{1}{2} \sum_{l \neq 1} (ECT_{li} + ECT_{lo}) \cdot (\log T_{li} - \log T_{lo})^2$$

$$- \frac{1}{3} \sum_k \rho_{k11} (\log w_{ki} - \log w_{ko}) \cdot (\log T_{1i} - \log T_{1o})^2$$

$$+ \theta_{io}. \qquad (3.41)$$

Similarly, the cost-efficiency difference decomposition formula (3.17) becomes

$$CED_{i,o} = -\frac{1}{2}[ECQ_i + ECQ_o - 2] \cdot \Delta \log Q$$

$$-\frac{1}{2}(ECT_{1i} + ECT_{1o} - 2) \cdot (\log T_{1i} - \log T_{1o})$$

$$-\frac{1}{2}\sum_{l\neq 1}(ECT_{li}+ECT_{lo})\cdot(\log T_{li}-\log T_{lo})^2$$

$$-\frac{1}{3}\sum_k \rho_{k11}(\log w_{ki}-\log w_{ko})\cdot(\log T_{1i}-\log T_{1o})^2$$

$$-\theta_{io}. \tag{3.42}$$

Appendix 3.A: Equality of total factor productivity and cost-efficiency growth rates

We have

$$C=\sum_{k=1}^K w_k\cdot x_k, \tag{3.A.1}$$

where C is total cost and x_k, w_k are quantities and prices (respectively) of the kth input. Differentiating (3.A.1), we obtain

$$dC=\sum_k w_k\, dx_k+\sum_k x_k\, dw_k \tag{3.A.2}$$

or

$$\frac{dC}{C}=\sum_k\left[\frac{w_k x_k}{C}\right]\frac{dx_k}{x_k}+\sum_k\left[\frac{w_k x_k}{C}\right]\frac{dw_k}{w_k}. \tag{3.A.3}$$

Subtracting dq/q (proportionate change in actual output) from both sides of (3.A.3) and rearranging yields

$$\frac{dC}{C}-\frac{dq}{q}-\sum_k S_k\frac{dw_k}{w_k}=-\left[\frac{dq}{q}-\sum_k S_k\frac{dx_k}{x_k}\right], \tag{3.A.4}$$

where S_k is the cost share of the kth input in total cost.

Equation (3.A.4) can be rewritten as

$$-\left[d\ln\left(\frac{C}{q}\right)-\sum_k S_k\, d\ln w_k\right]=d\ln q-\sum_k S_k\, d\ln x_k. \tag{3.A.5}$$

The left-hand side of (3.A.5) is the Divisia index of cost efficiency growth, and the right-hand side is the Divisia index of total factor productivity growth.

CHAPTER 4

Data base sources and method of construction

The basic sources of much of the data used are the various censuses of manufacturers in each of the countries studied. From these sources we acquired data on output, labor and materials inputs, and investment. For Germany, we relied on a data bank compiled by Klaus Conrad at the University of Mannheim. Data on capital services, the prices of output and inputs, capacity utilization, and technical change were acquired from other sources detailed in Appendix 4.C. A number of problems were encountered, including the benchmarking of the cost of production across countries as well as accounting for the very different types of motor vehicles produced.

4.1   Coverage of the data

Although the coverage of the 3-digit motor vehicles data is reasonably similar across the four countries, there are some discrepancies. In Canada, unlike Japan, automotive products foundries, aluminum casting plants, auto glass plants, and motorcycle production are not included in automotive sector data. In the United States, unlike Japan, automotive stamping, vehicular lighting equipment, engine electrical equipment, and motorcycle production are not included. For Germany, the only major difference (relative to Japan) is that repair work is included in the definition of the automotive industry. It is not possible to determine accurately the quantitative impact of these discrepancies, but we estimate they amount to 5–10% of the value of gross output for Canada and for the United States. Any bias imparted by omission of the listed subindustries should be reasonably small.

4.1.1   *Standard Industrial Classification (SIC) codes in the United States, Japan, Canada, and Germany*

In the United States and Japan, the SIC code treats the automotive industry in this way:

2-digit level: transportation equipment

3-digit level: motor vehicles, aircraft, shipbuilding, etc.

4-digit level: assembly, parts and accessories, etc.

Although the Canadian and German SICs are similar in concept, there is no 3-digit aggregation of the entire automotive industry. Rather, each of what would be 4-digit industries in the United States or Japan are separate 3-digit industries in Canada, and the U.S./Japanese–style 3-digit aggregate must be created by summing these industries.[1] For Germany, however, the motor vehicle industry is at the 2-digit level, comparable to the 3-digit level in the United States and Japan; separate industries (assembly, parts, etc.) are at the 4-digit level and are summed to arrive at the vehicle industry. In general, this discussion will refer to the automotive industry as a whole at the 3-digit level and to separate categories for assembly, parts, and so forth at the 4-digit level, although this is not strictly correct for Canada or Germany.

Two facets of the SIC system render the Canadian coverage of the automotive industry incomplete (and also affect, to some extent, data for the United States, Japan, and Germany). First, a number of parts production plants are classified under industries outside of the automotive sector. Automotive products foundries are classified as 294 (foundries), aluminum casting plants as 296 (aluminum castings), auto glass plants as 3562 (glass products other than containers), and so on. Note that the SIC is applied to establishments or factories, rather than to firms. Thus General Motors–owned plants in Canada are classified in various separate industries: motor vehicles, parts, foundries, aluminum castings, glass, and electronics.

Second, factories for which automotive parts represent a significant proportion of their output are classified as more general, nonautomotive industries if that proportion is less than 50%. Thus, a number of major parts producers, and many more smaller ones, are not captured by the automotive categories of the SIC.

The following table shows the broad definition of the U.S. automotive SIC.[2]

2-digit	37	Transportation equipment
3-digit	371	Motor vehicles

---

[1] Canadian 4-digit automotive industries (for which there is usually little information available) would therefore be 5-digit industries in the U.S./Japanese scheme (e.g., Canadian 3255: motor vehicle wheels and brakes).

[2] Includes assembly of trucks and any production of truck chassis or bodies by an automobile manufacturer.

Table 4.1. *SIC code numbers, non–U.S.*

Level	Number	Description
Japan		
2-digit	36	Transportation equipment
3-digit	361	Motor vehicles
4-digit	3611	Automobiles and motorcycles (assembly)
	3612	Motor vehicle bodies
	3613	Motor vehicle parts
Canada		
2-digit	32	Transportation equipment
3-digit	323	Motor vehicles (assembly)
	324	Truck bodies and trailers
	325	Motor vehicle parts
Germany		
2-digit	33	Motor vehicles
4-digit	3311	Motor vehicles and engines
	3314	Motor vehicle parts
	3316	Chassis and trailers
	3390	Other (motorcycles, etc.)

4-digit	3711	Motor vehicles and passenger car bodies (assembly)
	3713	Truck and bus bodies
	3714	Motor vehicle parts and accessories
	3715	Truck trailers

There have been a number of changes in the definitions of these codes over the time period of this study.[3] In addition, there are a number of automotive-product SICs not included under transportation equipment; for example, 2396 (automotive apparel and trimmings), 3647 (vehicular lighting equipment), and 3694 (engine electrical equipment). Other categories – including 3465 (automotive stampings) and 3592 (carburetors, pistons, rings, and valves) – were created in the 1972 SIC from more general nonautomotive categories and cannot be traced farther back. Once again, some automotive production is classified under other more general industries. SICs in the other three countries are listed in Table 4.1.

[3] Code 3712, passenger car bodies, was absorbed into 3711 in the 1967 SIC code revision. Motor homes were removed from 3713 in 1977, and some other subcategories of 3713 were moved to 3715.

4.1.2 *Establishing international comparability*

The category most closely comparable across countries is the 4-digit "assembly" category; in all four countries, all major plants are covered. The definitions of this SIC category are very similar for Canada and the United States, but the Japanese and German assembly categories differ in at least one important way: the inclusion of motorcycle production.

The international comparability of the parts production category is much poorer than for assembly. Industry coverage varies substantially among countries,[4] and each national industry produces a much different physical mix of parts. The Canadian industry does not produce a high volume of parts used in vehicle assembly, unlike industries in the United States, Japan, and Germany. Over the study period, moreover, the U.S. parts industry produced much larger engines and many more automatic transmissions than the Japanese or German industries; the German industry produced many more diesel engines than producers in the other three countries.

4.2 Construction of the variables within each country

4.2.1 *Real capacity output per plant*

Nominal gross actual output was computed as the sum of value added plus the cost of materials (total activity). We ensured that changes in finished goods inventories were correctly accounted for in all countries, and that in Japan account was taken of KD kits (autos exported as kits that are then assembled in the country where they are sold).

For the United States and Canada, the materials data includes materials purchased strictly for resale. This wholesaling activity is particularly important in Canada owing to the Canada–U.S. Auto Pact, which led to the import of finished vehicles for resale. This could lead to a significant distortion because such finished imports have little Canadian value added. Resale materials were therefore subtracted from total materials before gross output was computed.

Real actual output is calculated as nominal output divided by the implicit price deflator for output. For the automobile industry, quality adjustment of the implicit price deflator is important to ensure comparability across countries and time. In all four countries the government statistical

---

[4] For example, automotive stampings are included in Canadian SIC 325 but not in U.S. SIC 3714.

agencies adjust the motor vehicles price index to take account of the changing nature of vehicles (e.g., accessories, pollution control equipment, etc.). In comparing price indexes across countries, no quality adjustment is made for the possibility that Japanese or German cars may be more reliable or that additional real resources may be required to build in reliability. To the extent that this latter phenomenon is important, our results underestimate Japanese or German cost and efficiency advantages.

Capacity output is measured by real actual output divided by the capacity utilization rate (see Section 4.2.5 for the construction of this rate). The average output per plant was computed as a weighted average (weighted by proportion of total output) of the average output in seven size classes of plants.[5] The weighting procedure was used so that the large number of plants in the smallest size classes would not distort the measurement of the mean output per plant. The "effective" number of plants is total output divided by average output per plant, and this number is used to compute cost per plant. Size class data is available in each year for Canada, Japan, and Germany. For the United States such data is available only for census years; the average plant size for other years was obtained by interpolation.

4.2.2   Labor input

The cost of the labor input was defined as total compensation, or wages and salaries plus fringe benefits. Wages and salaries were available for each country from its published census data base. For the United States, Japan, and Germany, the ratio of total compensation to wages for production workers was provided in an unpublished series by the U.S. Bureau of Labor Statistics (BLS). For Canada, this ratio was available as a time series only for the 2-digit transportation equipment industry. Data for one year, 1971, was available for the Canadian motor vehicle industry; because motor vehicles activity is 85–90% of transportation equipment activity, we used the 2-digit ratio scaled to coincide with the motor vehicles ratio in 1971. For all four countries, the ratio of total compensation to wages and salaries for nonproduction workers was assumed to be the same as for production workers.

The price of labor was defined as total compensation divided by hours worked. Census data in the United States and Canada provide data on the number of employees distinguished by production and nonproduction categories, as well as the number of hours worked for production

---

[5] The size classes are based on the number of workers employed in a plant.

workers. We assumed that nonproduction workers worked the same number of hours per year as did production workers. For Japan, the annual census of manufacturers provides data on the total number of employees and hours worked by both production and nonproduction workers. For Germany, hours worked were available in the Conrad data.

4.2.3 *Materials input*

The cost of materials was defined as materials purchased (for Japan and Germany) and materials purchased minus goods purchased strictly for resale (for the United States and Canada); this data is available in the annual censuses in the United States, Japan, and Canada.[6] For Germany, materials inputs were in the Conrad data base. The wholesaling correction for Japan and Germany was assumed to be negligible.

The price of materials was measured as the implicit price deflator for materials. For the United States, this index was obtained from unpublished 1983 data of Norsworthy and Zabala (NZ) for the period 1961–78 and of the Public Research Institute for 1979–80. We extended the index to 1984 by estimating a price prediction equation, obtained by regressing the index over the period 1961–80 on the steel price index, the durables price index, and a time trend. The coefficients from these equations were then used, along with data on the independent variables, to predict materials prices for 1981 through 1984. Materials price indexes were available for Canada from census data and for Japan from the *Price Indexes Annual* of the Bank of Japan. Materials price indexes for Germany were obtained from Conrad.

4.2.4 *Capital input*

As indicated earlier, capital stock series are not provided in census data and had to be taken from other sources or constructed. The capital stock for the Canadian motor vehicle industry, as previously defined, was available to 1984 from Statistics Canada. For the United States, estimates for the period 1961–80 were obtained from NZ and from the U.S. Office of Business Analysis (OBA) for the period 1976–84. For the period 1981–4, we extended the NZ series by taking the 1976–80 average ratio of NZ estimates to OBA estimates and then applying this ratio to the OBA estimates for 1981–4.

---

[6] The lack of materials data in the German annual survey of manufacturers was a major reason why we did not construct our own data series for Germany.

In 1980, U.S. producers began to rationalize capacity by closing plants, but this reduction is not reflected in the OBA estimates of the capital stock of this industry. We therefore reduced the U.S. capital stock, as calculated previously for the period 1980–4, by the percentage change in productive capacity due to the plant closings. Details on the capacity of plants that were closed were obtained from various issues of *Wards Auto-motive Yearbook*.

Capital stock data does not exist for Japan. We computed our own estimate using the perpetual inventory method. For our capital stock benchmark we used an estimate available from the Ministry of International Trade and Industries (MITI) for transportation equipment in 1962 (when the industry was very small), scaled down by the gross output levels of motor vehicles relative to transportation equipment. We employed a depreciation rate of 10%. Our estimated capital stock grows at the same rate over the period 1964–70 (23.8% per annum) as the series constructed by Tsurumi and Tsurumi (1983) from individual firm data. (They provide information for this period only.) Capital stock data for Germany was provided by Conrad and was also estimated using the perpetual inventory method.

The appropriate price of capital is the ex ante neoclassical user cost of capital services

$$P_K = Q_K \cdot (r + d) \frac{1 - uz}{1 - u},$$

where Q_K is the capital asset price, r is the ex ante rate of return, d is the depreciation rate, u is the corporate tax rate, and z is the present value (for tax purposes) of the depreciation allowances on an investment of 1 unit of currency.

The industry-specific capital service price series available for the U.S. motor vehicle industry had been estimated by the residual method, an inappropriate ex ante measure for such a highly cyclical industry. We have instead constructed a user cost-of-capital series by combining the rate of return and tax effects for U.S. total manufacturing – which are not subject to such cyclical variations, and which may be calculated from Norsworthy and Malmquist (1983) – with the motor vehicles–specific capital asset price index. In our previous equation,

$$P_K(\text{motor vehicles}) = P_K(\text{manufacturing}) \cdot \frac{Q_K(\text{motor vehicles})}{Q_K(\text{manufacturing})}.$$

This construction implies that we assume ex ante rates of return, depreciation rates, and tax effects for motor vehicles and manufacturing to be equal in a particular year. We believe this assumption is preferable to the only other available assumptions: that ex ante and ex post rates of return are equal, or that tax effects are the same across countries. The Norsworthy and Malmquist (NM) data was published only to 1977, and was updated to 1980 using internal U.S. Bureau of the Census data. The U.S. capital service price series was extrapolated to 1984, assuming no change in tax parameters, by using the motor vehicles asset price index (provided by BLS), the long-term bond rate (provided by OBA), and the depreciation rate implicit in the capital stock estimates. Given the assumption of constant tax effects, the updating formula is

$$\Delta \log P_K = \Delta \log Q_K + \Delta \log(r + d).$$

The capital service price for Japan was constructed in the same way as for the United States, except that the NM data was available to 1978 and hence extrapolation was used for the period 1979–84. The motor vehicles asset price deflator was kindly provided by Masahiro Kuroda of Keio University from his unpublished data base; the long-term bond rate was provided by the Bank of Japan; and the depreciation rate was assumed, as in the generation of capital stock data, to be 10%. For Canada, the method of combining the specific asset price series for motor vehicles with overall manufacturing data on tax rates, rate of return, and depreciation data was applied to the complete sample. Unpublished estimates of the user cost of capital for 1961–81 Canadian manufacturing were kindly provided by Michael Denny of the University of Toronto. This data was updated to 1984 by using a Divisia aggregation of unpublished Economic Council of Canada estimates for durable and nondurable manufacturing sectors. The motor vehicles asset price deflator was provided by Statistics Canada.

For Germany, the user cost-of-capital series for the period 1964–77 was provided by M. I. Nadiri of New York University. The series was extrapolated for the periods 1961–4 and 1978–81 by using data on the percentage change in the user cost of capital; this data was provided by E. R. Berndt of the Massachusetts Institute of Technology.

As with most studies of this type, our capital data (stock and price) is undoubtedly the most problematic of the data we have constructed. This difficulty accounts for certain restrictions that we impose in estimation – for example, concavity of the cost function – since the concavity violations that did occur were associated with capital substitution effects.

4.2.5 Capacity utilization

Rather than using a "peak-to-peak" method to determine potential output and hence capacity utilization, we have endeavored to fashion a more "engineering-like" approach to calculating capacity utilization. Capacity utilization (CU) rates were calculated from data for total vehicle assembly by first dividing actual output by potential output, where potential output is defined as follows. Maximum (potential) output was measured in the United States and Canada as the second highest weekly nameplate output calculated from individual plant data in *Wards Weekly*; for Japan and Germany, maximum monthly output was compiled from (more aggregate) data provided by the Japanese Automobile Manufacturers Association (JAMA) and the Verband der Automobilindustrie (VDA), respectively. For Japan and Germany, the count of motorcycles and other vehicles was value weighted, so that fluctuations in motorcycle production would not distort the comparative data. For all four countries, a CU rate was calculated as the ratio of actual output of vehicles to the maximum or potential output on a calendar-year basis.

The so-called normal or full CU rate was defined as the average utilization rate (ratio of actual to maximum output) for Japan 1969–80, because yearly CU rates there were reasonably constant over that period. Actual CU rates were normalized by setting this average rate equal to unity.

4.2.6 *Technology index*

For each country, we estimated a technological change indicator: the "capital stock" of research and development (R&D). This stock was constructed by converting annual R&D expenditures to a real capital stock using the perpetual inventory method and the country-specific consumer price index; a depreciation rate of 15% was assumed. Our data on R&D expenditures goes back to 1957 for the United States, Canada, and Germany, and back to 1967 for Japan. We established a benchmark R&D stock by assuming that in 1967 the technology available to Japan and Germany could be represented by the R&D stock in North America, and therefore normalized the stock in each country by setting the 1967 value at unity.

Because of the way in which the R&D stock index was constructed, we have only a tentative link to the effect of the level of R&D stock on the level of production costs. We believe our R&D variable is more sensibly viewed as a method of tracing country-specific unexplained technical change. From this point of view, the variable is similar to a time trend and was used because it consistently outperformed a time trend in the regression analysis.

4.2.7 *Output mix*

Canadian, U.S., Japanese, and German automobile production were divided into size class categories, which were assigned a category weight corresponding to the classification in FTC (1984). For Canada, the United States, and Germany, average category weights were then computed by finding the weighted average of the production of the various size classes from actual production figures. For Japan, a slightly more complicated procedure was adopted. Detailed production data was available only for the years 1978–80. However, for all other years, production data by cylinder-size category was available from JAMA *Motor Vehicle Statistics*. The detailed Japanese automobile data used in the construction of the U.S.–Japan comparative price index (see Appendix 4.A) was also used to predict weight categories from cylinder-size categories by regressing category weight on cylinder size. Data for 1978 and 1979 as computed by this method was compared to actual category weights, to be certain that the margin for error in the indirect calculation of category weights was not too large. The margin of error was in the range of 2% and was deemed satisfactory. Average category weights for auto production in all four countries are listed in Table 4.2.

4.3   Construction of intercountry price-level comparisons

The output-price deflators used to convert nominal output into real output are indexes that are normalized to be unity in a particular year for each country. The same normalization occurs for materials and capital prices. In order to obtain intercountry comparisons of cost and efficiency, benchmark prices must be calculated in a particular year to bridge the individual country price indexes for outputs and inputs.

4.3.1   *Output price*

We used 1979 as the benchmark year for output-price comparisons among the U.S., Japan, Canada, and Germany, because detailed price data was available for that year from FTC (1984). We first divided all automobile production into twelve categories: standard and luxury versions of mini, subcompact, compact, midsize, full-size and large autos. Average wholesale prices were determined for each of these twelve categories (see following paragraph), and a translog relative aggregate price index was calculated from the price and quantity data on the twelve categories.[7]

---

[7] The implied aggregate relative Japan–U.S. price for 1975 was virtually identical to the one calculated by Kravis, Heston, and Summers (1982). Our relative Germany–U.S. price was substantially below the estimate of Kravis et al.; their estimate implies unreasonably large relative prices in the last few years of the sample.

Table 4.2. *Product mix variable*

Year	Canada	U.S.	Japan	Germany
1961	3,244	3,272		2,461
1962	3,134	3,259		2,460
1963	3,192	3,280		2,448
1964	3,195	3,308		2,447
1965	3,218	3,320		2,456
1966	3,500	3,469		2,457
1967	3,527	3,482	1,917	2,479
1968	3,547	3,517	1,931	2,464
1969	3,403	3,630	1,952	2,550
1970	3,141	3,489	1,986	2,585
1971	3,276	3,611	2,042	2,588
1972	3,064	3,652	2,064	2,666
1973	3,177	3,680	2,089	2,659
1974	3,312	3,578	2,097	2,632
1975	3,572	3,618	2,121	2,606
1976	3,735	3,670	2,214	2,596
1977	3,569	3,605	2,240	2,606
1978	3,392	3,357	2,240	2,672
1979	3,251	3,205	2,228	2,687
1980	3,205	2,954	2,219	2,651
1981	3,184	2,874	2,231	2,684
1982	3,092	2,869	2,237	
1983	2,945	2,884	2,230	
1984	3,053	2,850	2,228	

Note: Figures represent average category weight (in pounds) of auto production; see Section 4.2.7.

Calculation of price data for the twelve individual categories was problematic because in each country there was at least one category for which no production data existed. Thus it was necessary to create equations for predicting the price that would have existed in a particular country had automobiles of a particular class actually been produced in that country. (See Appendix 4.A for details.)

Price-prediction equations were formed for the United States, Canada, and Japan by using relatively simple hedoniclike price relationships between price and category weight; estimates were derived from observations on individual models of automobiles. *Consumer Reports* was used to obtain information on 1979 automobile retail prices, classification, and typical profit margins for North American sales. Retail prices and category weights for Japanese-produced automobiles were kindly provided by Makoto Ohta from his unpublished data base. For Germany, various assumptions linking German prices to U.S. prices were used; for details, see Appendix 4.A. To complete the benchmark construction, we assumed that intercountry relative 1979 prices of all motor vehicle products other than automobiles were in the same proportion as our calculated average automobile price.

4.3.2 *Capital service price*

Capital service prices were linked by computing relative asset prices. For the United States and Japan, estimates of purchasing power parities (PPP) for 1975 investment in nonresidential construction, nonelectrical machinery, and electrical machinery were obtained from Kravis et al. (1982). The weights used to combine these PPP numbers into a PPP for the aggregate capital stock were the proportions of 1975 Japanese capital stock falling into these three categories (data provided by M. Kuroda). For Canada–U.S. comparisons, a more indirect method had to be adopted because no PPP numbers are available for Canada. We assumed that in the period 1966–80 (post–Auto Pact but before the large depreciation of the Canadian dollar), integration of North American production facilities resulted, on average, in equal (common-currency) asset prices for facilities in the two countries. This rough equality would occur because firms could purchase equipment in either country, and structure costs (net of subsidy) for Canadian plants would need to be cost-competitive with U.S. plants in order to induce location in Canada. Scaling the Canadian asset price index so that it equals (on average) the U.S. index yields the required bridge of the data.

For Germany, we could not obtain a breakdown of the relationship between different assets such as that used to bridge the Japan–U.S. PPP price of capital. Instead, the following approach was used: We computed the gross real return to capital in each year for Germany, using the residual method. We then determined the year (1976) in which this calculated real return per unit of capital most closely approximated the average real return over the sample. For that year, the residual return was assumed to be the user cost of capital services; the user cost of capital for other years was obtained by linking the cost-of-capital index to this benchmark year. Our procedure implies that the user cost of capital contains any excess (long-run average) profits that result from the exercise of market power (if any) by firms in the automobile industry.

4.3.3   *Materials price*

No direct source exists for comparisons of U.S.–Japan or U.S.–Germany materials price, so we constructed such comparisons for 1974 as follows. Toder et al. (1978) present data on relative prices of nonautomotive materials for 1974. To obtain a price comparison of the intracountry, intra-industry materials flow in 1974, we assumed that the relative materials price was proportional to the relative industry output price. The relative shares of inter- and intraindustry materials flows for the United States can be obtained from census data (we used U.S. census data for 1977). These U.S. shares were then used to weight the logarithms of U.S.–Japan (and U.S.–Germany) nonautomotive and automotive relative materials prices to obtain the logarithm of an aggregate relative price of materials for 1974; Appendix 4.B contains the detailed calculations. A benchmark Canada–U.S. materials price comparison is available for 1967 from Emerson (1975), and was used in this study.

Appendix 4.A: Output-price prediction

4.A.1   *Estimation of the equation for output-price prediction,*
1979 U.S. automobile production

Wholesale prices of U.S. auto producers were assumed to be determined by the equation

$$P_i = a + bW_i + cL_i, \tag{4.A.1}$$

where

P_i = wholesale price of the ith automobile;
W_i = category weight of the ith automobile;
L_i = 1 if the ith automobile is a luxury car,
     = 0 otherwise.

The actual wholesale price of the ith automobile is unobserved, since it is based on *Consumer Reports* 1979 wholesale–retail margins for basic (i.e., with minimal options) versions of the automobile. However, we do know that the actual average wholesale price for all U.S. automobile production in 1979 was $5,975 (FTC 1984). Let $\hat{P}_i = \alpha P_i$, where $\hat{P}_i$ is the observed wholesale price from *Consumer Reports*. Then

$$\hat{P}_i = \alpha P_i = \alpha a + \alpha b W_i + \alpha c L_i. \tag{4.A.2}$$

Aggregating (4.A.1) over all automobiles produced in the United States in 1979 yields

$$\bar{P} = a + b\bar{W} + c\bar{L}, \tag{4.A.3}$$

where

$\bar{P} = \$5,975$ (U.S. dollars);
$\bar{W} =$ average category weight $= 3,205.5$ lb.;
$\bar{L} =$ proportion of U.S.-produced automobiles that are luxury automobiles $= 0.0781$.

Substituting (4.A.3) into (4.A.2), we obtain

$$\hat{P}_i = \alpha[\bar{P} - b\bar{W} - c\bar{L}] + \alpha b W_i + \alpha c L_i. \tag{4.A.4}$$

Equation (4.A.4) was estimated for 1979 by nonlinear least squares using data on retail prices, retail–wholesale margins, and category weights for all U.S.-produced autos as recorded in *Consumer Reports*. The sample size was 166, and the parameter estimates were as follows (standard errors in parentheses):

$$a = 470.0 \ (393.3), \qquad c = 6268.1 \ (253.3),$$

$$b = 1.565 \ (0.124), \qquad \alpha = 0.7504 \ (0.0069).$$

Note that these results imply that prices increased more than proportionately to category weight, and that the wholesale price of a basic U.S.-produced auto was, on average, 75% of the wholesale price of a U.S.-produced auto complete with the actual options purchased. Using these values, the price-prediction equation for U.S. production is:

$$P_i = 470.0 + 1.565(W_i) + 6268.2(L_i). \tag{4.A.5}$$

Table 4.A.1 presents the price–quantity data obtained by applying equation (4.A.5).

4.A.2 *Estimation of the equation for output-price prediction, 1979 Canadian automobile production*

We assumed that the basic functional relationship between wholesale prices and category weights was the same for Canada as for the United States. However, the actual average wholesale price and mix of automobiles produced differed in the two countries. For Canada, $b = 1.565$ and $c = 6268.2$

Table 4.A.1. *Disaggregated price–quantity data,*
U.S. automobile production, 1979

Category	Category weight (lbs.)	Predicted wholesale price (U.S.$)	Quantity produced
Mini			
Standard	1,800	3,286	0
Luxury	1,800	n.c.[a]	0
Subcompact			
Standard	2,250	3,990	1,094,644
Luxury	2,250	n.c.	0
Compact			
Standard	2,650	4,616	1,300,759
Luxury	2,650	n.c.	0
Midsize			
Standard	3,250	5,555	3,219,836
Luxury	3,250	n.c.	0
Full-size			
Standard	3,600	6,103	1,705,186
Luxury	3,600	12,371	238,454
Large			
Standard	4,200	7,042	443,846
Luxury	4,200	13,310	419,349

[a] n.c. means "not computed."

(equation 4.A.1), but $a = \bar{P} - b\bar{W} - c\bar{L}$ (from 4.A.3) $= 252.3$, where $\bar{P} = \$5,339$ (U.S.), $\bar{W} = 3,250.8$ lb., and $\bar{L} = 0.000055$. The price-prediction equation for Canadian production is:

$$P_i = 252.3 + 1.565(W_i) + 6268.2(L_i). \qquad (4.A.6)$$

Table 4.A.2 presents the price–quantity data obtained by applying equation (4.A.6).

4.A.3 Estimation of the equation for output-price prediction, 1979 Japanese automobile production

Estimation of the Japanese price-prediction equation was more difficult than for the United States and Canada, owing to the lack of a classification

Table 4.A.2. *Disaggregated price–quantity data,*
Canadian automobile production, 1979

Category	Category weight (lbs.)	Predicted wholesale price (U.S.$)	Quantity produced
Mini			
Standard	1,800	3,069	0
Luxury	1,800	n.c.[a]	0
Subcompact			
Standard	2,250	3,773	22,312
Luxury	2,250	n.c.	0
Compact			
Standard	2,650	4,399	191,102
Luxury	2,650	n.c.	0
Midsize			
Standard	3,250	5,337	375,046
Luxury	3,250	n.c.	0
Full-size			
Standard	3,600	5,885	388,641
Luxury	3,600	12,153	0
Large			
Standard	4,200	6,824	1,752
Luxury	4,200	13,092	54

[a] n.c. means "not computed."

source such as *Consumer Reports* for automobiles sold in Japan. In addition, Japanese retail prices include a commodity tax that varies by classification.

We begin by describing the calculation of the wholesale price of individual models produced in Japan. From M. Ohta's data base, we obtained retail prices and actual weights of all models sold in Japan. Similar data was obtained from *Consumers Reports* for Japanese production sold in the United States. For sales in the United States, initial estimates of wholesale prices were obtained in the same way as for U.S. production. For Japanese sales, the wholesale price can be obtained as:

$$\text{Wholesale Price} = \frac{\text{Retail Price}}{1 + \text{CT} + \text{DM}}, \qquad (4.A.7)$$

where

CT = commodity tax rate;
DM = dealer markup.

Values for CT and DM were based on unpublished JAMA data and assumed to be given by:

	Small	Large	Luxury
CT	0.160	0.160	0.205
DM	0.255	0.255	0.265

where

Small = all cars with category weight ≤ 2650 lb.;
Large = all cars with category weight > 3250 lb.;
Luxury = all cars with retail price $> \$10,000$ U.S.

Our first task was to estimate the parameter α, the ratio of the estimated and actual wholesale prices. The price-prediction equation specified was

$$P_i = a + (b_0 DW_0 + b_1 DW_1 + b_2 DW_2 + b_3 DW_3) \cdot W_i + cDu, \qquad (4.A.8)$$

where

$$DW_0 = \begin{cases} 1 & \text{if } W_i = 1,800 \text{ or } 2,250, \\ 0 & \text{otherwise;} \end{cases}$$

$$DW_1 = \begin{cases} 1 & \text{if } W_i = 2,650, \\ 0 & \text{otherwise;} \end{cases}$$

$$DW_2 = \begin{cases} 1 & \text{if } W_i = 3,250, \\ 0 & \text{otherwise;} \end{cases}$$

$$DW_3 = \begin{cases} 1 & \text{if } W_i = 4,200, \\ 0 & \text{otherwise;} \end{cases}$$

$$Du = \begin{cases} 1 & \text{if auto sold in United States,} \\ 0 & \text{otherwise.} \end{cases}$$

There is no DW for $W_i = 3600$ because there was no Japanese production in this category in 1979.

From FTC (1984) we can obtain the actual average wholesale price of Honda, Nissan, and Toyota combined production in 1979. This average price is $4,336 (U.S.).

Aggregating (4.A.3) over all automobiles produced by Honda, Nissan, and Toyota, we obtain the equation

$$\bar{P} = a + \sum_{j=0}^{3} b_j \bar{W}_j \cdot S_j + cSu, \qquad (4.A.9)$$

where

$\bar{P} = 4{,}336$, the average price (Honda, Nissan, Toyota);

$\bar{W}_j = $ the category weight, $j = 1, 2, 3$;

$W_0 = 2{,}199$, the averaged category weight over the 1,800-lb. and 2,250-lb. classes;

$S_j = $ the share in production of the jth category, $j = 0, \ldots, 3$ (i.e., $S_0 = .8636$, $S_1 = .0814$, $S_2 = .0542$, $S_3 = .0008$);

$Su = 0.2926$, the share of Japanese production sold in the United States.

Equation (4.A.9) can be solved for a and substituted into (4.A.8). Finally, recalling that the observed wholesale price $\hat{P}_i$ can be expressed as $\hat{P}_i = \alpha P_i$, the estimated equation becomes

$$P_i = \alpha \left[\bar{P} + \sum_{j=0}^{3} b_j (W_i \cdot DW_j - \bar{W}_j \cdot S_j) + c(Du - Su) \right]. \qquad (4.A.10)$$

Equation (4.A.10) was estimated for Honda, Nissan, and Toyota production for 1979. The sample size was 141, and the parameter estimates were as follows (standard errors in parentheses):

$b_0 = 2.019 \ (1.048)$, $\quad b_3 = 3.712 \ (0.599)$,

$b_1 = 2.355 \ (0.894)$, $\quad c = 232.6 \ (178.7)$,

$b_2 = 2.687 \ (0.736)$, $\quad \alpha = 0.935 \ (0.018)$.

The purpose of this exercise is to estimate α. The results imply that, on average, the wholesale price of a basic Japanese-produced auto is 93.5% of the price of a Japanese-produced auto complete with the actual options purchased. This compares with $\alpha = 0.75$ for the United States, and reflects the fact that much optional equipment on U.S. autos is standard equipment on Japanese autos.

We now assume that $\alpha = 0.935$ applies to all Japanese production, and not just to Honda, Nissan, and Toyota. Therefore, wholesale prices used to estimate a price-prediction equation for all Japanese production are computed as $\hat{P}_i/0.935$.

From the data presented here, it can be seen that 86% of Japanese production for 1979 was in the 1,800-lb. or 2,250-lb. class; other classes had a relatively small number of observations. We decided to estimate first a price-prediction equation for standard autos using only the 1,800-lb. and 2,250-lb. classes. The sample size was 139, and the equation estimated was

$$P_i = bW_i, \quad W_i = 1{,}800 \text{ or } 2{,}250. \qquad (4.A.11)$$

The estimate of b was 1.778 (0.026). The estimates of a and c were insignificantly different from zero, so these parameters were omitted.

Using (4.A.11), prices were estimated for the remaining classes. These estimated prices were compared with actual prices to separate the autos from the three heaviest classes (2,650-lb., 3,250-lb., 4,200-lb.) into standard versus specialty autos. (All 1,800-lb. and 2,250-lb. autos were deemed to be standard automobiles.) Specific models were classified as specialty models if their actual price P_i exceeded their estimated price (calculated from 4.A.11) by two standard deviations. After careful consideration, it was decided that the Japanese specialty automobiles had no North American counterparts and hence no comparable prices could be calculated. These autos were deleted from the sample used to compute the 1979 aggregate relative prices; the deleted automobiles represent 11% of the autos produced in Japan in 1979. Table 4.A.3 presents the price–quantity data obtained by applying these procedures.

4.A.4   Estimation of output-price predictions, 1979 German automobile production

It was not possible to estimate for Germany an equation for output-price prediction, owing to the lack of a sufficient range of observations on individual models. There was, however, sufficient information to compute average wholesale prices for mini, subcompact, and compact standard categories, as well as the midsize luxury category. It was also possible to construct an average wholesale price for the combined full-size + large luxury category. Hence, for Germany we have one less category than was the case for the other three countries.

The calculated average prices are contained in Table 4.A.4. For the midsize and full-size + large standard classes, we assumed that the wholesale prices were in the same proportion (1.24) to U.S. prices as were the weighted average of mini, subcompact, and compact standard categories. In order to compute the German–Canadian relative price index (see Section 4.A.5), we needed a predicted Canadian price for the midsize luxury category (for which production in Canada is zero). We thus assumed that the German–Canadian wholesale price for this category was in the same proportion (1.31) as the weighted average of the other categories.

This procedure yielded a Canadian wholesale price of $7,266 (U.S.) for the midsize luxury class. Table 4.A.4 presents the price–quantity data used to calculate the German relative output price index.

Table 4.A.3. *Disaggregated price–quantity data,
Japanese automobile production, 1979*

Category	Category weight (lbs.)	Predicted wholesale price (U.S.$)	Quantity produced
Mini			
Standard	1,800	3,201	423,509
Luxury	1,800	n.c.[a]	0
Subcompact			
Standard	2,250	4,001	4,480,536
Luxury	2,250	n.c.	0
Compact			
Standard	2,650	4,713	105,586
Luxury	2,650	n.c.	0
Midsize			
Standard	3,250	5,780	0
Luxury	3,250	n.c.	0
Full-size			
Standard	3,600	6,402	0
Luxury	3,600	14,090[b]	0
Large			
Standard	4,200	7,469	0
Luxury	4,200	15,157[c]	3,247

[a] n.c. means "not computed."
[b] Luxury premium in this class set equal to the calculated full-size premium.
[c] Production-weighted average price of President and Century.

4.A.5 Calculation of intercountry relative price indexes

Let p_{ij}, q_{ij} be the predicted wholesale price and quantity (respectively) of the jth automobile type produced in country i during 1979. Let $s_{ij} = (p_{ij} \cdot q_{ij})/\sum_j (p_{ij} \cdot q_{ij})$ be the revenue share of the jth automobile type produced in country i. A multilateral translog intercountry price index is obtained from the formula

$$\log p^i - \log p^0 = \sum_j \frac{1}{2}(s_{ij} + s_{0j}) \cdot (\log p_{ij} - \log p_{0j}), \qquad (4.A.12)$$

where 0 represents the base country.

Table 4.A.4. *Disaggregated price–quantity data,*
German automobile production, 1979

Category	Category weight (lbs.)	Predicted wholesale price (U.S.$)	Quantity produced
Mini			
Standard	1,800	4,022	146,306
Luxury	1,800	n.c.[a]	0
Subcompact			
Standard	2,250	4,648	1,170,451
Luxury	2,250	n.c.	0
Compact			
Standard	2,650	6,112	1,572,794
Luxury	2,650	n.c.	0
Midsize			
Standard	3,250	6,888	0
Luxury	3,600	9,518	694,955
Full-size and large			
Standard	4,200	8,732	0
Luxury	4,200	19,893	73,153

[a] n.c. means "not computed."

Equation (4.A.12) is the same form of the translog index as used by
Denny, Fuss, and May (1981) to calculate Canadian interregional unit
cost comparisons. Table 4.A.5 contains the results of applying equation
(4.A.12) to the data in Tables 4.A.1–4, with Canada chosen as the base
country.

Appendix 4.B: Calculation of the 1974 U.S.–Japan relative price index for materials

Let

P_M^J/P_M^U = materials relative price index to be calculated;

P_R^J/P_R^U = relative price index for materials purchased outside the automobile industry;

P_Q^J/P_Q^U = Japan–U.S. output relative price index (from Table 4.A.5);

P_Q^J/P_Q^C = Japan–Canada output relative price index (from Table 4.A.5);

Table 4.A.5. *Relative aggregate output prices*

Year	Canada	U.S.	Japan	Germany
1961	0.87	0.77		0.51
1962	0.87	0.83		0.55
1963	0.88	0.84		0.56
1964	0.89	0.85		0.56
1965	0.90	0.86		0.56
1966	0.90	0.86		0.58
1967	0.82	0.87	0.87	0.58
1968	0.93	0.90	0.85	0.58
1969	0.95	0.92	0.84	0.60
1970	0.97	0.92	0.81	0.65
1971	1.00	0.94	0.81	0.70
1972	1.02	0.95	0.91	0.79
1973	1.05	0.98	1.05	0.99
1974	1.14	1.04	1.13	1.09
1975	1.24	1.22	1.21	1.30
1976	1.35	1.26	1.19	1.29
1977	1.48	1.45	1.42	1.57
1978	1.66	1.68	1.95	2.01
1979	1.80	1.87	1.92	2.36
1980	2.00	2.05	1.89	2.50
1981	2.24	2.41	2.04	2.15
1982	2.40	2.65	1.91	
1983	2.54	2.70	1.99	
1984	2.68	2.89	2.11	

s_1 = cost share (of total cost of materials) of those materials purchased outside the automobile industry;

s_2 = cost share (of total cost of materials) of those materials inputs into auto manufacturing sources from within the domestic auto industry;

s_3 = cost share (of total cost of materials) of those materials inputs into auto manufacturing sources from within foreign auto industries.

It would have been preferable to apply the translog aggregation procedure used in Appendix 4.A, but cost share data for Japan was not available. Instead, we have used an aggregation procedure in which the shares of one country (here the United States) are used as weights. The aggregation formula is

$$\log\left(\frac{P_M^J}{P_M^U}\right) = s_1 \log\left(\frac{P_R^J}{P_R^U}\right) + s_2 \log\left(\frac{P_Q^J}{P_Q^U}\right) + s_3 \log\left(\frac{P_Q^J}{P_Q^C}\right). \quad (4.B.1)$$

In equation (4.B.1) we assume that (a) interindustry relative materials input prices are equal to relative industry output prices; (b) all foreign-sources interindustry materials inputs into the U.S. industry came from Canada in 1974; and (c) for Japan, the interindustry foreign and domestic input prices in 1974 were equal. The relative price data used was:

$P_R^J/P_R^U = 1.089$ (from Toder et al. 1978);
$P_Q^J/P_Q^U = 1.134/1.044$ (from Table 4.A.5);
$P_Q^J/P_Q^C = 1.134/1.144$ (from Table 4.A.5);
$\left.\begin{array}{l} s_1 = 0.400 \\ s_2 = 0.563 \\ s_3 = 0.037 \end{array}\right\}$ (from the 1977 U.S. *Census of Manufacturers*).

Using this data and equation (4.B.1), we obtain the Japan–U.S. relative materials price index for 1974:

$$\frac{P_M^J}{P_M^U} = 1.084.$$

Appendix 4.C: Data

4.C.1   *Data sources: Canada*

Gross output in current dollars and gross output deflator; materials input and materials price deflator:

> Statistics Canada. *Real Domestic Product by Industry, 1961–1971.* Catalogue #61-516 (July 1977).
> Statistics Canada. *Gross Domestic Product by Industry, 1984.* Catalogue #61-213, annual (September 1985).
> Statistics Canada. Industry Division. Unpublished revision to 1984, Catalogue #61-213 (August 1987).

Adjustment for goods for resale:

> Statistics Canada. *Motor Vehicle Manufacturers.* Catalogue #42-209, annual. Various issues (1961–6).
> Statistics Canada. *Motor Vehicle Parts and Accessories Manufacturers.* Catalogue #42-210, annual. Various issues (1961–6).

Statistics Canada. Industry Division. Unpublished data on goods purchased for resale in SIC 324 and SIC 325.

Total hours paid:

Statistics Canada. *Manufacturing Industries of Canada.* Catalogue #31-203, annual. Various issues (1961–84).

Total hours worked:

Statistics Canada. Direct from Industry Division. Annual (1961–84).

Total wages and fringe benefits:

Statistics Canada. Input–Output Division. Unpublished data.

Statistics Canada. *Estimates of Labour Income.* Catalogue #72-005, quarterly. Various issues (1974II–1984IV).

Statistics Canada. *Labour Costs in Canada, Manufacturing, 1971.* Catalogue #72-612 (February 1975).

U.S. Bureau of Labour Statistics. Office of Productivity and Technology. "International Comparison of Labour Compensation in the Motor Vehicle Industry." Unpublished data (1983, 1985, 1987).

Number of plants:

Statistics Canada. *Motor Vehicle Manufacturers.* Catalogue #42-209, annual. Various issues (1961–80).

Statistics Canada. *Motor Vehicle Industries.* Catalogue #42-219, annual. Various issues (1981–4).

Statistics Canada. *Truck Body and Trailer Manufacturers.* Catalogue #42-217, annual. Various issues (1961–84).

Statistics Canada. *Motor Vehicle Parts and Accessories Manufacturers.* Catalogue #42-210, annual. Various issues (1961–84).

Capital input; capital stock:

Statistics Canada. Wealth and Capital Stock Division. Unpublished data (1961–84).

Garston, Gordon J. "Canada's Capital Stock." Economic Council of Canada, Discussion Paper #226 (February 1983).

Asset price deflators for motor vehicles and manufacturing:

Statistics Canada. Wealth and Capital Stock Division. Unpublished data (1961–84).

User cost of capital:

Rao, Someshwar. "User Cost and Capital Stock Data Base, 1957–1984." Economic Council of Canada, Ottawa (unpublished).

Denny, Michael. "User Cost of Capital, 1961–1981." University of Toronto (unpublished).

Capacity output:

> Wards Communication Inc. *Wards Automotive Reports*. Detroit, weekly (January 1961–July 1985).
> Motor Vehicle Manufacturers Association. *World Motor Vehicle Data*. Detroit, annual. Various issues.
> Canadian Motor Vehicle Association. Unpublished data.

R & D stock; expenditures on R & D:

> Statistics Canada. *Industrial Research and Development Expenditures in Canada, 1959*. Catalogue #13-516 (April 1961).
> Statistics Canada. *Industrial Research and Development Expenditures in Canada, 1961*. Catalogue #13-520 (November 1963).
> Statistics Canada. *Industrial Research and Development Expenditures in Canada, 1962*. Catalogue #13-524 (November 1965).
> Statistics Canada. *Industrial Research and Development Expenditures in Canada, 1963*. Catalogue #13-527 (November 1967).
> Statistics Canada. *Industrial Research and Development Expenditures in Canada, 1965*. Catalogue #13-532 (February 1970).
> Statistics Canada. *Industrial Research and Development Expenditures in Canada, 1971*. Catalogue #13-203 (January 1974).
> Statistics Canada. Science and Technology Canada, Science Statistics Centre. *Research and Development in Canadian Industry* (1974).
> Statistics Canada. Science and Technology Statistics Division. *Science Statistics*. Catalogue #88-001, monthly (April 1984).
> Statistics Canada. Science and Technology Canada, Science Statistics Centre. *Industrial Research and Development Statistics, 1984*. Catalogue #88-202, annual (July 1986).

Price deflator for R & D; consumer price index:

> Statistics Canada. *Prices and Price Indexes*. Catalogue #62-002, monthly. Various issues (to 1974).
> Statistics Canada. *Consumer Prices and Price Indexes*. Catalogue #62-010, quarterly. Various issues (1975–84).

Output mix; production by auto model and category weights:

> Wards Communication Inc. *Wards Automotive Yearbook*. Detroit, annual. Various issues (1961–86).
> Canadian Motor Vehicle Manufacturers Association. *Facts and Figures of the Automotive Industry in Canada*. Toronto, semiannual. Various issues (to December 1986).

4.C.2   *Data sources: United States*

Gross output in current dollars and gross output deflator; materials input in current dollars; total hours worked and paid:

U.S. Department of Commerce. Bureau of Industrial Economics. Direct from Bureau data base (1961–80).

U.S. Department of Commerce. Undersecretary for Economic Affairs, Office of Business Analysis. Direct from Office data base (1981–4).

U.S. Department of Commerce. Bureau of the Census. *Census of Manufacturers.* Various issues.

U.S. Department of Commerce. Bureau of the Census. *Annual Survey of Manufacturers.* Washington, D.C., annual (non-census years). Various issues.

Materials price deflator:

Norsworthy, J. R., and Zabala, C. A. "Output Measurement and Productivity Growth in the U.S. Auto Industry." Bureau of the Census, unpublished background paper (April 1983).

The Public Research Institute, Centre for Naval Analysis. Alexandria, VA, unpublished data base (1983).

U.S. Department of Commerce. Bureau of the Census. *Statistical Abstract of the United States.* Various issues.

Adjustment for goods for resale:

Statistics Canada. *Motor Vehicle Manufacturers.* Catalogue #42-209, annual. Various issues (to 1980).

Statistics Canada. *Motor Vehicle Industry.* Catalogue #42-219, annual. Various issues (1981–4).

Crain Automotive Group. *Automotive News Market Data Book.* Detroit, annual. Various issues.

Wards Communication Inc. *Wards Automotive Yearbook.* Detroit, annual. Various issues.

Motor Vehicle Manufacturers Association. *World Motor Vehicle Data.* Detroit, annual. Various issues.

Statistics Canada. *Exports by Countries.* Catalogue #65-003, Semiannual. Various issues.

Motor Vehicle Manufacturers Association. U.S. Information on U.S. Tariffs on Motor Vehicles. Washington, D.C. Direct from Association data base (1961–85).

Bank of Canada. *Bank of Canada Review.* Ottawa, monthly. Various issues.

Number of plants:

U.S. Department of Commerce. Bureau of the Census. *Census of Manufacturers.* Various issues.

Total wages and fringe benefits:

U.S. Department of Labor. Bureau of Labor Statistics, Office of Productivity and Technology. Unpublished data.

Capital input:

Norsworthy, J. R., and Zabala, C. A. "Output Measurement and Productivity Growth in the U.S. Auto Industry." Bureau of the Census, unpublished background paper (April 1983).

U.S. Department of Commerce. Bureau of Economic Analysis. "Fixed Private Capital in the United States." *Survey of Current Business* 65(7): 36–59 (July 1985).

U.S. Department of Commerce. Bureau of Economic Analysis. "Fixed Reproducible Tangible Wealth in the United States: Revised Estimates." *Survey of Current Business* 66(1): 51–75 (January 1986).

Asset price deflators for motor vehicles and manufacturing:

U.S. Department of Commerce. Bureau of Economic Analysis. Washington, D.C., unpublished data base (1961–85).

User cost of capital:

Norsworthy, J. R., and Malmquist, H. "Input Measurement and Productivity Growth in Japanese and U.S. Manufacturing." *American Economic Review* 73(5): 947–67 (December 1983).

Department of Commerce. Bureau of the Census. *Statistical Abstract of the United States,* Washington, D.C., annual. Various issues.

Capacity output:

Wards Communication Inc. *Wards Automotive Reports.* Detroit, weekly (January 1961–July 1985).

Motor Vehicle Manufacturers Association. *World Motor Vehicle Data.* Detroit, annual. Various issues.

Crain Automotive Group. *Automotive News.* Detroit, weekly. Various issues.

Wards Communication Inc. *Wards Automotive Yearbook.* Detroit, annual. Various issues.

R & D stock; expenditures on R & D:

U.S. National Science Foundation. Washington, D.C., unpublished data (1957–84).

Price deflator for R & D; consumer price index:

Department of Commerce. Bureau of the Census. *Statistical Abstract of the United States,* Washington, D.C., annual. Various issues.

Output mix:

Wards Communication Inc. *Wards Automotive Yearbook.* Detroit, annual. Various issues.

4.C.3 *Data sources: Japan*

Gross output in current yen; material input in current yen; total hours paid; number of plants:

> Ministry of International Trade and Industry. Minister's Secretariat, Research and Statistics Department. *Census of Manufacturers: Report by Industry*. Tokyo, annual. Various issues.

Gross output in constant yen; material input in constant yen:

> Bank of Japan. Research and Statistics Department. *Price Indexes Annual*. Tokyo. Various issues.

Total hours worked:

> United Nations. International Labour Office. *Yearbook of Labour Statistics*. Geneva. Various issues.

Total wages and fringe benefits:

> U.S. Department of Labor. Bureau of Labor Statistics, Office of Productivity and Technology. Unpublished data.

Capital stock (investment):

> Ministry of International Trade and Industry. Minister's Secretariat, Research and Statistics Department. *Census of Manufacturers: Report by Industry*. Tokyo, annual. Various issues.

Asset price deflator and user cost of capital:

> Kuroda, Masahiro. University of Tokyo, unpublished data base (1957–79).
> Bank of Japan Research and Statistics Department. *Price Indexes Annual*. Tokyo. Various issues.
> Norsworthy, J. R., and Malmquist, H. "Input Measurement and Productivity Growth in Japanese and U.S. Manufacturing." *American Economic Review* 73(5): 947–67 (December 1983).
> International Monetary Fund. *International Financial Statistics*. Washington, D.C., monthly. Various issues.

Capacity output:

> Japan Automotive Manufacturers Association. *Motor Vehicle Statistics of Japan*. Tokyo, annual. Various issues.
> Bank of Japan. Research and Statistics Department. *Japanese Statistical Yearbook*. Tokyo, annual. Various issues.

R & D stock; R & D expenditures:

> Bank of Japan. Research and Statistics Department. *Japan Statistical Yearbook*. Tokyo, annual. Various issues.

Saxonhouse, Gary R. "Economic Statistics and Information Concerning the Japanese Auto Industry." U.S. Department of Transportation, National Highway Traffic Safety Administration, Office of Research and Development Report No. DOT-HS-805-481. Washington, D.C. (December 1980).

Price deflator for R & D; consumer price index:

OECD. *Main Economic Indicators.* Paris, monthly. Various issues.

Output mix:

Japan Automotive Manufacturers Association. *Motor Vehicle Statistics of Japan.* Tokyo, annual. Various issues.
Japan Automotive Manufacturers Association. Car Characteristics and Used Price Data. Tokyo, unpublished data.
Motor Vehicle Manufacturers Association. *World Motor Vehicle Data.* Detroit, annual. Various issues.

4.C.4   *Data sources: Germany*

Gross output in current marks and gross output deflator; materials input and materials price deflator; labor hours worked and total hourly compensation; capital stock in constant marks:

Conrad, Klaus. Unpublished data base using annual input–output tables (1960–81).

Number of plants:

Verband der Automobilindustrie e. V. *Tatsachen und Zahlen.* Frankfurt, annual. Various issues.

User cost of capital:

Nadiri, M. I. New York University, unpublished data set.
Berndt, E. R. Cambridge, Massachusetts Institute of Technology, unpublished data set.

Capacity output:

Verband der Automobilindustrie e. V. *Tatsachen und Zahlen.* Frankfurt, annual. Various issues.

R & D stock; R & D expenditures:

OECD. *Science and Technology Indicators: Resources Devoted to R & D.* Paris (1984).
Volkswagen A. G. Wolfsburg, Germany, unpublished data set.

Price deflator for R & D:

> International Monetary Fund. *International Financial Statistics.* Washington, D.C., monthly. Various issues.

Output mix:

> Verband der Automobilindustrie e. V. *Tatsachen und Zahlen.* Frankfurt, annual. Various issues.

4.C.5   *Data used to bridge country-specific price indexes*

Output price:

> Consumers Union of the United States. *Consumer Reports* 45(4) (April 1979).
> Federal Trade Commission. Report of the Bureaus of Competition and Economics Concerning the General Motors/Toyota Joint Venture (3 volumes). Washington, D.C., mimeo (1983).
> Ohta, Makoto. Sakura, Japan, University of Tsukuba, unpublished data base.

Materials price:

> Toder, E. J., Cordell, N. S., and Burton, E. *Trade Policy and the U.S. Automobile Industry.* New York: Praeger Publishers (1978).
> Emerson, David L. *Production, Location and the Automotive Agreement.* Ottawa: Economic Council of Canada (1975).

Capital price:

> Kravis, Irving B., Heston, Alan, and Summers, Robert. *World Product and Income.* The Statistical Office of the United Nations and the World Bank. London: Johns Hopkins University Press (1982).
> Kuroda, Masahiro. University of Tokyo, unpublished data base (1957–79).

4.C.6   *Listing of data used in estimation*

Our study focused on the automotive industries of four countries, as detailed in the following chart:

Country	SIC codes
United States	371 (motor vehicles)
Canada	323 (motor vehicle assembly) + 324 (truck and trailer bodies) + 325 (parts and accessories)
Japan	361 (motor vehicles)
Germany	33 (motor vehicles)

Table 4.C.1. *Range of data*

Country	Number of observations	Years
United States	31–54	1961–84
Canada	61–84	1961–84
Japan	98–114	1968–84
Germany	121–141	1961–81

A plus-sign after the code descriptor indicates that the data used is the aggregate of the three subindustries listed. The range of the data is listed in Table 4.C.1.

Key to variables: Tables 4.C.2–6 provide explicit values for the following variables:

$$CST = \text{cost per plant (thousands of Canadian dollars)};$$
$$SL = \text{cost share of labor};$$
$$SK = \text{cost share of capital};$$
$$SM = \text{cost share of materials};$$
$$PL = \text{price of labor (Canadian dollars)};$$
$$PK = \text{price of capital (Canadian dollars)};$$
$$PM = \text{price of materials (Canadian dollars)};$$
$$Q = \text{capacity output (thousands of 1971 Canadian dollars)};$$
$$T1 = \text{capacity utilization rate}$$
$$T2 = \text{R\&D stock (thousands of 1971 Canadian dollars)};$$
$$T3 = \text{output mix}$$
$$EXRCU = \text{actual exchange rate between United States and Canada (\$Can./\$U.S.)};$$
$$EXRJU = \text{actual exchange rate between United States and Japan (yen/\$U.S.)};$$
$$EXRGU = \text{actual exchange rate between United States and Germany (mark/\$U.S.)}.$$

The variables PL, PK, PM, Q, T2, and T3 are normalized so that Canada 1971 = 1. All monetary variables are converted to Canadian dollars using actual exchange rates. Price indexes are first bridged using PPP rates and other methods (see Appendix 4.A for details).

Table 4.C.2. *Exchange rates*

Year	EXRCU	EXRJU	EXRGU
1961	1.01300	359.98560	4.018
1962	1.06900	360.05347	4.000
1963	1.07900	360.14697	3.986
1964	1.07900	360.14697	3.975
1965	1.07800	359.93286	3.994
1966	1.07700	361.89502	3.999
1967	1.07900	362.20215	3.986
1968	1.07700	360.32104	3.992
1969	1.07700	358.28320	3.925
1970	1.04400	358.02441	3.647
1971	1.01000	347.07861	3.482
1972	0.99100	303.15063	3.189
1973	1.00000	270.63599	2.673
1974	0.97800	291.59204	2.588
1975	1.01700	296.50122	2.460
1976	0.98600	296.36304	2.518
1977	1.06300	265.95117	2.322
1978	1.14100	208.05977	2.009
1979	1.17100	218.10384	1.833
1980	1.16900	225.45796	1.818
1981	1.19900	219.99992	2.252
1982	1.23400	248.48965	2.424
1983	1.23200	237.37946	2.551
1984	1.29500	237.35318	2.840

Table 4.C.3. *United States*

Year	CST	SL	SK	SM	PL	PK	PM	Q	T1	T2	T3
1961	141,020.06250	0.16174	0.23058	0.60768	0.71842	0.74454	0.84182	0.67132	0.93778	0.45312	0.99869
1962	167,024.81250	0.15917	0.20896	0.63187	0.78603	0.87660	0.87693	0.74421	0.98293	0.52161	0.99460
1963	189,665.50000	0.15863	0.20929	0.63207	0.81915	0.95336	0.85743	0.81707	1.00873	0.59053	1.00113
1964	195,895.93750	0.17012	0.21482	0.61506	0.87024	1.00836	0.88744	0.88996	0.93712	0.65959	1.00961
1965	238,777.56250	0.16853	0.20951	0.62196	0.91721	1.08571	0.90737	0.96280	1.05415	0.72193	1.01322
1966	252,697.43750	0.17641	0.21591	0.60768	0.97622	1.06947	0.92611	1.05868	0.97911	0.78496	1.05884
1967	232,675.62500	0.17899	0.22841	0.59260	1.03279	0.96597	0.95091	1.10856	0.83258	0.83524	1.06275
1968	271,798.87500	0.18553	0.19787	0.61659	1.08026	0.97257	0.97794	1.14406	0.97074	0.88847	1.07331
1969	262,419.31250	0.19847	0.17112	0.63041	1.16519	0.81940	1.00904	1.17962	0.91556	0.93260	1.10786
1970	232,347.31250	0.21081	0.18345	0.60574	1.21946	0.74247	1.01944	1.21513	0.74291	0.96295	1.06476
1971	288,340.05250	0.20537	0.15855	0.63608	1.33842	0.79517	1.03701	1.25073	0.94377	1.00000	1.10221
1972	311,857.62500	0.20905	0.16459	0.62637	1.40825	0.86537	1.05990	1.28622	0.96015	1.05007	1.11460
1973	353,190.81250	0.21691	0.14272	0.64037	1.52309	0.84804	1.11872	1.32777	1.03934	1.12437	1.12312
1974	315,554.93750	0.22452	0.13239	0.64310	1.68751	0.68390	1.27193	1.36934	0.81856	1.16452	1.09196
1975	342,250.31250	0.21202	0.14382	0.64416	1.99784	0.80768	1.53149	1.41096	0.72590	1.17770	1.10426
1976	438,295.43750	0.20750	0.13069	0.66181	2.09287	0.95968	1.58499	1.45254	0.91851	1.21067	1.12022
1977	567,475.06250	0.20734	0.13005	0.65262	2.48567	1.18458	1.82928	1.49410	0.98780	1.26348	1.10023
1978	680,973.25000	0.20832	0.14565	0.64604	2.96068	1.53430	2.11848	1.55447	0.96215	1.32668	1.02454
1979	717,896.31250	0.20764	0.17492	0.61744	3.33997	1.83729	2.41214	1.61488	0.83901	1.39045	0.97833
1980	659,229.31250	0.21645	0.22821	0.55534	4.03771	2.12036	2.65307	1.58216	0.61983	1.43275	0.90142
1981	794,864.25000	0.20376	0.22225	0.57399	4.30081	2.23575	2.94044	1.68798	0.62971	1.43888	0.87703
1982	795,381.06250	0.19956	0.22679	0.57365	4.60478	2.32869	3.11074	1.71510	0.57713	1.43151	0.87569
1983	1,091,435.00000	0.19081	0.18201	0.62717	4.58921	2.40431	3.17422	1.91784	0.77046	1.44154	0.88030
1984	1,488,488.00000	0.19382	0.15550	0.65078	4.82020	2.55727	3.43487	2.14249	0.89500	1.47031	0.86968

Table 4.C.4. *Canada*

Year	CST	SL	SK	SM	PL	PK	PM	Q	T1	T2	T3
1961	94,012.18750	0.18829	0.19312	0.61859	0.54005	0.50751	0.82675	0.43943	0.83658	0.45312	0.99002
1962	102,739.43750	0.17879	0.16179	0.65942	0.54808	0.51517	0.82632	0.49232	0.85714	0.52161	0.95636
1963	126,665.62500	0.17610	0.13980	0.68410	0.56946	0.53123	0.83869	0.59019	0.90057	0.59053	0.97430
1964	112,573.56250	0.17917	0.13467	0.68616	0.59747	0.53707	0.84790	0.55637	0.83046	0.65959	0.97497
1965	115,017.50000	0.17945	0.13553	0.68502	0.64302	0.56852	0.85724	0.52610	0.90037	0.72193	0.98208
1966	128,504.37500	0.17160	0.16155	0.66684	0.67578	0.62746	0.87615	0.59746	0.84639	0.78496	1.06812
1967	145,494.81250	0.15869	0.18057	0.66074	0.70270	0.69297	0.89615	0.73538	0.77772	0.83524	1.07654
1968	174,957.37500	0.15399	0.16847	0.67754	0.78478	0.76260	0.92596	0.77158	0.87561	0.88847	1.08247
1969	198,495.25000	0.14944	0.16555	0.68501	0.84040	0.82839	0.94696	0.81490	0.92839	0.93260	1.03858
1970	217,100.00000	0.15310	0.20860	0.63830	0.93167	0.93585	0.97999	0.97333	0.75974	0.96295	0.95874
1971	248,672.43750	0.15514	0.19510	0.64975	1.00000	1.00000	1.00000	1.00000	0.85774	1.00000	1.00000
1972	295,305.81250	0.16615	0.15870	0.67515	1.05467	0.86781	1.01289	1.18108	0.89263	1.05007	0.93517
1973	311,395.18750	0.16973	0.14405	0.68622	1.13105	0.90990	1.07210	1.16373	0.94215	1.12437	0.96963
1974	379,293.81250	0.16978	0.14125	0.68897	1.30193	0.95054	1.17226	1.43894	0.85322	1.16452	1.01093
1975	441,784.87500	0.15032	0.16660	0.68308	1.46090	1.21904	1.32568	1.62425	0.76104	1.17770	1.09031
1976	468,875.68750	0.15640	0.16900	0.67459	1.66798	1.44104	1.45772	1.37244	0.86947	1.21067	1.13987
1977	515,475.81250	0.16864	0.16905	0.65231	1.80793	1.51842	1.59372	1.34867	0.90383	1.26348	1.08924
1978	577,144.75000	0.16119	0.15217	0.68664	2.07849	1.56527	1.78200	1.39783	0.88034	1.32668	1.03516
1979	600,015.50000	0.14649	0.15542	0.69809	2.21900	1.74421	1.93002	1.51695	0.77294	1.39045	0.99216
1980	689,223.43750	0.13899	0.20311	0.65790	2.46403	2.02921	2.17573	1.70655	0.62831	1.43275	0.97818
1981	807,065.12500	0.13828	0.25288	0.60884	2.71804	2.56475	2.40633	1.75680	0.61335	1.43888	0.97171
1982	882,228.62500	0.13149	0.23892	0.62959	2.99402	2.41411	2.56670	1.92207	0.58348	1.43151	0.94357
1983	1,061,190.00000	0.13228	0.20135	0.65637	3.04542	2.39533	2.62268	1.99185	0.71789	1.44154	0.89895
1984	1,259,683.00000	0.13550	0.18880	0.67570	3.27223	2.81142	2.80741	1.90402	0.84791	1.47031	0.93173

Table 4.C.5. *Japan*

Year	CST	SL	SK	SM	PL	PK	PM	Q	T1	T2	T3
1968	73,631.12500	0.11205	0.17817	0.70978	0.16703	0.64360	0.75758	0.36160	1.03328	0.86011	0.58935
1969	84,156.62500	0.11564	0.17852	0.70584	0.20459	0.66781	0.77737	0.41894	1.00395	0.92373	0.59573
1970	97,683.43750	0.11307	0.18874	0.69819	0.22845	0.64418	0.79045	0.50078	1.00118	0.98817	0.60629
1971	114,883.60250	0.11491	0.17584	0.70925	0.26663	0.61678	0.78173	0.57462	0.99917	1.09991	0.62310
1972	133,208.56250	0.12054	0.18255	0.69691	0.34175	0.79709	0.88437	0.58945	0.99539	1.22730	0.62991
1973	164,786.18750	0.12891	0.14976	0.72133	0.46645	0.78032	1.13884	0.63299	1.02693	1.36998	0.63742
1974	173,927.12500	0.13343	0.13338	0.73319	0.56840	0.67793	1.37832	0.64853	0.95287	1.53196	0.63989
1975	209,469.75000	0.13648	0.14589	0.71763	0.71006	0.82337	1.43652	0.74758	0.93092	1.68009	0.64721
1976	226,593.56250	0.13873	0.14035	0.72091	0.74910	0.88322	1.46824	0.75855	1.02738	1.79566	0.67584
1977	312,923.56250	0.13448	0.12326	0.74226	0.96635	0.97643	1.84257	0.91845	1.00040	1.90687	0.68366
1978	487,711.37500	0.13371	0.12040	0.74589	1.50543	1.39231	2.55245	0.99607	1.03726	2.06945	0.68363
1979	516,463.68750	0.13215	0.13185	0.73599	1.57188	1.56232	2.55859	1.12267	0.98224	2.29336	0.67999
1980	545,847.18750	0.12201	0.13423	0.74376	1.46026	1.65562	2.75341	1.15368	1.00904	2.50559	0.67722
1981	622,375.12500	0.11955	0.14119	0.73926	1.76460	1.78520	2.94215	1.22762	0.99902	2.72558	0.68085
1982	607,810.12500	0.12270	0.15568	0.72162	1.74959	1.66890	2.67885	1.32739	0.94913	3.03912	0.68268
1983	665,757.12500	0.12554	0.16161	0.71285	1.92507	1.77892	2.81699	1.41196	0.94944	3.35649	0.68060
1984	718,970.43750	0.12136	0.16062	0.71803	2.03006	1.91563	2.97512	1.41212	0.95476	3.65702	0.67999

114

Table 4.C.6. *Germany*

Year	CST	SL	SK	SM	PL	PK	PM	Q	T1	T2	T3
1961	74,042.06250	0.28039	0.12219	0.59742	0.20624	0.30127	0.81561	0.64131	0.96488	0.95376	0.75098
1962	80,523.68750	0.27451	0.13143	0.59406	0.24599	0.33557	0.86499	0.66929	0.91883	0.87023	0.75074
1963	85,323.50000	0.26158	0.13717	0.62124	0.25966	0.35328	0.88054	0.67151	0.93767	0.81226	0.74717
1964	97,114.25000	0.25323	0.13307	0.61370	0.28112	0.37130	0.88799	0.75884	0.93662	0.77977	0.74689
1965	101,760.87500	0.26037	0.13299	0.60664	0.31839	0.38199	0.89988	0.81025	0.90104	0.77117	0.74955
1966	107,840.00000	0.26021	0.14180	0.59799	0.34694	0.39793	0.91486	0.86790	0.86128	0.78817	0.74989
1967	107,061.43750	0.25877	0.16287	0.57836	0.36527	0.40189	0.90125	1.02458	0.69593	0.83524	0.75663
1968	117,703.87500	0.24428	0.14770	0.60802	0.37295	0.41098	0.89241	0.95774	0.83721	0.91220	0.75190
1969	130,330.06250	0.25351	0.13102	0.61546	0.43385	0.43728	0.93365	0.89287	0.97325	1.02229	0.77833
1970	155,009.25000	0.22802	0.12604	0.64595	0.47183	0.50548	1.02369	0.89840	1.01825	1.14166	0.78892
1971	197,098.68750	0.26779	0.13821	0.59400	0.62254	0.54430	1.08142	0.91741	0.99000	1.16669	0.78993
1972	205,822.12500	0.27792	0.14593	0.57614	0.75944	0.59341	1.17929	1.05643	0.94604	1.34785	0.81358
1973	282,015.31250	0.28905	0.13857	0.57238	1.06368	0.74401	1.50290	1.08353	0.98895	1.39066	0.81157
1974	284,764.00000	0.29911	0.15359	0.54730	1.18760	0.81232	1.71183	1.11460	0.83616	1.42620	0.80842
1975	334,372.75000	0.29372	0.15044	0.55584	1.47159	0.95950	1.96325	1.11159	0.86128	1.45810	0.79527
1976	355,723.18750	0.27526	0.15868	0.56605	1.48518	1.14561	1.93004	1.07586	0.97848	1.50853	0.79231
1977	445,356.93750	0.29143	0.14424	0.56433	2.03912	1.38364	2.29913	1.07452	1.02558	1.57864	0.79530
1978	607,617.68750	0.28269	0.14177	0.57554	2.55876	1.75114	2.89536	1.19106	1.01302	1.67796	0.81550
1979	737,848.31250	0.30477	0.14849	0.54673	3.52470	2.30557	3.42046	1.14639	1.03395	1.81382	0.81993
1980	819,863.06250	0.32541	0.16316	0.51144	4.16678	2.61354	3.64182	1.22736	0.94918	1.95478	0.80922
1981	751,343.87500	0.31704	0.18285	0.50011	3.74854	2.46473	3.09415	1.31257	0.93767	2.10001	0.81926

CHAPTER 5

Empirical results: estimation of the cost function

The cost function was estimated using annual pooled three-digit automobile production data from Canada (1961–84), United States (1961–84), Japan (1968–84), and Germany (1961–81). A detailed description of the data was presented in Chapter 4.

However, there is one variable, output, whose construction must be discussed in some detail because of the substantial bias that can result when the normal procedures are applied in the context of international comparisons. The output used in the estimation is real gross output, where the various physical outputs are aggregated using real comparative wholesale prices as weights. The procedure of using prices (rather than the theoretically correct marginal costs) as aggregation weights imparts a bias to the calculation of real comparative outputs when markups differ across the outputs being aggregated, and when the mix of outputs being produced differs among countries. Calculation of the bias requires a detailed knowledge of production, wholesale prices, and markups. We have this data for a major portion of output for one year (1979), and can calculate the magnitude of the bias for that year. Table 5.1 contains the information required for the automobile-production portion of output. Note the very different mix of production in the U.S., Japan, and Germany, as well as the difference in markups for different categories of automobiles. The distribution of production in Canada is sufficiently similar to the distribution in the United States that the bias imparted to U.S.–Canada comparisons in 1979 is negligible. Hence the biases inherent in comparisons of Canada with Japan and Germany will be eliminated as a byproduct of eliminating the U.S.–Japan and U.S.–Germany biases.

It will be helpful to understand the magnitude of the bias if we use the United States and Japan as an example. To facilitate an understanding of bias calculations, we assume initially that production is subject to constant returns to scale and that marginal costs are equal in the two countries. Then we would wish our index of relative average cost to be unity. Measured relative average cost (MRAC) (Japan/U.S.) is given by the formula

Table 5.1. *Data used to calculate measured relative average cost bias for 1979*

Category of automobile	Proportion of production			Wholesale price (U.S.$)			Assumed markups[a]
	U.S.	Japan	Germany	U.S.	Japan	Germany	
Mini	0.00	0.08	0.04	3,286	3,201	4,022	1.15
Subcompact	0.13	0.89	0.32	3,990	4,001	4,648	1.16
Compact	0.15	0.02	0.43	4,616	4,713	6,112	1.17
Midsize							
Standard	0.38	0.00	0.00	5,555	5,780	6,888	1.21
Luxury	0.00	0.00	0.19	n.c.[b]	n.c.	9,518	1.37
Full-size and large	0.34	0.01	0.02	7,861	15,157	19,893	1.37

[a] Price–marginal cost markups for categories other than Minis are taken from Bresnahan (1981, table 5, column 2). They are calculated on the basis of 1977 U.S. data.
[b] n.c. means "not computed."

$$MRAC = \frac{\dfrac{\Sigma(MC_i) \cdot Q_i/Q}{\Sigma(P_i/P_Q) \cdot Q_i/Q} \text{ (Japan data)}}{\dfrac{\Sigma(MC_i) \cdot Q_i/Q}{\Sigma(P_i/P_Q) \cdot Q_i/Q} \text{ (U.S. data)}} \tag{5.1}$$

where MC_i is marginal cost for the ith size class and hence $C = \Sigma(MC_i) \cdot Q_i$; Q_i/Q is the proportion of production in the ith size class; and P_Q is the aggregate price index (1.87 for the United States and 1.92 for Japan, from Table 4.A.5). Assuming that the markup for minis is 0.15, and substituting the data from Table 5.1 into equation (5.1), we have

$$MRAC = \frac{\left(\dfrac{3426}{4063}\right) \cdot (1.92)}{\left(\dfrac{4734}{5995}\right) \cdot (1.87)} = 1.10. \tag{5.2}$$

Thus MRAC is approximately 10% above the correct value (1.00). This bias would disappear in two cases. First, suppose price–marginal cost margins were equal across size classes; that is, let $P_i^U = \theta_U \cdot MC_i$ and $P_i^J = \theta_J \cdot MC_i^J$. Then

$$MRAC = \left(\frac{\theta_U}{\theta_J}\right) \cdot \left(\frac{P_Q^J}{P_Q^U}\right) \approx 1.00, \tag{5.3}$$

since $\theta_U/\theta_J = P_Q^U/P_Q^J$ for relative aggregate price indexes to be consistent with equal marginal costs. Second, suppose the output mix is the same in the two countries; that is, let $(Q_i/Q)^U = (Q_i/Q)^J$. Since $MC_i^U = MC_i^J$ by assumption,

$$MRAC = \frac{\Sigma(p_i^U) \cdot (Q_i/Q)^U}{\Sigma(p_i^J) \cdot (Q_i/Q)^J} \cdot \frac{P_Q^J}{P_Q^U} \approx 1.00. \tag{5.4}$$

We now relax the assumptions of constant returns to scale and inter-country equal marginal costs. If λ is the degree of returns to scale, then $\Sigma(MC_i) \cdot Q_i = \lambda^{-1} \cdot C$ or $C = \lambda \Sigma(MC_i) \cdot Q_i$. Let x be the Japanese advantage in marginal costs that produces the actual MRAC of 0.884. Using the returns to scale estimated in 1979 for Japan ($\lambda = 1.06$) and the United States ($\lambda = 1.05$), together with the data from Table 5.1, x can be computed from

$$MRAC = \frac{\dfrac{3426(1.06)}{4063} \cdot x \cdot (1.92)}{\dfrac{4734(1.05)}{5995} \cdot (1.87)} = 0.884, \tag{5.5}$$

which implies

$$x = 0.799. \tag{5.6}$$

Hence marginal costs in 1979 were 25% (1/0.799) lower in Japan than in the United States. The true relative average cost was $(0.799) \cdot (1.06)/1.05 = 0.807$. Therefore, the Japanese cost advantage in 1979 is underestimated by 8 percentage points, a sizable bias. The U.S. efficiency disadvantage would also be underestimated by approximately the same amount.

In an analogous manner we can compute the bias associated with the Germany–U.S. average cost comparisons. The actual measured relative average cost for 1979 is 1.175. Let y be the German disadvantage (relative to the U.S.) that produces the actual MRAC of 1.175. Then y can be computed from

$$\text{MRAC} = \frac{\dfrac{4165(1.10)}{6483} \cdot y \cdot (2.36)}{\dfrac{4734(1.05)}{5995} \cdot (1.87)} = 1.175, \tag{5.7}$$

which implies

$$y = 1.092. \tag{5.8}$$

Marginal costs in 1979 were 9% higher in Germany than in the United States. The true relative average cost was $(1.092) \cdot (1.10)/1.05 = 1.144$. The bias is approximately 3 percentage points, which is less than the Japan–U.S. bias because in 1979 Germany and the United States produced a more similar mix of automobiles. As noted previously, since the United States and Canada produced very similar mixes of autos, the Canada–U.S. bias was negligible in 1979.

The biases can be estimated for years other than 1979 by adding indicators of the output mix to the set of explanatory variables of the cost function, and by constraining the parameters to reproduce the actual 1979 biases. As described in Section 4.2.7, the output-mix variable (T_{3it}) was computed as an index, where typical weights were assigned to different classes of automobiles (mini, subcompact, compact, etc.) and an average weight computed for actual production. This variable fluctuated fairly tightly around 2,200 for Japan, 2,600 for Germany, and 3,500 for Canada and the United States, although it trended upward in Japan and downward in North America (see Table 4.2). From initial estimation results, it became clear that the output-mix data showed insufficient variation within each country to estimate second-order effects involving T_{3it}. Therefore, the cost–output-mix elasticity was assumed to be constant over time for each country, although the elasticity could differ among countries. The effect of including an output-mix variable is to add terms of the form

$$(\theta_3 + \theta_{3i} D_{ii}) \cdot \log T_{3it} \tag{5.9}$$

to the cost function. The biases calculated previously for 1979 imply constraints on the parameters θ_3, θ_{3i}. The calculations of these parameter constraints are contained in Appendix 5.A.

Equations $(3.22 + 3.32)$ and $(3.29 + 3.33)$ were estimated with constraints (3.25) imposed, using the Zellner iterative technique, to obtain maximum likelihood estimates. Initial estimation results implied the existence of positive serial correlation in the share equations, and also that regularity conditions for the cost function were not satisfied at a number of data points. The cost function was not concave for Japan in several years. A first-order autocorrelation specification for share equations was adopted (see Berndt and Savin 1975), and the minimal parameter constraints necessary to ensure local regularity over the sample were imposed. Since the regularity constraints are not nested in the basic specification, no formal testing was undertaken. However, the imposition of the constraints led to only a moderate decline in the log-likelihood function. The parameter constraints for Japan consistent with the output-mix bias calculated for 1979 had virtually no effect on the maximized log likelihood. The parameter constraint for Germany consistent with the output-mix bias was rejected at the 5% level. However, we retained this parameter constraint because we felt it was important to correct for this output-mix bias.

Appendix 5.B presents a discussion of the pretesting and choice of regression used in the cost and efficiency analysis. We begin by estimating the cost function and share equations restricted only by the adding-up, symmetry, and envelope-condition constraints (regression 1). We arrive at the final preferred structure (regression 6), which incorporates the cost bias–correction constraints for Japan and Germany, the concavity constraints, and constraints on certain capacity output parameters (detailed in Appendix 5.B). The parameter estimates, along with asymptotic standard errors and the usual diagnostic summary statistics, can also be found in Appendix 5.B. Parameter estimates of the regressions leading to the final regression (6) are also contained in this appendix, as well as test statistics on the viability of the constraints imposed.

Using the parameter estimates from regression 6 (final preferred structure), we verified that the inequality condition (3.34) required by the envelope theorem is satisfied at each data point in the sample. The importance

Table 5.2. *Own-factor price elasticities*

Input	Canada	U.S.	Japan	Germany
Capital	−0.08 (0.07)	−0.14 (0.06)	−0.13 (0.05)	−0.04 (0.08)
Materials	−0.07 (0.01)	−0.11 (0.01)	−0.05 (0.01)	−0.13 (0.01)
Labor	−0.28 (0.03)	−0.36 (0.03)	−0.15 (0.03)	−0.40 (0.02)

Notes: Computed at the mean data point for each country. Figures in parentheses are approximate standard errors.

Table 5.3. *Elasticities of substitution (Allen–Uzawa)*

Inputs	Canada	U.S.	Japan	Germany
Capital–materials	0.09 (0.10)	0.09 (0.10)	0.18 (0.08)	−0.14 (0.13)
Capital–labor	0.14 (0.07)	0.39 (0.05)	−0.02 (0.05)	0.47 (0.05)
Labor–materials	0.37 (0.04)	0.46 (0.03)	0.21 (0.03)	0.57 (0.03)

Notes: Computed at the mean data point for each country. Figures in parentheses are approximate standard errors.

of including the third-order capacity utilization terms is readily evident from the empirical results. Each of the parameters ρ_{k11} $(k=1,2,3)$ is statistically significant. The signs of the parameters are the correct ones, indicating that as underutilized capacity is used more intensively, the cost share of capital declines and the cost shares of labor and materials increase. (Recall that when capacity is underutilized, $T_1 < 1$ and $\log T_1 < 0$.)

Own-factor price elasticities and elasticities of substitution are contained in Tables 5.2 and 5.3. These tables indicate that, conditional on the state of technology, the possibilities for factor substitution in automobile production are not substantial. Table 5.4 provides estimates of capacity output elasticities, scale elasticities, and technical change elasticities, all calculated assuming full capacity utilization. This table also

Table 5.4. *Elasticities of capacity output, scale, utilization, and technical change*

Elasticity	Canada	U.S.	Japan	Germany
Cost–output	0.85	0.91	0.94	0.91
	(0.04)	(0.04)	(0.05)	(0.03)
Scale	1.17	1.09	1.07	1.10
	(0.05)	(0.05)	(0.05)	(0.04)
Cost–capacity utilization	0.69	0.80	0.93	0.86
	(0.03)	(0.04)	(0.05)	(0.03)
Cost–technical change	−0.07	−0.20	−0.35	−0.15
	(0.06)	(0.04)	(0.05)	(0.02)
Capital–output	0.61	0.69	0.71	0.65
	(0.09)	(0.09)	(0.08)	(0.08)
Materials–output	0.96	1.03	1.04	1.04
	(0.03)	(0.05)	(0.05)	(0.04)
Labor–output	0.59	0.71	0.59	0.75
	(0.06)	(0.06)	(0.07)	(0.04)
Capital–technical change	0.16	0.01	−0.13	0.10
	(0.10)	(0.08)	(0.09)	(0.09)
Materials–technical change	−0.11	−0.24	−0.39	−0.20
	(0.10)	(0.04)	(0.05)	(0.03)
Labor–technical change	−0.12	−0.24	−0.41	−0.17
	(0.08)	(0.06)	(0.08)	(0.06)

Notes: Computed at the mean data point for each country. Figures in parentheses are approximate standard errors.

contains cost–capacity utilization elasticities, calculated at the actual mean capacity utilization rates. Table 5.4 demonstrates that production in all four countries is subject to increasing returns to scale at the mean data point. The capacity utilization elasticity shows that costs increase proportionately less than actual output (potential output held constant), so that there are short-run increasing returns to utilization. Increasing research and development expenditures appear to have more of a cost-reducing impact in Japan than elsewhere, although – since the elasticities vary with the data – this cannot be determined for certain from the mean elasticities.

The input–capacity output elasticities indicate that the production function is nonhomothetic, with capacity expansion using proportionately less capital and labor than materials. Technology improvements result in more capital-intensive production processes. Technical change, rather than changes in relative factor prices, appears to be the major source of substitution of capital for other inputs (cf. Table 5.3).

In the remaining chapters we will use this estimated cost-function structure to calculate the differences in unit costs over time and between countries, as well as to determine the sources of these differences.

Appendix 5.A: Calculation of constraints on cost bias parameters

The cost bias term can be calculated as if it were one of the technological condition terms in the decomposition equation (3.14). It takes the form

$$\log(\text{average cost bias}) = -\tfrac{1}{2}(ECT_{3i} + ECT_{30}) \cdot (\log T_{3i} - \log T_{30}), \quad (5.A.1)$$

where

$$ECT_{3i} = \theta_3 + \theta_{3,i}. \qquad (5.A.2)$$

For 1979, $T_{3,U} = 0.978$, $T_{3,J} = 0.680$, $T_{3,G} = 0.820$.

For the Japan–U.S. comparision, the average cost bias is $(0.807/0.884)$. Equation (5.A.1) takes the form

$$\log(0.807/0.884) = -\tfrac{1}{2}(2\theta_3 + \theta_{3,U} + \theta_{3,J}) \cdot [\log(0.680) - \log(0.978)]$$

or

$$2\theta_3 + \theta_{3,U} + \theta_{3,J} = -0.5. \qquad (5.A.3)$$

For the Germany–U.S. comparison, the average cost bias is $(1.144/1.175)$. Hence equation (5.A.1) takes the form

$$\log(1.144/1.175) = -\tfrac{1}{2}(2\theta_3 + \theta_{3,U} + \theta_{3,G}) \cdot [\log(0.820) - \log(0.978)]$$

or

$$2\theta_3 + \theta_{3,U} + \theta_{3,G} = -0.3. \qquad (5.A.4)$$

Appendix 5.B: Discussion of pretesting and choice of regression in the analysis of cost and efficiency

As noted in the text, a number of hypothesis tests were conducted to arrive at the final estimated structure. In this appendix we present the parameter estimates and the various statistical tests.

There was one final change in the specification of the cost function. A very sharp decline in total factor productivity (TFP) growth occurred in

Japan after 1980. From an average annual rate of 3.8% during the 1970–80 period, TFP growth fell to only 1.0% during 1981–4. We allowed for the possibility that this change would affect the paramters by specifying a shift in the first-order technical change term for Japan. The term $(\theta_2 + \theta_{2i} D_{ii}) \cdot \log T_{2it}$ in the cost function was replaced by

$$(\theta_2 + \theta_{2i} D_{ii} + \theta_{2J8} \cdot D_{J8}) \cdot \log T_{2it},$$

where $D_{J8} = 1$ for Japan 1981–4 and 0 otherwise. As expected, θ_{2J8} was positive and statistically significant at the 1% level.

5.B.1   *Key to regressions*

Regression (1) – restricted only by the adding-up and symmetry constraints, and by the envelope-condition constraints (from Chapter 3).

Regression (2) – (1) plus cost bias-correction constraints:

$$2\theta_3 + \theta_{3,U} + \theta_{3,J} = -0.5 \text{ (Japan)};$$

$$2\theta_3 + \theta_{3,U} + \theta_{3,G} = -0.3 \text{ (Germany)}.$$

Regression (3) – (2) plus the following:

$$\beta_{1,J} = 0, \quad \beta_{1,G} = 0, \quad \mu_{11} = 0.$$

Regression (4) – (1) plus the following concavity constraints:

$$\delta_{33} = S_L(1 - S_L), \qquad \delta_{23} = -S_M \cdot S_L,$$

where S_L, S_M are Japan's 1969 shares.

Regression (5) – (4) plus the cost bias correction constraint.

Regression (6) – final preferred structure, equal to (5) plus the following:

$$\beta_{1,J} = 0, \quad \beta_{1,G} = 0, \quad \mu_{11} = 0.$$

Table 5.B.1 presents the empirical results corresponding to regressions (1) through (6).

5.B.2   *Order of variables*

Factor prices w_{it}:   Technical conditions T_{it}:

(1) capital;   (1) capacity utilization rate;
(2) materials;   (2) index of the stock of R & D;
(3) labor.   (3) output mix.

Table 5.B.1. *Estimation results*

Parameter	Regressions					
	(1)	(2)	(3)	(4)	(5)	(6)
α_0	12.827 (0.009)	12.825 (0.009)	12.821 (0.009)	12.828 (0.009)	12.826 (0.009)	12.821 (0.009)
$\alpha_{0,U}$	−0.161 (0.014)	−0.153 (0.014)	−0.145 (0.013)	−0.167 (0.014)	−0.159 (0.014)	−0.148 (0.013)
$\alpha_{0,J}$	−0.311 (0.215)	−0.162 (0.083)	−0.104 (0.036)	−0.297 (0.214)	−0.176 (0.083)	−0.118 (0.036)
$\alpha_{0,G}$	0.013 (0.119)	−0.260 (0.024)	−0.234 (0.019)	0.022 (0.119)	−0.265 (0.024)	−0.234 (0.019)
α_1	0.166 (0.005)	0.166 (0.005)	0.166 (0.005)	0.167 (0.005)	0.167 (0.005)	0.167 (0.005)
$\alpha_{1,U}$	0.036 (0.007)	0.036 (0.007)	0.036 (0.007)	0.030 (0.006)	0.030 (0.006)	0.029 (0.006)
$\alpha_{1,J}$	−0.033 (0.013)	−0.032 (0.013)	−0.032 (0.013)	−0.006 (0.011)	−0.005 (0.011)	−0.004 (0.011)
$\alpha_{1,G}$	0.017 (0.008)	0.017 (0.008)	0.017 (0.008)	0.029 (0.008)	0.029 (0.008)	0.029 (0.008)
α_2	0.676 (0.006)	0.676 (0.006)	0.676 (0.006)	0.675 (0.006)	0.675 (0.006)	0.675 (0.006)
$\alpha_{2,U}$	−0.052 (0.009)	−0.052 (0.009)	−0.051 (0.009)	−0.059 (0.008)	−0.059 (0.009)	−0.058 (0.009)
$\alpha_{2,J}$	−0.024 (0.020)	−0.025 (0.020)	−0.028 (0.020)	−0.012 (0.014)	−0.012 (0.014)	−0.013 (0.014)
$\alpha_{2,G}$	−0.176 (0.012)	−0.176 (0.012)	−0.178 (0.012)	−0.177 (0.010)	−0.177 (0.010)	−0.177 (0.010)
α_3	0.158 (0.004)	0.158 (0.004)	0.158 (0.004)	0.158 (0.004)	0.158 (0.004)	0.158 (0.004)
$\alpha_{3,U}$	0.016 (0.006)	0.016 (0.006)	0.015 (0.006)	0.030 (0.005)	0.030 (0.005)	0.029 (0.005)
$\alpha_{3,J}$	0.056 (0.016)	0.058 (0.016)	0.061 (0.016)	0.017 (0.008)	0.017 (0.008)	0.018 (0.008)
$\alpha_{3,G}$	0.159 (0.008)	0.159 (0.008)	0.160 (0.008)	0.148 (0.005)	0.148 (0.005)	0.148 (0.005)
β_1	0.933 (0.050)	0.917 (0.052)	0.846 (0.034)	0.945 (0.055)	0.929 (0.052)	0.845 (0.034)
$\beta_{1,U}$	0.002 (0.054)	0.007 (0.056)	0.063 (0.043)	−0.004 (0.054)	0.002 (0.056)	0.069 (0.043)

Table 5.B.1 *(cont.)*

Parameter	Regressions					
	(1)	(2)	(3)	(4)	(5)	(6)
$\beta_{1,J}$	0.028	−0.094	0	0.023	−0.093	0
	(0.159)	(0.158)		(0.158)	(0.157)	
$\beta_{1,G}$	−0.220	−0.148	0	−0.241	−0.167	0
	(0.082)	(0.081)		(0.081)	(0.081)	
θ_1	0.933	0.917	0.846	0.945	0.929	0.845
	(0.050)	(0.052)	(0.034)	(0.050)	(0.052)	(0.034)
$\theta_{1,U}$	0.002	0.007	0.063	−0.004	0.002	0.069
	(0.054)	(0.056)	(0.043)	(0.054)	(0.056)	(0.043)
$\theta_{1,J}$	0.028	−0.094	0	0.023	−0.093	0
	(0.159)	(0.158)		(0.158)	(0.157)	
$\theta_{1,G}$	−0.220	−0.148	0	−0.241	−0.167	0
	(0.082)	(0.081)		(0.081)	(0.081)	
θ_2	−0.171	−0.148	−0.070	−0.188	−0.165	−0.070
	(0.064)	(0.066)	(0.054)	(0.063)	(0.066)	(0.054)
$\theta_{2,U}$	−0.041	−0.074	−0.132	−0.032	−0.068	−0.141
	(0.061)	(0.062)	(0.052)	(0.061)	(0.062)	(0.052)
$\theta_{2,J}$	−0.091	−0.006	−0.152	−0.067	0.022	−0.131
	(0.170)	(0.165)	(0.051)	(0.169)	(0.164)	(0.051)
$\theta_{2,G}$	0.037	0.118	−0.021	0.061	0.146	−0.015
	(0.088)	(0.079)	(0.041)	(0.087)	(0.146)	(0.042)
θ_3	−0.272	−0.263	−0.288	−0.278	−0.269	−0.291
	(0.079)	(0.082)	(0.083)	(0.079)	(0.082)	(0.084)
$\theta_{3,U}$	0.082	0.040	0.054	0.102	0.054	0.059
	(0.098)	(0.100)	(0.096)	(0.097)	(0.099)	(0.097)
$\theta_{3,J}$	−0.458	−0.014	0.021	−0.394	−0.015	0.024
	(0.459)	(0.110)	(0.112)	(0.457)	(0.110)	(0.112)
$\theta_{3,G}$	1.301	0.186	0.221	1.355	0.185	0.224
	(0.477)	(0.110)	(0.112)	(0.475)	(0.110)	(0.112)
δ_{11}	0.116	0.117	0.117	0.112	0.113	0.113
	(0.009)	(0.008)	(0.008)	(0.010)	(0.010)	(0.010)
δ_{22}	0.157	0.158	0.160	0.161	0.162	0.162
	(0.017)	(0.017)	(0.017)	(0.008)	(0.008)	(0.008)
δ_{33}	0.128	0.129	0.131	0.088	0.088	0.088
	(0.012)	(0.012)	(0.012)	(0.005)	(0.005)	(0.005)
μ_{11}	0.217	0.123	0	0.238	0.145	0
	(0.204)	(0.209)		(0.203)	(0.209)	

Table 5.B.1 *(cont.)*

Parameter	Regressions					
	(1)	(2)	(3)	(4)	(5)	(6)
ϕ_{11}	1.157	1.091	0.839	1.193	1.127	0.834
	(0.253)	(0.262)	(0.151)	(0.252)	(0.262)	(0.152)
ϕ_{22}	−0.074	−0.258	−0.250	−0.071	−0.259	−0.260
	(0.220)	(0.213)	(0.124)	(0.219)	(0.212)	(0.124)
ϕ_{12}	−0.114	0.026	0.079	−0.134	0.006	0.077
	(0.203)	(0.205)	(0.070)	(0.202)	(0.205)	(0.071)
δ_{12}	−0.073	−0.073	−0.073	−0.093	−0.093	−0.093
	(0.010)	(0.010)	(0.010)	(0.010)	(0.010)	(0.010)
δ_{13}	−0.044	−0.044	−0.044	−0.020	−0.020	−0.019
	(0.006)	(0.006)	(0.006)	(0.002)	(0.002)	(0.002)
δ_{23}	−0.084	−0.085	−0.087	−0.069	−0.069	−0.069
	(0.012)	(0.012)	(0.012)	(0.004)	(0.004)	(0.004)
λ_{11}	−0.039	−0.040	−0.038	−0.037	−0.037	−0.035
	(0.011)	(0.011)	(0.011)	(0.011)	(0.011)	(0.011)
λ_{21}	0.075	0.075	0.075	0.080	0.080	0.076
	(0.014)	(0.014)	(0.014)	(0.014)	(0.014)	(0.014)
λ_{31}	−0.036	−0.036	−0.036	−0.043	−0.043	−0.041
	(0.007)	(0.007)	(0.007)	(0.007)	(0.007)	(0.007)
Ω_{11}	−0.039	−0.040	−0.038	−0.037	−0.037	−0.035
	(0.011)	(0.011)	(0.011)	(0.011)	(0.011)	(0.011)
Ω_{21}	0.075	0.075	0.075	0.080	0.080	0.076
	(0.014)	(0.014)	(0.014)	(0.014)	(0.014)	(0.014)
Ω_{31}	−0.036	−0.036	−0.036	−0.043	−0.043	−0.041
	(0.007)	(0.007)	(0.007)	(0.007)	(0.007)	(0.007)
Ω_{12}	0.056	0.056	0.055	0.036	0.036	0.035
	(0.012)	(0.012)	(0.012)	(0.011)	(0.011)	(0.011)
Ω_{22}	−0.016	−0.015	−0.012	−0.030	−0.029	−0.027
	(0.017)	(0.017)	(0.017)	(0.014)	(0.014)	(0.014)
Ω_{32}	−0.040	−0.041	−0.044	−0.006	−0.007	−0.007
	(0.013)	(0.013)	(0.013)	(0.008)	(0.008)	(0.008)
τ_{11}	0.217	0.123	0	0.238	0.145	0
	(0.204)	(0.209)		(0.203)	(0.209)	
τ_{12}	−0.114	0.026	0.079	−0.134	0.006	0.077
	(0.203)	(0.205)	(0.070)	(0.202)	(0.205)	(0.071)
ρ_{111}	0.172	0.171	0.173	0.172	0.171	0.173
	(0.025)	(0.025)	(0.025)	(0.025)	(0.025)	(0.025)

Table 5.B.1 *(cont.)*

| Parameter | Regressions | | | | | |
	(1)	(2)	(3)	(4)	(5)	(6)
ρ_{211}	−0.138	−0.137	−0.141	−0.135	−0.134	−0.137
	(0.028)	(0.028)	(0.028)	(0.029)	(0.029)	(0.029)
ρ_{311}	−0.033	−0.033	−0.032	−0.037	−0.037	−0.036
	(0.007)	(0.007)	(0.007)	(0.007)	(0.007)	(0.007)
$\theta_{2,J8}$	0.084	0.105	0.108	0.083	0.103	0.107
	(0.024)	(0.022)	(0.022)	(0.024)	(0.022)	(0.022)
Autocorrelation	0.613	0.615	0.615	0.613	0.616	0.617
parameter	(0.037)	(0.037)	(0.037)	(0.043)	(0.043)	(0.043)
Log likelihood	796.044	792.827	789.771	787.771	784.390	780.740
R^2						
Cost	0.995	0.994	0.994	0.995	0.994	0.994
Capital share	0.990	0.990	0.990	0.988	0.988	0.988
Materials share	0.968	0.968	0.968	0.967	0.967	0.967
D.W.[a]						
Cost	1.299	1.162	1.088	1.310	1.161	1.076
Capital share	1.908	1.915	1.914	1.773	1.784	1.787
Materials share	1.759	1.759	1.769	1.758	1.760	1.771

[a] Durbin–Watson statistic.

5.B.3　*Hypothesis testing*

Table 5.B.2 presents hypothesis tests for the regressions in order to test the constraints that we imposed. The likelihood-ratio test is performed, and the result is compared to the criticial values of the chi-squared statistic for the corresponding number of restrictions at the 1% and 5% levels.

The output bias constraint imposed on both Japan and Germany is just rejected at the 5% level, but accepted at the 1% level. As mentioned in Chapter 4, there are a number of problems with the German data that could not be corrected for. The output bias constraint is not rejected (at the 5% level) when imposed only on Japan. Even though it is rejected in the German data, we felt it important to correct for the bias and so the constraint was maintained.

Although the concavity constraints were rejected at both the 5% and 1% levels by the data, the cost and efficiency comparisions were unaffected

Table 5.B.2. *Hypothesis tests*

Constraints	Log likelihood	Test statistics	Critical χ^2_F
(1) Initial maintained hypothesis	796.044		
(2) $2\theta_3 + \theta_{3,U} + \theta_{3,J} = -0.5$ $2\theta_3 + \theta_{3,U} + \theta_{3,G} = -0.3$	792.827	(2) versus (1): 6.434	$\chi^2_1(5\%) = 5.99$ $\chi^2_1(1\%) = 9.21$ $\chi^2_3(5\%) = 7.81$
(3) $2\theta_3 + \theta_{3,U} + \theta_{3,J} = -0.5$ $2\theta_3 + \theta_{3,U} + \theta_{3,G} = -0.3$ $\beta_{1,J} = 0,\ \beta_{1,G} = 0,\ \mu_{11} = 0$	789.991	(3) versus (2): 5.672 (3) versus (1): 12.106	$\chi^2_5(5\%) = 11.07$ $\chi^2_5(1\%) = 15.09$
(4) Concavity constraints:[a] $\delta_{33} = SL(1 - SL)$ $\delta_{23} = -SM \cdot SL$	787.771	(4) versus (1): 16.546	$\chi^2_2(5\%) = 5.99$ $\chi^2_2(1\%) = 9.21$
(5) Concavity constraints + $2\theta_3 + \theta_{3,U} + \theta_{3,J} = -0.5$ $2\theta_3 + \theta_{3,U} + \theta_{3,G} = -0.3$	784.390	(5) versus (4): 6.762 (5) versus (1): 23.308	$\chi^2_2(5\%) = 5.99$ $\chi^2_2(1\%) = 9.21$ $\chi^2_4(5\%) = 9.49$ $\chi^2_4(1\%) = 13.28$
(6) Concavity constraints + $2\theta_3 + \theta_{3,U} + \theta_{3,J} = -0.5$ $2\theta_3 + \theta_{3,U} + \theta_{3,G} = -0.3$ $\beta_{1,J} = 0,\ \beta_{1,G} = 0,\ \mu_{11} = 0$	780.740	(6) versus (5): 7.3 (6) versus (4): 14.062 (6) versus (1): 30.608	$\chi^2_3(5\%) = 7.81$ $\chi^2_5(5\%) = 11.07$ $\chi^2_7(5\%) = 14.07$ $\chi^2_7(1\%) = 18.482$

[a] *SL* and *SM* are constrained by equation (3.29), where the right-hand side variables take on Japan 1969 values.

by their imposition. Given the robustness of the results of interest, we decided to impose the constraints to insure a theoretically valid estimated cost function over the complete sample.

Imposition of the zero constraints on the second-order parameters μ_{11}, β_{1J}, and β_{1G} were not rejected by the data at the 5% and 1% level, and the constrained structure resulted in a proportion of fixed costs in total costs at full capacity utilization for the United States that was closer to the actual proportion observed in the data. See Fuss and Waverman (1990, p. 235) for additional details.

The final preferred regression (6) used in our analysis includes the concavity and output bias constraints, as well as the zero restrictions $\mu_{11} = \beta_{1J} = \beta_{1G} = 0$.

CHAPTER 6

Productivity growth in the automobile industry, 1970–1984: a comparison of the United States, Japan, Germany, and Canada

6.1 Introduction

In this chapter we calculate and analyze the automobile industry's cost and productivity experience during the 1970s and early 1980s in the United States, Japan, Germany, and Canada. Using our econometric cost-function methodology, we are able to isolate the major source of short-run disequilibrium in this industry – variations in capacity utilization – and analyze its effect on cost and total factor productivity (TFP) growth. The importance of analyzing variations in capacity utilization is confirmed by the fact that failure to correct for this source of productivity change over the period 1970–84 would have led to a 20% overestimate of long-run TFP growth in Canada and a 22% overestimate for the United States.

Even after correcting for capacity utilization differences, the Japanese productivity "miracle" is evident from our results (see Table 6.5). During the 1970s, total factor productivity in the Japanese automobile industry grew at an average rate of 3.9% per annum. By way of contrast, the Canadian and U.S. automobile industries both experienced average per-annum TFP growth rates of only 1.2%, less than one-third of the Japanese rate. The TFP growth of the German auto sector in the 1970s was slightly more than that achieved in North America, averaging 1.4% per annum, a growth rate far below that achieved in Japan.

The large difference between the TFP growth rates of the North American and Japanese automobile industries is in sharp contrast to Norsworthy and Malmquist's (1983) results for total manufacturing, where the Japanese advantage was much less pronounced.

The comparatively much more rapid efficiency gain in Japan is a major reason why long-run average cost, as measured in each country's own currency, grew at only a 3.2% annual rate for Japanese automobile production, whereas long-run average cost increased at a 7.3% rate in Canada,

131

at an 8.2% rate in the United States, and at a 6.7% rate in Germany (see Table 6.1). The source of the Japanese relative decrease in unit costs is also clear from Table 6.1 – rapid technical change.

In the 1980s, the TFP growth rate story changes. The United States and Canada have annual (capacity utilization–adjusted) growth rates of TFP of 0.7% and 0.4% per year, respectively, whereas Japan's TFP growth rate drops to 1.3% per year.[1]

6.2   Growth rates of cost and productivity and their decomposition

Tables 6.1–6.5 present the empirical results on cost and productivity, which are the focus of this chapter. Table 6.1 contains our analysis of increases in actual unit production costs over the 1970–84 period. The actual annual percentage cost increase in a common currency (Canadian dollars) is shown in column 1. This figure is calculated as the average of the increases over each of three periods: 1970–84, 1970–80, and 1980–4. Over the 1970–80 period, average cost (in Canadian dollars) increased by an annual rate of 10.1% in the United States, 9.3% in Japan, 15.6% in Germany, and 8.1% in Canada. Relative to the United States, both Canada and Japan improved their cost-competitive positions, but the relative improvements were not particularly large. The United States, Japan, and Canada did experience significant improvements in their position relative to Germany. In the 1980–4 period, Japan improved significantly vis-à-vis the United States and Canada; the Japanese annual increase in unit costs was 60% of that in the United States and half of that in Canada (all measured in Canadian currency).

The pattern of cost increases in each country's own currency tells a dramatically different story. Over the period 1970–80, the Japanese cost increase is only 3.2% per year, compared with 8.9% for the United States, 6.8% for Germany, and 8.1% for Canada. These differences are due to substantial appreciation of the Japanese yen and the German mark relative to the U.S. and Canadian dollars, and a smaller appreciation of the U.S. dollar relative to the Canadian dollar.

Over the entire 1970–84 period, again in Canadian dollars, annual unit costs increased by 6.8% in Canada, 7.9% in the United States, and 7.0% in Japan. Relative to the United States, Canada and Japan improved their competitive positions.

---

[1] Our German data ends in 1981, so we cannot compare the performance of the German auto sector to that of the other three countries in this latter period.

Table 6.1. *Unit production cost increases and their sources*

Years	Average annual unit production cost increase (%)				Sources of increase (%)					
	Can.$	U.S.$	Yen	Mark	Price of labor	Price of capital	Price of materials	Scale economies	Technical change	Capacity utilization
United States										
1970–84	7.9	6.2			1.7	1.2	4.6	−0.3	−0.8	−0.3
1970–80	10.1	8.9			2.4	1.8	5.1	−0.2	−1.1	0.7
1980–84	2.6	0.0			0.4	0.4	2.4	−0.5	−0.2	−2.6
Japan										
1970–84	7.0		2.4		1.3	0.6	3.6	−0.4	−2.7	0.0
1970–80	9.3		3.2		1.5	0.6	5.0	−0.6	−3.3	0.0
1980–84	1.6		0.3		0.7	0.4	0.5	−0.2	−1.1	0.1
Germany										
1970–80	15.6			6.8	4.0	1.3	2.7	−0.3	−1.1	0.1
Canada										
1970–84	6.8				1.4	1.4	5.2	−0.7	−0.3	−0.3
1970–80	8.1				1.6	1.5	5.3	−0.8	−0.5	0.8
1980–84	3.5				1.1	1.5	4.3	−0.4	−0.1	−2.9

Note: Costs are estimated costs derived from the cost function.

The pattern of cost increases in each country's own currency is again different: the Japanese average annual cost increase is only 2.4%, compared with 6.2% for the United States and 6.8% for Canada. These differences – between calculations in one currency versus each country's own currency – are due to changes in exchange rates. (Table 2.22 contains the time path of the relevant exchange rates that had such a large impact on intercountry differences in unit-cost growth rates.)

The 1980–4 period saw a narrowing of the rate of average cost increases measured in each country's own currency. The best performance is in the United States, where average unit production costs remained constant, followed closely by Japan, with Canada experiencing higher unit-cost growth.

Table 6.1 also contains a decomposition of average unit production cost increases; the decomposition in Table 6.1 and subsequent tables is with respect to average costs as measured in the country's *own* currency. (The formulas used to calculate the decomposition were presented in Chapter 3.) Any element listed under "Sources of increase" in Table 6.1 can be interpreted as follows. Consider the number 3.6 under "Price of materials" for Japan in the period 1970–84. If all the variables affecting unit production costs in Japan had remained constant at the geometric average of their 1970 and 1984 levels, *except for the price of materials,* unit production costs in Japan would have increased by 3.6% per annum because of the increase in the price of materials between 1970 and 1984. Similarly, the number −0.8 under the heading "Technical change" in the first row of Table 6.1 implies that if all variables except for the actual changes in the technical-change variable (stock of R & D) had been constant, U.S. unit production cost would have fallen by 0.8% per annum over the 1970–84 period. For the tables in this chapter, each element listed under "Sources" is a set of discrete comparative statics results for variations in each of the exogenous variables affecting average production costs.

In all countries except Germany, the major determinant of average cost increases over the 1970–80 period was the substantial increase in materials prices. In Germany, materials prices grew as well, but not at the same rates as in North America and Japan. In Germany, average annual increases in labor costs were the major contributor to average cost increases.

Technical change has been the major source of cost reduction in Japan, the United States, and Germany, whereas for Canada the major source of cost reduction was the realization of economies of scale associated with larger plant size. The size and pattern of the impact of technical change deserves some comment. In the 1970–80 period, technical change was reducing Japanese unit production costs at a 3.3% annual rate but U.S. and German unit production costs at only a 1.1% annual rate. This differential of 2.2% per year would (when compounded) yield a 26-percentage-point differential between unit costs and productivity in Japan and unit costs and productivity in the United States and Germany. In the period 1980–4, the contribution of technical change to unit cost reduction fell to 1.1% per annum in Japan and to only 0.2% in the United States, so the gap has not narrowed appreciably.

As we have already discussed in detail, capacity utilization rates have varied considerably from year to year in the North American automotive industry. We have also pointed out that the Japanese motor vehicle industry's capacity utilization (CU) rate has been relatively constant over the entire period at nearly full utilization. The German motor vehicle sector has also had relatively steady and high rates of capacity utilization. The effect on unit production costs of variations in CU are evident. In North America this effect is most pronounced when comparing the periods 1970–80 and 1980–4. In the United States, average unit production costs increased by 0.7% per year from 1970–80, but decreased by 2.7% per year from 1980–4 due to the CU effect *alone*. The results for Canada are even more pronounced. Note, however, that variations in CU have no noticeable effect on unit production costs in Japan and Germany.

In order to analyze cost increases on a more permanent long-run basis, we present in Table 6.2 results for a form of hypothetical long-run equilibrium. In this table, we assume that CU rates for all four countries are constant at their normal rate for all years. As expected, the growth rates of U.S. and Canadian costs become less variable over the periods analyzed. Two points are important. First, in the 1970s the gap between the Japanese industry and its North American competitors is not closed. Second, during 1980–4 the lower U.S. unit cost increase relative to Japan (suggested by Table 6.1) is reversed, since it was entirely a CU phenomenon. In the crucial sense of long-run equilibrium, the U.S. auto industry's unit costs continued to exceed the Japanese in the early 1980s. Canadian unit costs grew at a very high rate.

Table 6.3 presents data on decomposition of the long-run equilibrium in a slightly altered way. The components of TFP growth are aggregated (using equation 3.17 with $T_1 = 1$) and compared with the aggregate of factor price effects. This table portrays two facts in a graphic way. First, the Japanese motor vehicle industry has consistently experienced lower rates of aggregate factor-price increases than have its competitors. Second, the

Table 6.2. *Unit production cost increases and their sources: long-run equilibrium*

Years	Average annual unit production production cost increase (%)				Sources of increase (%)				
	Can.$	U.S.$	Yen	Mark	Price of labor	Price of capital	Price of materials	Scale economies	Technical change
United States									
1970–84	8.2	6.6			1.7	1.1	4.9	−0.3	−0.7
1970–80	9.5	8.2			2.3	1.5	5.6	−0.2	−1.0
1980–84	5.3	2.6			0.4	0.3	2.6	−0.5	−0.2
Japan									
1970–84	7.0		2.3		1.3	0.6	3.6	−0.5	−2.7
1970–80	9.3		3.2		1.5	0.6	4.9	−0.6	−3.3
1980–84	1.5		0.2		0.7	0.4	0.5	−0.2	−1.1
Germany									
1970–80	15.5			6.7	4.0	1.4	2.7	−0.3	−1.1
Canada									
1970–84	7.1				1.4	1.3	5.4	−0.7	−0.3
1970–80	7.3				1.5	1.3	5.7	−0.8	−0.4
1980–84	6.5				1.1	1.3	4.6	−0.4	−0.1

Table 6.3. *Unit production cost increases: long-run equilibrium*

	Average annual unit production cost increase (%)				Sources of increase (%)	
Years	Can.$	U.S.$	Yen	Mark	Factor prices	TFP growth
United States						
1970–84		6.6			7.7	−1.0
1970–80		8.2			9.5	−1.2
1980–84		2.6			3.3	−0.7
Japan						
1970–84			2.3		5.5	−3.1
1970–80			3.2		7.2	−3.9
1980–84			0.2		1.5	−1.3
Germany						
1970–80				6.7	8.2	−1.4
Canada						
1970–84	7.1				8.1	−1.0
1970–80	7.3				8.5	−1.2
1980–84	6.5				7.0	−0.4

Japanese industry – to a much greater extent than North American and German producers – has used productivity growth to minimize unit production cost increases stemming from factor-price increases. This effect was particularly pronounced during the 1970–80 period. Not one of the other three countries has had a particularly sterling record in offsetting its rising factor prices with productivity improvements.

Tables 6.4 and 6.5 examine changes in total factor productivity in the four countries.[2] From 1970 to 1980 TFP grew by only 0.6% in the United States and 0.5% in Canada, compared with a TFP growth rate of 3.8% for Japan. The German industry did better than North America but far worse than Japan. However, TFP growth appears to be considerably faster in the United States and Canada than in Japan during the 1980–4 period. This latter result is quite misleading, however, because it is actually a

[2] In contrast with Tables 6.1-6.3, the "Sources of growth" columns in Tables 6.4 and 6.5 are organized according to conventional growth accounting procedures. They measure the proportions of TFP growth that can be attributed to the various effects.

Table 6.4. *Total factor productivity (TFP) growth*

Years	Average annual TFP growth rate (%)	Percentage contributions to growth		
		Scale economies	Capacity utilization	Technical change
United States				
1970–84	1.3	22	22	56
1970–80	0.6	32	−103	171
1980–84	3.2	15	79	6
Japan				
1970–84	3.0	15	−1	86
1970–80	3.8	15	0	85
1980–84	1.0	13	−5	92
Germany				
1970–80	1.3	22	−6	84
Canada				
1970–84	1.3	54	20	26
1970–80	0.5	176	−185	109
1980–84	3.3	11	86	3

phenomenon of variable CU rates; this points to the importance of accounting for CU variations in a highly cyclical industry. In Table 6.5, CU effects are removed and the true underlying trends in efficiency are revealed. Over the 1970–84 period, North American long-run TFP growth rates were about 1% per annum, only about *one-third of the TFP growth rate for Japan.*

The contributions of the various sources of "equilibrium"[3] TFP growth (Table 6.5) over the 1970–80 period were very similar for the United States, Japan, and Germany; approximately 80–85% was due to technical change and 15–20% due to the growth of the average plant size in the presence of increasing returns to scale. For Canada during 1970–80, 68% of TFP growth was due to scale economies and only 32% due to technical change. The 1970–84 period was similar to the 1970–80 period, except that TFP grew less rapidly in the three countries (no German data is available for 1980–4), with Japan maintaining a 3:1 edge. However, the contributing

---

[3] A glance at the "Percentage contributions" portion of Table 6.4 indicates how including short-run effects such as capacity utilization can hamper interpretation of the results.

Table 6.5. *Total factor productivity (TFP) growth:*
long-run equilibrium

Years	Average annual TFP growth rate (%)	Percentage contributions to growth	
		Scale economies	Technical change
United States			
1970–84	1.0	29	71
1970–80	1.2	17	83
1980–84	0.7	73	27
Japan			
1970–84	3.1	15	85
1970–80	3.9	15	85
1980–84	1.3	13	87
Germany			
1970–80	1.4	21	79
Canada			
1970–84	1.0	71	29
1970–80	1.2	68	32
1980–84	0.4	82	18

sources of growth diverge dramatically in the 1980–4 period: 73% of the contribution to U.S. TFP growth is due to scale effects, with an even higher percentage in Canada. The 1980–4 results may not represent a long-run trend, for a number of reasons. The period is a fairly short one for calculations of this type, and it saw very large modernization investments in North America and the closing of a number of existing plants. Scale may not have increased, but the use of *kanban* ("just-in-time" inventory management techniques) may have led to agglomeration effects that appear here as scale improvements.

It is also of some interest to compare our TFP growth rate results with previous estimates. To our knowledge, there are no previous estimates of TFP growth in the Canadian auto sector. Previous estimates for the United States, Germany, and Japan are presented in Table 6.6. Conrad and Jorgenson's (1985) and Jorgenson, Kuroda, and Nishimizu's (1987) estimated TFP growth rates are below ours for both the United States and Japan, and the difference for Japan is quite large. Part of the difference can be attributed to their adjustment of labor hours for educational

Table 6.6. *Comparison of estimates of annual average total factor productivity growth rates (%)*

Country	Conrad and Jorgenson (1985)	Jorgenson, Kuroda, and Nishimizu (1987)	Griliches and Mairesse (1985)[a]	This study[b]
1970–9				
United States	0.9			2.2
Japan	0.6			3.5
Germany	1.8			1.9
1973–9				
United States		−0.2		1.2
Japan		1.4		3.6
1973–80				
United States			−0.7	−0.4
Japan			4.4	3.9

[a] Transportation equipment industry.
[b] Calculated using the Tornqvist index for purposes of comparison.

attainment, which tends to increase the rate of growth of the labor input, thus lowering measured TFP growth. But this adjustment alone cannot account for the magnitude of the difference. Our results are quite similar to those of Griliches and Mairesse (1985), who estimated TFP growth using data drawn from a sample of individual firms from the two-digit transportation equipment industry. Since 1973 was a peak and 1980 a trough year in the North American automobile business cycle, their negative number for the United States is due largely to the effects on TFP of the decline (to 0.62 from 1.04) in capacity utilization, and is thus a short-run measure. Our estimate of the long-run underlying TFP growth rate over the period 1973–80 is an increase of 1.1% per annum.

The only other German study available for comparison purposes is Conrad and Jorgenson (1985). The close agreement between our study and that of Conrad and Jorgenson is of no particular significance, since we have relied heavily on Conrad's data base for Germany.

6.3 Conclusions

In this chapter we have calculated and analyzed the automobile industry's cost and productivity experience during the 1970s in the United States,

Japan, Germany, and Canada. Percentage cost increases in a common currency (Canadian dollars) differed less significantly than the increases in each country's own currency, owing to currency realignments. The appreciation of the Japanese yen during the 1970s masked the superior performance of the Japanese auto industry relative to the North American and German industries during that period. Of course, rates-of-growth analysis cannot determine whether Japan was just catching up to North American and German productivity levels or actually pulling ahead. A levels analysis is required to answer that important question: such an analysis appears in Chapter 7.

Of substantial importance is the finding that a major source of Japanese productivity growth was technical change, and that differentials in technical change between Japan and its German and North American competitors were large over the period under study.

Finally, we have emphasized the importance of taking account of variations in capacity utilization when analyzing TFP growth rates for a cyclical industry such as the automobile industry. Failure to do so would have led to a 20% overestimate of TFP growth in Canada during the 1970s and a 22% overestimate for the United States.

CHAPTER 7

International comparisons of automobile industry cost and productivity levels: Japan, Germany, and the United States

7.1 Introduction

In this chapter we compare and analyze the relative levels of unit cost and productivity between the United States and Japan over the period 1970–84, and between Germany and both Japan and the United States over the period 1970–80. (Comparisons between Canada and the United States, and between Canada and both Germany and Japan, are presented in Chapter 8.) We also examine cost and productivity levels for the three countries in 1979 and 1980. A comparison for 1979 is the one that has been used for most accounting cost studies (see Chapter 2), and we contrast our results with those earlier studies. In 1980, the North American automobile industry for the first time lobbied for protection against a perceived large Japanese cost advantage.

Our results indicate a Japanese cost advantage of 19.3% over American producers for 1979; these results are considerably less unfavorable to North American automobile production than were those of most analysts surveyed in Chapter 2.

Our empirical results for 1980 show a substantial Japanese cost advantage over American car producers, on the order of 35%. However, the large change in relative costs between 1979 and 1980 was primarily due to substantial reductions in capacity utilization rates in North America, rather than to any abrupt deterioration of long-run comparative productivity levels. Depreciation of the Japanese yen relative to its purchasing power parity (PPP) equilibrium also contributed to the North American disadvantage. In 1984, the Japanese cost advantage over U.S. producers was still at 1980 levels.

For 1979, we find that Japanese auto producers had a larger cost advantage over German auto producers than over U.S. auto producers; in 1979, U.S. producers had lower per unit production costs than German auto producers. In 1980, the Japanese cost advantage over Germany jumped,

142

primarily because of factor-price movements (including exchange-rate appreciation) in Germany.

The sources of these cost advantages – Japan over the United States and the United States over Germany – are somewhat surprising. In 1979, the Japanese cost efficiency advantage over the United States was 65% of its unit production cost advantage, but in 1984 less than 50%. In 1979, divergence of the actual exchange rate from its Fundamental Equilibrium Exchange Rate (FEER) level explained only 3% of the Japanese cost advantage over the United States; in 1984 this explained 16% of the cost advantage. In 1979, U.S. producers were less efficient than German producers in the manufacture of equivalent automobiles, but U.S. factor-price advantages dominated its relative technical inefficiency.

7.2   Adjustment of the allocation formulas for exchange-rate effects

In a number of the intercountry comparisons presented here, it is instructive to isolate changes in cost differences due to exchange-rate fluctuations from those due to relative movements in factor prices and efficiencies within each country. To do so, we must establish "standard" exchange rates to measure fluctuations around the standard, and we need to adjust the allocation formulas so that fluctuations of the exchange rate around this standard rate become another source of unit-cost differences.

For comparisons between Japan, the United States, and Germany, we establish "equilibrium" exchange rates based on the concept of a fundamental equilibrium exchange rate (FEER) as calculated by Williamson (1983, 1985). The FEERs were combined with relative inflation rates (as measured by industrial price indexes) to produce PPP currency exchange rates, which are denoted as the equilibrium rates. A comparison of costs calculated at the equilibrium rates with those calculated at actual exchange rates provides a measure of the cost difference attributable to exchange-rate fluctuations away from the equilibrium rates. (Table 2.12 presents the actual and equilibrium exchange rates between the United States and Japan for 1977–84, and between the United States and Germany for the period 1977–81.) Details of the calculation procedure, along with data for the period 1977–84, are contained in Appendix 7.A. Earlier data could not be obtained because Williamson did not calculate FEERs before 1977.

Once the equilibrium exchange rates have been calculated, we are in a position to adjust the allocation formulas in order to separate out exchange-rate effects. The results of this adjustment are to provide factor-price effects that measure cost differentials when factor prices are computed at equilibrium exchange rates.

7.3   International comparison of cost and productivity levels: empirical results

In this section we present the empirical results on cost and productivity level comparisons between Japan, the United States, and Germany, using equations (3.41) and (3.42) as modified in Section 7.2. The results are presented in Tables 7.1–7.12. For each set of comparisons (Japan–U.S., Germany–U.S., Germany–Japan) we provide four tables: (1) actual levels of unit-cost differences and their sources; (2) equilibrium levels (holding capacity utilization at normal levels); (3) actual levels adjusted for exchange-rate disequilibria; and (4) equilibrium levels adjusted for exchange-rate disequilibria.

7.3.1   *U.S.–Japan comparisons*

Table 7.1 contains the unit production cost differences between Japanese and U.S. automobile production over the period 1970–84. As in Chapter 6, the unit production cost difference is in a common currency – Canadian dollars. From Table 7.1 we can see that unit production costs of Japanese automobile producers were 34% less in 1970 than unit costs in the U.S. industry. This Japanese cost advantage varied over the 1970s: it declined in 1974, rose in 1975, declined again by 1978, and rose substantially in 1979. In 1980 there was a rapid deterioration in the American position, leading to a substantial advantage to Japan (on the order of 35%), a Japanese advantage not witnessed since 1970. The Japanese advantage rose again in 1982 and fell back to 1980 levels in 1984.

Recall from Chapter 6 the method of interpreting data listed in columns under the heading "Sources of difference." The number −23.0 under "Price of labor" in the first row of Table 7.1 has the following interpretation: If all variables affecting cost, other than the price of labor, were equal in the two countries at the geometric average of their values in the two countries in the year 1970, then total unit production costs in Japan would have been 23.0% lower than in the United States. Similarly, the number 9.7 under "Cost efficiency" indicates that if all factor prices had been equal in the two countries at the 1970 geometric means, unit production costs would have been 9.7% higher in Japan than in the United States in 1970.

Table 7.1. *Unit-cost difference and its sources (%): Japan–United States*

Year	Unit production cost difference[a]	Sources of difference							
		Price of labor	Price of capital	Price of materials	Cost efficiency	Scale economies	Capacity utilization	Country-specific efficiency	Residual
1970	−34.1	−23.0	−2.5	−15.6	9.7	8.4	−6.0	7.6	−5.4
1974	−12.5	−17.1	−0.1	5.8	1.6	4.8	−2.1	−1.0	−1.6
1975	−21.2	−16.7	0.3	−4.3	−4.9	4.1	−4.6	−4.2	3.6
1978	−6.3	−10.8	−1.3	13.8	−8.1	2.8	−0.4	−10.2	1.9
1979	−19.3	−11.9	−2.4	4.1	−12.5	2.2	−2.0	−12.6	3.1
1980	−35.1	−15.2	−4.1	2.5	−22.1	1.8	−10.3	−14.7	0.1
1982	−43.6	−15.5	−5.6	−9.3	−22.1	1.3	−12.2	−12.5	0.2
1984	−35.4	−13.0	−4.3	−9.4	−17.2	1.8	−0.6	−18.1	3.5

[a] [(Japan/U.S.) −1] ×100.

In Chapter 5 we argued that the technical-change variable is properly viewed as a method of tracking the country-specific unexplained technical change. From this point of view, consistency requires that we aggregate the technical-change effect with the country-specific efficiency effect, forming a single decomposition effect that we will also call the *country-specific efficiency effect*. That has been done in creating the tables for this chapter. Hence the number 7.6 in the column "Country-specific efficiency" means that if all variables – excepting the technical change variable and the U.S. and Japanese dummy variables – had been equal in the two countries, then unit production costs would have been 7.6% higher in Japan in 1970.

Several features stand out in Table 7.1. First, we see the deterioration in the country-specific efficiency (CSE) effect from an American advantage of 7.6% in 1970 to an American *dis*advantage of 18.1% in 1984. This should not be surprising, given the results from Chapter 6: Total factor productivity grew at a 3.8% rate in Japan and only a 0.6% rate in the United States over the period 1970–80.[1] Second, between 1970 and 1974 the deterioration in the American CSE advantage was more than compensated for, in terms of relative production costs, by the substantial advantage gained by the United States in factor prices. The American deterioration in CSE was, by 1979, too great to be compensated for by factor prices, which rose relatively faster in Japan than in the United States. Third, the abrupt deterioration between 1979 and 1980 in U.S. unit costs was caused by a worsening of all of the main effects on the unit production cost difference, but was primarily caused by a large increase in the capacity utilization (CU) cost disadvantage. The importance of the CU effect in determining cost differences in 1980 will be a constant theme throughout this chapter.

Note that, in 1970, American motor vehicle producers enjoyed plant scale advantages and CSE advantages over Japanese auto producers. The *entire U.S. unit-cost disadvantage in 1970 was a result of lower factor prices in Japan*. In contrast, although Japan in 1984 still held a substantial unit-cost advantage over the United States (35.4% as compared to 34.1% in 1970), *the Japanese advantage in 1984 was primarily due to more efficient production*. Factor-price advantages to Japan declined sharply over the 1970–84 period. For example, if only the price of labor had differed between the two countries, the Japanese advantage in unit production costs would have been 23.0% in 1970 and only 13.0% in 1984. If only

---

[1] The CSE term aggregates the technical change parameter and pure CSE. In Chapter 6 we noted substantially greater technical change in Japan than in the United States.

the price of materials had differed, a Japanese cost advantage of 15.6% in 1970 would have changed to a 2.5% disadvantage by 1980, and reverted to a 9.4% advantage in 1984.

As the data in Table 7.1 also indicates, 1980 and 1982 are years during which all major sources of cost differences moved against the United States. The major source of the sharp increase in the Japanese unit-cost advantage can be attributed to the deterioration in relative CU in the United States; this was not necessarily a source of long-run disadvantage.

We now turn to Tables 7.2 to 7.4, which separate out the effects of capacity utilization and exchange-rate fluctuation. Consider Table 7.2, which removes exchange-rate fluctuations around FEER from unit production costs. The number −11.4 under the heading "Price of labor" implies that had the U.S.–Japan exchange rate been at its PPP or equilibrium level, and all effects other than the price of labor were equal between the two countries, then unit production costs in 1978 would have been 11.4% lower in Japan than in the United States. The number 3.8 under the heading "Exchange-rate fluctuation" means that had all factors affecting cost differences been the same in the two countries, where input prices are evaluated at the equilibrium exchange rate, unit production cost in 1978 would have been 3.8% higher in Japan than in the United States, owing to exchange-rate fluctuations away from the equilibrium exchange rate.

From Table 7.2 it can be seen that the rise in the U.S. production cost disadvantage between 1980 and 1982 was caused by the substantial devaluation of the yen relative to its equilibrium value. Note that accounting separately for exchange-rate effects smooths out the sharp annual differences between the two countries in labor and capital prices appearing in Table 7.1, and that the U.S. advantage in materials prices still deteriorates over the 1978–84 period, but not to the extent as in Table 7.1. Most of the change in materials prices, in Table 7.1 seemingly to Japan's advantage, turn out in Table 7.2 to arise because of the devaluation of the yen.

As noted earlier, the other major determinant of the substantial post-1979 rise in the U.S. cost disadvantage was the CU effect. In Table 7.3, we examine "equilibrium" effects holding CU at its normal level. Making this change reduces the U.S. cost disadvantage in 1970, 1974, 1980, and 1982, years of significant capacity underutilization in the United States. The Japanese cost advantage in the 1980s is still substantial, rises monotonically between 1979 and 1984, and is a function of both factor-price advantages and real long-term efficiency differences.

In Table 7.4 we hold both CU and exchange rates at their equilibrium levels. As we have shown, the sharp increase in the unit production cost

Table 7.2. *Unit-cost difference and its sources (%), including exchange-rate fluctuations from purchasing power parity: Japan–United States*

Year	Unit production cost difference[a]	Sources of difference							
		Price of labor	Price of capital	Price of materials	Cost efficiency	Scale economies	Capacity utilization	Country-specific efficiency	Exchange-rate fluctuation
1978	−6.3	−11.4	−1.9	11.0	−8.1	2.8	−0.4	−10.2	3.8
1979	−19.3	−11.3	−1.9	6.4	−12.5	2.2	−2.0	−12.6	−3.3
1980	−35.1	−14.3	−3.1	6.1	−22.1	1.8	−10.3	−14.7	−5.3
1982	−43.6	−12.7	−2.4	1.1	−22.1	1.3	−12.2	−12.5	−15.9
1984	−35.4	−10.3	−1.4	1.6	−17.2	1.8	−0.6	−18.1	−16.1

[a] [(Japan/U.S.)−1]×100.

148

Table 7.3. *Unit-cost difference and its sources (%): Japan–United States (equilibrium – not adjusting for exchange-rate fluctuations)*

Year	Unit production cost difference[a]	Sources of difference					
		Price of labor	Price of capital	Price of materials	Scale economies	Country-specific efficiency	Cost efficiency
1970	−26.3	−22.3	−2.4	−15.9	8.4	6.5	15.5
1974	−9.2	−16.7	−0.1	5.9	4.8	−1.6	3.1
1975	−20.5	−16.2	0.2	−4.4	4.1	−5.0	−1.1
1978	−7.6	−10.8	−1.3	13.8	2.8	−10.2	−7.7
1979	−20.1	−11.6	−2.4	4.1	2.2	−12.9	−11.0
1980	−27.2	−14.5	−3.7	2.6	1.8	−15.2	−13.7
1982	−35.3	−14.8	−4.8	−9.8	1.3	−12.7	−11.6
1984	−37.0	−12.8	−4.2	−9.5	1.8	−18.1	−16.7

[a] [(Japan/U.S.) −1]×100.

Table 7.4. *Unit-cost difference and its sources (%): Japan–United States (equilibrium – adjusting for exchange-rate fluctuations)*

Year	Unit production cost difference[a]	Sources of difference					
		Price of labor	Price of capital	Price of materials	Scale economies	Country-specific efficiency	Cost efficiency
1978	-11.0	-11.4	-1.9	11.0	2.8	-10.2	-7.7
1979	-17.3	-11.1	-1.8	6.5	2.2	-12.9	-11.0
1980	-23.0	-13.7	-2.8	6.3	1.8	-15.2	-13.7
1982	-23.1	-12.1	-2.1	1.1	1.3	-12.7	-11.6
1984	-24.9	-10.1	-1.4	1.7	1.8	-18.1	-16.7

[a] [(Japan/U.S.) − 1] × 100.

disadvantage to the United States between 1979 and 1980 could, to a considerable extent, be attributed to the devaluation of the Japanese yen relative to its equilibrium level.[2] However, after accounting for CU and exchange-rate disequilibria, the United States still had an increasing cost disadvantage compared to Japan, culminating at 25% in 1984. It is important to note that the Japanese long-run cost advantage in 1984 consisted of both factor-price (labor) advantages and cost-efficiency advantages, the latter being more important than the former. It is the very substantial deterioration in the U.S. cost efficiency relative to Japan that accounts for most of the rise in the Japanese long-run cost advantage.[3] The primary reason for the rise in the U.S. cost-efficiency disadvantage was a substantial deterioration in the CSE effect.

As we have seen, exchange-rate fluctuations and variations in CU can strongly impact the relative levels of unit production costs and cost efficiency. For many purposes, it is more important to look at the long-run underlying trends in these cost differences. It is striking to note that while U.S. producers had a 44% actual unit-cost disadvantage in 1982 (Table 7.1), they had only a 23% equilibrium unit-cost disadvantage in that same year.

7.3.2   Germany–U.S. comparisons

In Tables 7.5–7.8 we examine the unit production cost differences between German and U.S. motor vehicle producers, beginning with the "actual" (nonequilibrium) calculations.

In 1963, we estimate that German motor vehicle producers had 44% lower unit production costs than their American counterparts. Approximately 40% of this advantage to the German producers was superior cost efficiency; the remainder was due to favorable factor prices in Germany, which experienced far lower prices of labor and capital. By 1974, unit production costs were 4% *higher* in Germany than the United States; this

---

[2] Table 7.A.1 of the appendix to this chapter shows that the U.S. inflation rate was approximately 7.5 percentage points greater than the Japanese rate, and yet the actual value of the yen fell from 218 yen/U.S.$ to 225 yen/U.S.$.

[3] In 1978, the Japanese motor vehicle producers had no net advantage in factor prices over American producers, because the substantial Japanese advantage in labor costs was offset by a large Japanese disadvantage in materials prices. In the 1978–84 period, the Japanese disadvantage in materials prices fell. Thus, over this six-year period, the Japanese advantage in factor prices actually grew. Of course, any lowering of the prices through more efficient production of the semifinished component of materials prices is not really a factor-price effect, even though it appears in the materials price effect due to data limitations.

Table 7.5. *Unit-cost difference and its sources (%): Germany–United States*

Year	Unit production cost difference[a]	Sources of difference							
		Price of labor	Price of capital	Price of materials	Cost efficiency	Scale economies	Capacity utilization	Country-specific efficiency	Residual
1963	−43.6	−21.9	−14.9	1.7	−18.6	2.1	0.9	−21.1	2.5
1970	−37.1	−19.9	−5.7	0.6	−17.0	2.6	−5.5	−14.3	−0.2
1974	3.7	−8.5	2.3	20.0	−10.2	1.6	−0.4	−11.2	2.7
1975	−0.5	−7.5	2.4	16.2	−12.6	1.8	−3.6	−10.9	3.3
1978	6.9	−3.6	2.0	20.6	−9.4	2.1	−0.5	−10.9	−0.6
1979	14.4	1.4	3.8	22.5	−10.5	2.8	−2.7	−10.5	−0.8
1980	3.0	0.8	4.0	18.9	−18.4	2.1	−11.0	−10.3	1.3

[a] [(Germany/U.S.) −1] × 100.

German disadvantage worsened until 1979, then fell sharply in 1980. What explains these sharp and discontinuous changes?

Between 1963 and 1974, German factor prices increased enormously as compared to the United States. In 1963, if the only difference between the United States and Germany were the price of labor, then unit costs of production would have been 22% lower in Germany; in 1974, this substantial German advantage would have fallen to 8.5%. In 1963, the German advantage in capital costs alone meant 15% lower unit production costs; in 1974 capital costs were a relative disadvantage to German producers. Materials prices also moved significantly against German auto producers in this 1963–74 period. In 1970 materials prices were the same in the two countries, but in 1974 materials costs alone would have accounted for 20% higher unit production costs in Germany. In addition, by 1974 the German cost-efficiency advantage of 1963 had fallen by 40%, basically owing to a German deterioration in country-specific efficiency.

Between 1975 and 1979, German unit production costs rose sharply relative to production costs in the United States, with all of the change due to factor-price movements. All factor prices were higher in Germany than in the United States in 1979; this German disadvantage in factor prices was partially offset by a German advantage in cost efficiency, particularly country-specific efficiency.

In 1980, German unit costs fell sharply in relation to unit costs in the United States. This one-year change (which we also saw between U.S. and Japanese producers) was due to CU and factor-price movements.

In Table 7.6, movements in exchange rates from FEER are distinguished. These movements provide some explanation for factor-price movements. For example, nearly half of the deterioration in German relative unit production costs between 1978 and 1979, as well as one-third of the improvement in German cost performance between 1979 and 1980, was due to changes in the mark–dollar relationship relative to FEERs.

Table 7.7 provides one version of long-run equilibrium results, holding CU at its normal level. Remember that low U.S. capacity utilization was evident in 1970, 1974, 1980, and 1982, and accounting for those low levels helped explain relatively poor performance by the U.S. motor vehicle industry when compared to Japan. Accounting for low U.S. capacity utilization in Table 7.5 does not, however, explain differences with Germany; in fact, it increases the U.S. advantage in 1979 and 1980. Already in Table 7.5 we saw that the American producers' production costs were lower than German production costs, even though the United States had lower CU rates; raising these rates to normal levels increases the U.S. advantage

Table 7.6. *Unit-cost difference and its sources (%), including exchange-rate fluctuations from purchasing power parity: Germany–United States*

| Year | Unit production cost difference[a] | Sources of difference | | | | | | |
		Price of labor	Price of capital	Price of materials	Cost efficiency	Scale economies	Capacity utilization	Country-specific efficiency	Exchange-rate fluctuation
1978	6.9	−4.1	1.7	19.0	−9.4	2.1	−0.5	−10.9	2.3
1979	14.4	−0.3	2.7	18.0	−10.5	2.8	−2.7	−10.5	6.2
1980	3.0	0.5	3.8	18.1	−18.4	2.1	−11.0	−10.3	1.2

[a] [(Germany/U.S.)−1] ×100.

Table 7.7. *Unit-cost difference and its sources (%): Germany–United States (equilibrium – not adjusting for exchange-rate fluctuations)*

Year	Unit production cost difference[a]	Sources of difference					Country-specific efficiency	Cost efficiency
		Price of labor	Price of capital	Price of materials	Scale economies			
1963	−45.4	−21.8	−14.8	1.7	2.1	−21.2	−19.5
1970	−33.2	−19.5	−5.4	0.6	2.6	−15.0	−12.8
1974	0.9	−8.3	2.1	20.7	1.6	−12.1	−10.8
1975	−1.0	−7.3	2.1	17.0	1.8	−12.0	−10.4
1978	7.9	−3.6	2.0	20.7	2.1	−11.0	−9.1
1979	18.3	1.4	3.7	22.7	2.8	−10.8	−8.3
1980	14.1	0.8	3.5	20.0	2.1	−11.3	−9.5

[a] [(Germany/U.S.) −1] × 100.

even more. Examining the long-run cost-efficiency differences (the last column in Table 7.7), we see a steady (but declining rate of) fall in the German advantage to 1979 and a slight rise in 1980.

Holding both exchange rates and CU at normal levels leads to the results shown in Table 7.8 (for three years of data only). The U.S. advantage in unit production costs is cut to 11% in 1979 (from 14% in Table 7.5) and rises to 12% in 1980 (from 3% in Table 7.5). The German motor vehicle industry's cost-efficiency advantages do not offset its factor-price disadvantages.

7.3.3   *Germany–Japan comparisons*

Tables 7.9–7.12 present the data on comparisons between Japanese and German unit costs of motor vehicle production and the sources of the differences. In Table 7.9, the annual nonequilibrium results are presented. In 1970, the cost of producing motor vehicles in Germany was 9% lower than the cost in Japan; in 1980, ten years later, unit production cost in Germany was 55% higher than the cost in Japan.

This rapid change in the relative position of these two countries (in terms of unit production cost) was already implicitly evident in our other two comparisons, where we showed how Japan outpaced the United States in the 1970s and how the United States outpaced Germany. The German advantage over Japan in 1970 was based on a substantial efficiency advantage, offset somewhat by higher German labor and materials costs. In 1970, if all factor prices were held at their geometric mean levels, higher German technical efficiency would have led to unit production costs one-third below those in Japan. This German cost efficiency advantage was mainly due to country-specific efficiency, but scale economies also added to the German advantage.

Throughout the 1970s, the Japanese rapidly closed this efficiency gap so that by 1980 the German cost-efficiency advantage was down to 3.7%. Combining this deterioration of the German advantage in technical efficiency with a relative increase in German labor and capital costs leads to the results graphically portrayed in the first column of Table 7.9: German unit costs rocketed relative to Japanese costs in the 1970s.

Table 7.10 disaggregates exchange-rate misalignments around FEER. As can be seen, the appreciation of the mark relative to the yen between 1978 and 1979 added significantly to the German disadvantage in unit costs. In 1979, exchange-rate disequilibria alone meant that German unit costs were 10.3% higher than those in Japan (holding all other factors at

Table 7.8. *Unit-cost difference and its sources (%): Germany–United States (equilibrium – adjusting for exchange-rate fluctuations)*

| Year | Unit production cost difference[a] | Sources of difference | | | | | | |
		Price of labor	Price of capital	Price of materials	Scale economies	Country-specific efficiency	Cost efficiency
1978	5.5	−4.1	1.7	19.0	2.1	−11.0	−9.1
1979	11.0	−0.3	2.7	18.2	2.8	−10.8	−8.3
1980	12.0	0.5	3.3	19.1	2.1	−11.3	−9.5

[a] [(Germany/U.S.) −1] × 100.

Table 7.9. *Unit-cost difference and its sources (%): Germany–Japan*

Year	Unit production cost difference[a]	Sources of difference							
		Price of labor	Price of capital	Price of materials	Cost efficiency	Scale economies	Capacity utilization	Country-specific efficiency	Residual
1970	−9.3	13.7	−3.9	19.0	−33.8	−5.3	−0.1	−30.1	5.5
1974	12.8	16.6	2.5	15.3	−21.6	−3.9	1.9	−19.9	4.4
1975	20.1	16.9	2.2	22.3	−17.6	−3.0	1.2	−16.0	−0.2
1978	9.9	12.0	3.3	8.5	−10.3	−1.3	0.1	−9.2	−2.4
1979	37.2	19.2	6.2	20.0	−6.0	−0.2	−0.3	−5.6	−3.8
1980	54.6	23.9	7.5	19.0	−3.7	−0.4	0.5	−3.8	1.3

[a] [(Germany/Japan) −1] ×100.

Table 7.10. *Unit-cost difference and its sources (%), including exchange-rate fluctuations from purchasing power parity: Germany–Japan*

Year	Unit production cost difference[a]	Sources of difference							
		Price of labor	Price of capital	Price of materials	Cost efficiency	Scale economies	Capacity utilization	Country-specific efficiency	Exchange-rate fluctuation
1978	9.9	12.4	3.6	9.4	−10.3	−1.3	0.1	−9.2	−1.4
1979	37.2	16.6	4.5	12.9	−6.0	−0.2	−0.3	−5.6	10.3
1980	54.6	21.9	6.3	14.3	−3.7	−0.4	0.5	−3.8	6.9

[a] [(Germany/Japan) −1]×100.

their mean geometric levels). In 1978, unit costs were 1.4% lower in Germany due to exchange-rate disequilibria.

In Table 7.11, we remove CU factors to arrive at the first of our versions of long-run equilibrium differences. Because CU rates were high in Germany as well as in Japan (see the "Capacity utilization" column in Table 7.9), accounting for these differences does little to alter the unit-cost comparisons.

Finally, we account for disequilibria in both exchange rates and capacity utilization (Table 7.12). In this long-run equilibrium view of unit-cost differentials, the German disadvantage in 1980 was 42%, primarily because of higher factor prices in Germany. In 1980, the technical efficiency of producing cars was still slightly greater in Germany than in Japan.

7.4   Conclusions

The results presented in this chapter go a long way toward clarifying the Japanese competitive threat to U.S. and indeed (as will be seen from the comparisons to Canada in Chapter 8) to North American automobile production, and in analyzing the developments of the German industry as a purveyor of fine cars exported to North America. A Japanese relative cost advantage vis-à-vis North American producers is not a recent phenomenon. U.S. producers began the decade of the 1970s with unit production cost disadvantages as compared to Japanese producers. However, U.S. cost disadvantages at that time were due primarily to the existence of lower factor prices in Japan. In 1970, U.S. producers enjoyed country-specific efficiency advantages over Japanese producers. By the end of the decade the U.S. producers' disadvantage in production costs worsened, even though Japanese factor prices increased relative to those in the United States. The U.S. cost-efficiency advantage of 1970 was replaced by a significant and growing disadvantage. However, U.S. car producers fared better against their German counterparts, not because of any spectacular improvement in the relative efficiency of the U.S. producers, but because of rapidly escalating factor prices in Germany. Thus, in 1980 German small cars were not effective competitors in the U.S. market, while Japanese small cars certainly were.

Our results also shed light on the very large actual unit production cost increases in the United States between 1979 and 1980, which led to North American quotas on Japanese imports beginning in 1981. To some extent, these increases reflect a continuing deterioration in the North American

Table 7.11. *Unit-cost difference and its sources (%): Germany–Japan (equilibrium – not adjusting for exchange-rate fluctuations)*

| Year | Unit production cost difference[a] | Sources of difference | | | | | |
		Price of labor	Price of capital	Price of materials	Scale economies	Country-specific efficiency	Cost efficiency
1970	−13.9	13.7	−3.9	19.0	−5.3	−30.1	−33.8
1974	5.7	16.2	2.4	15.6	−3.9	−20.0	−23.1
1975	18.8	16.5	2.1	22.7	−3.0	−16.1	−18.6
1978	12.5	12.1	3.3	8.5	−1.3	−9.2	−10.4
1979	43.2	19.2	6.2	20.0	−0.2	−5.6	−5.7
1980	51.7	23.7	7.5	19.1	−0.4	−3.8	−4.2

[a] [(Germany/Japan) −1] × 100.

Table 7.12. *Unit-cost difference and its sources (%): Germany–Japan (equilibrium – adjusting for exchange-rate fluctuations)*

Year	Unit production cost difference[a]	Sources of difference					
		Price of labor	Price of capital	Price of materials	Scale economies	Country-specific efficiency	Cost efficiency
1978	14.1	12.5	3.6	9.3	-1.3	-9.2	-10.4
1979	29.8	16.6	4.5	12.9	-0.2	-5.6	-5.7
1980	41.9	21.8	6.2	14.4	-0.4	-3.8	-4.2

[a] [(Germany/Japan) −1] × 100.

Table 7.13. *Japanese percentage cost advantage, 1979–80 (based on Table 2.20)*

	Strict weights		Liberal weights	
	1979	1980	1979	1980
U.S. average cost	$5,743	$6,893	$5,743	$6,893
Japanese average cost[a]	5,757	5,994	4,931	5,117
Japanese advantage	−14	899	803	1,776
Japanese cost advantage (%)	−0.30	15.0	16.3	34.7

[a] Calculated using weighted average of Toyota, Datsun, and Honda costs, where weights are calculated from relative production (excluding transportation and tariff, estimated as $400).

position with regard to long-run efficiency differences. However, the bulk of the very sharp change in North American fortunes could be attributed to cyclical phenomena. The very low levels of capacity utilization experienced in 1980 in North America and the devaluation of the Japanese yen relative to its equilibrium level were the major causes of the cost deterioration. As noted in Chapter 1, the cost-competitive problems caused by low levels of CU are not really a reflection of inappropriate production *techniques* in any long-run sense. The major problem faced by North American producers was that they could not sell as many cars as their plants were designed to produce. In 1980 the primary field where North American producers could not compete with the Japanese was in the design of automobiles with appropriate quality and size characteristics, rather than in relative production costs.

Finally, it is useful to compare our results on U.S.–Japan comparisons with those presented by the Federal Trade Commission. Table 7.13 reproduces the relevant material from Table 2.28, putting the Japanese cost advantage into percentage form so that it can be compared with our results. Table 7.14 provides the direct comparison with our results. The FTC's liberal-weights results are quite close to our results; this provides support for the FTC's contention that the liberal-weights analysis is closer to the correct analysis. Comparing lines 3 and 4 of Table 7.14 shows the importance of separating out exchange-rate fluctuations and CU effects. The long-run equilibrium Japanese advantage we calculate is 90% of the unadjusted figure in 1979 and only 66% of the value in 1980. The very

Table 7.14. *Comparison of U.S.–Japan unit production cost calculations (Japanese cost advantage, %)*

	1979	1980
Federal Trade Commission (strict weights)	−0.3	15.0
Federal Trade Commission (liberal weights)	16.3	34.7
This study (Table 7.1)	19.3	35.1
This study – long-run equilibrium (Table 7.4)	17.3	23.0

Table 7.A.1. *Japan–U.S. Fundamental Equilibrium Exchange Rate (FEER) calculation*

Year	Real FEER[a] at beginning of year	Inflation rate (%) during year[b] U.S.	Japan	Nominal FEER[c] End of year	PPP[d] midyear
1984	193.5	0.4	0.7	194.0	195.45
1983	205.0	2.7	−1.1	196.9	201
1982	202.5	0.7	0.0	205.0	205
1981	199.9	5.2	2.1	204.7	207
1980	197.4	11.3	6.7	208.4	212
1979	194.9	15.4	19.3	215.0	210
1978	192.3	10.4	−1.2	205.3	217
1977	189.8	6.3	−1.4	227.9	236
1976	187.3	4.8	5.2	243.3	n.a.

Note: n.a. means "not available."
[a] Calculated from Williamson (1983, 1985).
[b] Source: wholesale price index from IMF, *International Financial Statistics* (various issues).
[c] Real FEER adjusted for inflation: $FEER \cdot (1+I^J) \cdot (1+I^U)^{-1}$, where I^J = Japanese inflation rate and I^U = U.S. inflation rate.
[d] PPP = purchasing power parity.

large observed 1980 cost disadvantage (compared to the long-run advantage) was primarily due to a devaluation of the yen and the very low CU rates in 1980 U.S. automobile production.

Thus Table 7.14 once again forcefully illustrates the need to decompose any observed cost advantage into its underlying causes. Failure to

Table 7.A.2. *Germany–U.S. Fundamental Equilibrium Exchange Rate (FEER) calculation*

Year	Real FEER[a] at beginning of year	Inflation rate (%) during year[b]		Nominal FEER[c]	
		U.S.	Germany	End of year	PPP[d] midyear
1982	1.96	0.7	5.2	1.98	1.93
1981	1.93	5.2	8.5	1.87	1.83
1980	1.91	11.3	6.3	1.79	1.84
1979	1.88	15.4	7.8	1.89	1.95
1978	1.86	10.4	2.2	2.02	2.06
1977	1.84	6.3	1.3	2.09	2.09
1976	1.81	4.8	4.2	2.08	n.a.

Note: n.a. means "not available."
[a] Calculated from Williamson (1983, 1985).
[b] Source: wholesale price index from IMF, *International Financial Statistics* (various issues).
[c] Real FEER adjusted for inflation: $\text{FEER} \cdot (1+I^G) \cdot (1+I^U)^{-1}$, where I^G = German inflation rate and I^U = U.S. inflation rate.
[d] PPP = purchasing power parity.

do so will often lead to a confusion between short-run effects (CU variations and exchange-rate fluctuations) and longer-run underlying effects due to secular movements in factor prices and cost-efficiency (productivity) levels.

Appendix 7.A: Calculation of equilibrium exchange rates

Tables 7.A.1 and 7.A.2 present the equilibrium exchange rates used as purchasing power parities between (1) Japan and the United States, and (2) Germany and the United States.

CHAPTER 8

International comparisons of automobile industry cost and productivity levels: Canadian with U.S., Japanese, and German production

A   THE CANADA–U.S. AUTO PACT OF 1965: A COST-FUNCTION
ANALYSIS OF COMPARATIVE COSTS AND EFFICIENCY IN
U.S.–CANADIAN AUTOMOBILE PRODUCTION

8.1   Introduction

From its inception, the automobile industry in Canada has been protected by a combination of tariffs and domestic content provisions. These
import substitution policies in the 1940s and 1950s induced U.S. multinationals to produce behind the Canadian tariff wall. The resulting Canadian auto industry was characterized by an excess number of models produced,[1] small scale, short production runs, and high costs.[2] There was
little trade in finished automobiles across the U.S. border; in 1962, for
example, 1% of cars produced in Canada were exported while 4% of cars
sold in Canada came from the United States.[3] In the late 1950s and early

[1] James M. Roche, president of General Motors Corporation, made the following state-
ment regarding GM Canadian production of motor vehicles in hearings before the House
Ways and Means Committee of Congress in 1965: "GM of Canada's Oshawa plant is
assembling this year [model year 1965] a total of 595 different passenger car and truck
models. By contrast, the most complex assembly operation in the United States has to
turn out only 256 models, less than half the Oshawa total. The Canadian operation is
further complicated by the fact that customers there have substantially the same choices
of colors and trim, equipment and accessory options as do those in the United States."
Quoted in Helmers (1967, p. 85).
[2] Wonnacott and Wonnacott (1967) examined the differentials in prices and several cost
components for U.S.- and Canadian-made cars in 1964. If it is assumed (as they did) that
the differences between Canadian and U.S. auto prices (which averaged 9.5% in 1964)
were due to differences in costs, then Wonnacott and Wonnacott (1967, p. 235) showed
that with the 60% Canadian-content rule, production in Canada resulted in a 13% cost
penalty. As a result, reducing the numbers of models produced and achieving higher
economies of scale in the reduced number produced would lower Canadian automotive
production costs appreciably.
[3] Many parts were imported into Canada from the United States, so that in 1962–4 the value
of parts imported from the United States was virtually the same as the value of Canadian
domestic parts production.

166

1960s, this high-cost autarkic industrial structure came under increasing pressure. Because of preferential British tariffs, domestic Canadian producers were threatened by low-cost British auto imports, and Canada faced a growing deficit in its balance of payments on auto trade. As Johnson (1983) remarked, "the post-war difficulties of the Canadian industry have to be viewed in a world context, as a facet of the difficulties created for the North American industry by the development, stimulated by dollar shortage, of a strongly export-oriented European motor industry equipped with the most advanced technology and enjoying the advantage of low wages."[4]

In 1961, in response to these problems, the Canadian government appointed a Royal Commission on the Auto Industry (The Bladen Commission). Implementing schemes to increase exports from Canada through duty remissions, a suggestion of the Bladen Report, led to objections from the U.S. auto-parts industry. Negotiations between the Canadian and U.S. governments resulted in the Auto Pact of 1965, partially freeing trade at the manufacturers' level between the two countries, subject to certain constraints and domestic-content provisions. Most writers viewed this pact as a move toward liberalized trade that would increase the efficiency of production in Canada; among dissenters, Harry Johnson (1963) was most vocal, claiming the Auto Pact increased protection.

As recently as 1980, the Canadian automobile industry was operating at approximately 60% of capacity, even though the industry was still protected by a combination of tariffs and domestic-content provisions. Thirty years after the 1950s European "threat," Canadian auto producers were threatened by lower-cost imports from a strong export-oriented Japanese (and, since 1984, Korean) auto industry. In 1983, a Federal Canadian Task Force on the Automobile Industry recommended increased protection for Canadian producers. As recently as late 1988, "voluntary" quotas were still in place in Canada against Japanese auto producers. A Hyundai auto plant announced in 1985 for Quebec was criticized as not guaranteeing minumum Canadian content.[5] In a different but related issue, Ford, GM, and Chrysler in 1987 initiated an antidumping inquiry into Hyundai's Canadian prices, an inquiry that resulted in a finding that no material injury to Canadian producers occurred through Hyundai's pricing policies. Finally, the Auto Pact itself was changed – and, in an important sense, protection against non–Auto-Pact manufacturers increased –

---

[4] This quote is especially ironic now: Replacing the word "European" with the word "Asian" would describe the period from 1979 to the present.

[5] See *The Globe & Mail,* November 20, 1985.

by the Canada–U.S. Free Trade Agreement (FTA) effective January 1, 1989.[6]

The U.S. auto industry has also experienced its share of difficulties. Unlike Canada, the United States has not protected its auto producers with high tariffs and domestic-content rules. (For much of the period, the U.S. tariff on parts and vehicles ranged from 2.9% to 8.5%, although a 25% tariff on light trucks was introduced in 1981.) However, in April 1981, the U.S. government imposed "voluntary" quotas on Japanese auto producers. These quotas, which are now administered by The Ministry of Industry and Trade in Japan, have been estimated to be equivalent to 18–20% ad valorem tariffs (Crandall 1984). Since 1981, various attempts have been made in the U.S. House and Senate to impose increased tariffs, formal quotas, and domestic-content provisions against all auto importers. The Japanese have attempted to stave off such protectionist legislation and to end quotas by opening production facilities in the United States (and Canada).

Table 8.1 provides some statistics on auto trade between Canada and the United States. The total value of auto vehicle and parts trade between Canada and the United States was some $366 million in 1961; in 1966, the year after the Auto Pact was implemented, this trade was valued at $2.2 billion. In 1961, Canada imported 16,574 vehicles from the United States, and exported a mere 175. In 1966, car exports from Canada to the United States numbered nearly 147,000 and, in 1984, over one million. In 1986, 1.2 million passenger cars were exported from Canada to the United States, while 690,000 were imported.

Auto parts have been a growing source of trade between Canada and the United States; although Canada is a net exporter of finished vehicles, Canada has always had a deficit in auto parts trade with the United States. This deficit in auto parts trade was the source of the overall Canadian deficit in auto trade with the United States under the Auto Pact for the periods 1965–9 and 1973–81. In 1986, $6 billion more of parts were imported into Canada from the United States than were exported; half of all imported parts were purchased by multinational enterprises.

Although Canada has a net surplus in overall automotive trade with the United States, few cars or parts are shipped to third countries. As a result, Canada has a substantial deficit in auto trade with European and Asian car producers. In 1986 this deficit exceeded the Canadian surplus in auto trade with the United States. Aside from exports to the United States under the Auto Pact, the Canadian industry is not export oriented.

[6] The FTA alters the 1965 Auto Pact rules and, in doing so, the Big Three's position, thus providing greater protection against Japanese producers.

Table 8.1. *Canadian auto trade (millions of Canadian dollars)*

Year	Canadian imports from U.S.[a]		Canadian exports to U.S.[a]		Net Canadian imports from U.S.[a]	Net Canadian imports, non-U.S.
	Motor vehicles	Parts	Motor vehicles	Parts	Motor vehicles and parts	Motor vehicles and parts
1961	65.5	292.0	0.4	8.7	348.4	89.0
1962	69.4	378.8	0.4	10.1	437.7	79.5
1965	153.5	797.9	80.6	150.2	720.6	22.3
1966	384.0	1,093.0	488.0	389.0	600.0	(31.6)
1973	2,082.0	3,553.0	3,060.0	2,171.0	404.0	388.0
1974	2,531.0	3,892.0	3,407.0	1,953.0	1,063.0	422.0
1975	3,126.0	4,552.0	3,790.0	2,045.0	1,843.0	82.0
1978	4,360.0	8,086.0	7,033.0	4,746.0	667.0	258.0
1979	5,699.0	8,659.0	6,706.0	4,488.0	3,164.0	259.0
1980	4,605.0	7,600.0	6,670.0	3,405.0	2,130.0	548.0
1982	3,748.0	9,676.0	11,116.0	4,902.0	(2,594.0)	647.0
1983	6,015.0	11,446.0	13,410.0	7,056.0	(3,005.0)	1,620.0
1984	8,124.0	15,446.0	18,965.0	10,287.0	(5,682.0)	2,877.0
1985	10,552.0	17,488.0	21,699.0	11,512.0	(5,171.0)	4,071.0
1986	11,452.0	17,680.0	22,232.0	11,577.0	(4,677.0)	5,687.0

[a] Includes all automotive trade, both within and outside the Auto Pact.

Sources: Statistics Canada, *Exports-Merchandise Trade* (Catalogue #65-202, various issues); Statistics Canada, *Imports-Merchandise Trade* (Catalogue #65-203, various issues); Motor Vehicle Manufacturers Association of Canada, *Facts and Figures of the Automotive Industry in Canada* (July 1987).

In this chapter, we examine the Canada–U.S. Auto Pact using the cost-function framework. First, we provide a number of hypotheses as to the effects of increased protection of the kind contained in the Auto Pact. Then, we empirically examine the impact of the 1965 Auto Pact on production costs in Canada. Our main conclusion is surprising. We find that the Auto Pact led to lower reductions in unit production costs in Canada vis-à-vis those in the United States than is commonly assumed. While the scale of Canadian output increased, we show that much of the increase in aggregate output could have occurred in a world without the Auto Pact. In addition, we find no evidence that the rationalization occurring in the Canadian auto industry after 1965 resulted in parity with the United States with respect to production efficiency.

8.2   Effects of protection on domestic costs of production

Eastman and Stykolt (1967) provided a diagram (reproduced here as Figure 8.1) to illustrate the impacts of protection on the structure and costs of domestic production. They built on Bain's (1956) earlier analysis of the impact of entry barriers on profitability.

In Figure 8.1, AB is the demand for automobiles in Canada, and $0G$ is the price (and cost) of cars sold in the world market. Ignoring transportation costs, a tariff GC leads to a landed cost of foreign cars in Canada of $0C$. The demand curve facing Canadian producers is $CDEB$. Assume that there are high scale economies and a high degree of product differentiation, but no other inherent reasons (such as national character) that would lead to higher costs of production in Canada than elsewhere. Assume also that the Canadian market is small – how small obviously depends on the relationship between minimum efficient scale (m.e.s.) and market size, a crucial point we will come back to later. Assume also that all domestic production results in import substitution by the same firms who also could import automobiles. An importer then has a choice: locate elsewhere in the world, ship to Canada, and face a cost in Canada of $0C$ (composed of the world price plus the Canadian tariff GC); or locate production in Canada, thus avoiding the Canadian tariff. The decision to locate in Canada would depend on the expected market share in Canada and the resulting costs of production. Eastman and Stykolt argue that where m.e.s. is high relative to both expected market share and market size, and where product differentiation and sunk capital barriers are also high, firms will enter at suboptimal scale and bear inefficient production costs rather than take the risk of entering at efficient scale. In Figure 8.1,

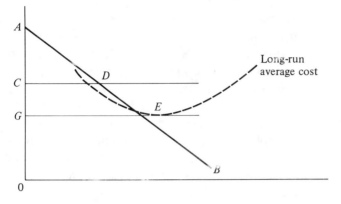

Figure 8.1. Effects of protection on domestic production costs.

these interdependent firm decisions result in production costs in Canada rising to $0C$. The Eastman–Stykolt policy advice is obvious: Lower tariffs unilaterally, so as to rationalize the industry.

Why is it in the Eastman–Stykolt story that no domestic auto plants are built at efficient scale in Canada from the 1940s to 1960s, but instead are all built at suboptimal size?[7] Given the precommitment necessary, the sunk nature of many of the industry- and firm-specific assets (e.g., dies for body panels), and the long lead times in constructing plants (3–5 years), each firm in the oligopoly is aware of the highly risky investment of a plant of m.e.s. if its rivals build equal-size plants. If all built plants are of m.e.s., a price war follows and all are worse off. If one alone builds an m.e.s. plant, its share of sales is still dependent on convincing marginal consumers (those buying another brand) to purchase its nameplate. Moreover, a successful entry at m.e.s. might incur antitrust action for monopolizing the industry. Multinational firms possibly could have built m.e.s. plants in Canada and exported, but did not do so because the only other country with similar consumer preferences (the United States) had a 6.5–8.5% tariff and Canadian costs of production were not sufficiently low that production in Canada could scale that tariff barrier.

In Canada in 1961, five producers produced 49 nameplates totalling 327,000 passenger vehicles. White (1971) estimates the m.e.s. for an assembly plant producing a single model in the early 1960s to be 200,000 cars per year, with a higher m.e.s. for stampings, engines, and transmissions. White argues that a risk-averse car producer would need two models, not

---

[7] Eastman and Stykolt do not analyze the auto industry in their book.

one.[8] *The total output of the Canadian assembly industry in 1961 was less than White's estimate of m.e.s. for a single firm,* and less than White's estimated m.e.s. for two plants.

The Canada–U.S. Auto Pact of 1965 was designed to increase the efficiency of Canadian auto production through rationalization, and it was expected this would also increase trade flows between the two countries. Beigie (1970, pp. 21–31) examines the rationalization of production by firms in the 1965–70 period. General Motors concentrated its Canadian production in Chevrolet, Ford phased out two chassis sizes in Canada, and Chrysler by 1968 was producing only two nameplates in Canada and one chassis size. Trade flows increased enormously between the two countries. Was the Auto Pact then a success?

8.3   The Canada–U.S. Auto Pact of 1965

Prior to the Auto Pact, Canada imposed substantial tariffs on the entry of assembled passenger cars, as well as on parts designated for use either in assembly operations or for the replacement (or "after-parts") market. These tariffs were designed "to protect the domestic Canadian industry from imports from the United States" (Bladen 1961, p. 6). Completed vehicles faced a 17.5% tariff.[9] Remission of duties on imported parts (but not for imported cars) occurred if the manufacturer maintained a 60% Canadian content in passenger cars and a 50% Canadian content in commercial vehicles.[10] In 1960, in the face of a large and growing deficit for auto trade, the Canadian federal government established the Bladen Commission on the Automobile Industry.

The Bladen Report was issued in April 1961 and recommended a duty-free zone for auto trade between Canada and the United States, subject to a number of contingency protection clauses for Canada. The cornerstone of the Bladen Report was the need to increase the scale of parts production in Canada, principally through their export.[11]

---

[8] In 1961, GM's five Canadian divisions produced 20 nameplates, 8 different chassis types, and 5 body styles. Chevrolet alone produced 36 combinations of chassis and body styles plus a variety of options and engine sizes. Ford produced 11 nameplates, 5 chassis types, and 4 body styles. Chrysler produced 14 nameplates, 4 chassis types, and 4 body styles.

[9] Vehicles and parts from the Commonwealth entered duty-free.

[10] For production over 20,000 units per year. For production between 10,000 and 20,000 units, the domestic content requirement was 50%; for production of under 10,000 units, 40%.

Because of the tariff barrier, most models were produced in Canada. This resulted in inefficient production, characterized by short production runs and higher prices than in the United States. See Beigie (1970).

[11] "Under the proposed plan, assembly is likely to increase but a relatively greater stimulus will be afforded to the production of parts" (Bladen 1961, p. 67).

In November 1962, the Canadian government instituted the first of two duty-remission schemes designed to increase the exports of Canadian-made parts. Exported parts earned a dollar-for-dollar remission of duty on imports of automatic transmissions or partially assembled engines. The second scheme expanded the allowable imports to all parts as well as finished vehicles (see Helmers 1967, p. 14). Parts manufacturers in the United States called these plans "unfair subsidies" and lobbied in Washington for countervailing legislation. While the U.S. House of Representatives was considering action against Canada, the Canadian government negotiated the Auto Pact that was signed and ratified in 1965.

The Auto Pact eliminated tariffs on completed vehicles and original equipment parts, conditional on those manufacturers who qualified for Auto-Pact status maintaining certain minimum production levels in Canada and minimum domestic content in North America. Hence the Auto Pact provided a mixture of trade liberalization and protection. On the one hand, vehicle manufacturers in both countries had potential duty-free access to Canadian and U.S. markets. On the other hand, since only "qualified" manufacturers had this access opportunity, the requisite production and domestic-content provisions might be expected to protect, at least to some extent, the inefficient Canadian industry.

The Auto Pact stipulated the following content and production requirements for manufacturers.

(1) For tariff-free entry of Canadian automobiles or original equipment parts into the U.S. market, a minimum of 50% North American (U.S. or Canadian) content.

(2) Only the Big Four (now the Big Three: GM; Ford; and Chrysler, which absorbed American Motors in 1988) were qualified to import cars duty-free into Canada. Volvo's eastern Canadian assembly facility has also obtained Auto Pact status, but Volvo's production was only 10,388 cars in 1986. For tariff-free entry of U.S. finished vehicles or original equipment parts into Canada, these qualified manufacturers had to satisfy the following criteria:

(a) Manufacturers must maintain a certain ratio between the net sales value of vehicles made in Canada and the net sales value of vehicles sold in Canada.

(b) The amount of Canadian value added for all classes of vehicles made in Canada must be at least as great as the amount that was achieved in the base year (1964).

(c) In each model year, the value added in Canada should amount to at least 60% of the growth in the value of cars sold in the base year; for commercial vehicles (e.g., trucks), the value added should amount to at least 50% of the growth in the value of commercial vehicles sold in the base year.

(d)   Vehicle manufacturers were collectively to increase the amount of value added in Canada between 1965 and 1968 by an additional $260 million beyond the requirements under (c).

All the above constraints potentially interfere with trade liberalization and thus provide protection. Provision 1 protects North American parts manufacturers from worldwide competitors. Provision 2 provides protection for Canadian parts producers and vehicle assemblers vis-à-vis U.S. producers. Provision 2(a) biases production in Canada toward assembly and away from parts production.

An observer of the provisions of the Auto Pact would be tempted to conclude that there could be an obvious reason why manufacturing efficiency did not improve substantially in Canada relative to the United States after 1965: The provisions of the pact prevented North American rationalization to the fullest extent desired by manufacturers. This conclusion would imply that manufacturers were constrained by the content provisions of the Auto Pact, an implication that is contrary to the evidence. At no time during the 1965–86 period have constraints 1, 2(b), (c), or (d) been binding constraints. In most years, manufacturers in aggregate have exceeded the minimum requirements by wide margins. Provision 2(a) was binding in 1980 and possibly 1968, but in all other years manufacturers comfortably exceeded the minimum requirements.

Hence it would appear that the "safeguards for Canada" built into the Auto Pact did not appreciably constrain the North American allocation of production facilities or the amount of value added produced in Canada. This fact would seem to contradict our result that Canadian production has remained inefficient relative to U.S. production. However, it is not relative efficiency that matters in the competition for production activity but rather relative costs. As we demonstrate, Canadian producers have remained cost-competitive primarily owing to lower factor prices and, in the latter part of the period, to currency devaluation.

Most commentators argued that this agreement – by eliminating U.S. tariffs, allowing the duty-free importation of finished cars into Canada, and allowing North American automobile manufacturers to meet the Canadian-content rule by exporting parts – would lead to a rationalization of the Canadian automobile industry (see Beigie 1970). The Eastman–Stykolt trap of low-scale, multiple models and high production costs could be escaped by allowing the manufacturers to rationalize *North American* auto production, concentrating production in Canada on a few models. A manufacturer could minimize Canadian tariffs by producing a limited number of models in Canada, importing other models into Canada, and exporting Canadian-made parts to the United States in order to meet the minimum-content provisions. This may have been Bladen's plan, but it did not occur. As shown earlier, Canada has continually had a large deficit in parts trade with the United States; the Canadian domestic-content provisions have been met by the export from Canada of finished vehicles, not parts.

Opponents of the Auto Pact saw it as a poor substitute for free trade, since the combination of continued tariffs on vehicles, reduced tariffs on some parts, and domestic-content provisions simply changed relative effective protection between parts and assembly. This dissenting view – that the Auto Pact would not necessarily improve efficiency or consumer welfare – is best articulated in Harry Johnson's (1963) article reviewing the Bladen Report.

Surprisingly, very few have attempted to estimate the productivity gains to Canada from the Auto Pact.[12] Beigie (1970) argues that increased efficiency did take place,[13] because the increase in Canada's share of North American auto production exceeded the increase in Canada's share of North American auto employment.[14] Alexander, however, finds little real efficiency gains in Canada, concluding that "efficiency gains may have been less than is commonly imagined" (1974, p. 29).

Two other elements must be added to the story. First and foremost, the Auto Pact limited duty-free imports to the four firms who were already producing finished vehicles in Canada.[15] The oligopolistic auto industry was thus offered increased protection against foreign competition (the British preferential tariff was raised by this "trade liberalization" pact),[16] as costs could be reduced behind an increased nominal tariff wall (Johnson 1963). The possibility of increased efficiency offered by the Auto Pact then depended on the behavior of oligopolists for its realization. If

---

[12] See Alexander (1974), Wilton (1972), and Emerson (1975).

[13] Beigie (1970, p. 5) states that it is "impossible to tell for sure whether the improvement in the Canadian efficiency has been sufficient to overcome the initial Canadian disadvantage."

[14] This is not necessarily evidence of productivity gains, because the Auto Pact did lead to the substitution of imported materials for Canadian labor and hence less vertical integration in Canada.

[15] The Canadian government did retain the right to add other firms to the list.

[16] The provisions covering the automobile industry in the FTA also raise barriers against "nonqualified" manufacturers – that is, Japanese and Korean producers.

the Eastman–Stykolt argument holds, then each oligopolist might be un-willing to substantially increase efficiency relative to his rivals', for fear of upsetting a delicate oligopoly equilibrium. In addition, as Johnson pointed out, nothing guaranteed that any efficiency improvements would be passed on to consumers.

A second element that must be considered in evaluating the Auto Pact is the realism of its goal of encouraging growth in the Canadian parts industry. It was hoped that opening the U.S. assembly market to Cana-dian parts producers would increase the scale and efficiency of their oper-ations. However, Canadian parts could not be imported duty-free for the U.S. replacement-parts market; this forced Canadian parts producers to sell to the four assemblers. Given the virulent opposition of the U.S. parts producers to the Canadian government's 1963 and 1964 duty-remission plan (see Helmers 1967, p. 14), a substantial use of Canadian parts in U.S. assembly may have been difficult to achieve.

Prior to the pact, Canadian parts producers were smaller and pro-duced a larger number of parts per firm, most at significantly lower vol-ume, than U.S. producers.[17] The opening up of trade was then a two-edged sword for the Canadian parts producers. Even as these Canadian producers gained access to U.S. markets, their U.S. counterparts were gaining access to the Canadian component of the models they were al-ready supplying in the United States. These American firms could then, at least in the short run, dominate their less efficient Canadian rivals. A Ford executive pointed this out[18] in his remarks at the 1965 hearings held (before the U.S. House Ways and Means Committee) to assess the poten-tial effects of the Auto Pact.

---

[17] Prior to the Auto Pact, Canadian parts manufacturers produced most of the parts for the full range of models assembled in Canada. Helmers (1967) surveys the Canadian metal-stamping firms producing for the automotive market and argues that protection prior to the Auto Pact resulted in a noncompetitive industry: "suppliers tended to spe-cialize in one, two or three general types of stampings, both medium-sized and small, year after year. The great variety of stampings required by the Canadian automobile manufacturers – from a relatively few approved vendors – tend to group the vendors according to types of stampings. This in turn reduced the number of firms competing for any single type of stamping" (p. 79).

[18] "Many automotive products now made inefficiently in Canada will in the future be sup-plied from efficient U.S. sources. . . . Let us assume that Ford of Canada is buying dozens of different kinds of wiring assemblies for its 290 models from a Canadian producer. It may well prove efficient under the new rules for this producer to sell only a few kinds of wiring assemblies to both Ford of Canada and Ford–United States. Our American sup-pliers of all the other types of wiring assemblies, then, would have access for the first time to a duty-free Canadian market, in addition to their retained American market."

The Auto Pact allowed the four qualified manufacturers to rationalize their Canadian production and sourcing so as to minimize total production costs. The Canadian-content provisions could be met by assembly and the purchase of most parts in Canada. Given that this was the inefficient pattern of operation prior to the Auto Pact, it was unlikely to continue after the pact was in force. Two other rationalization scenarios were possible. First, the manufacturers could have rationalized auto assembly, exporting and importing cars and purchasing Canadian parts for the entire model run then produced in Canada and destined for both the U.S. and Canadian markets. Alternatively, the manufacturers could expand assembly in Canada beyond the point required by rationalization, and only purchase Canadian parts necessary to meet (when combined with the value added in assembly) the Canadian-content rules and the conditions of the letters of agreement. Given the greater scale economies present in the production of many parts (especially complex parts such as engines or transmissions) than in assembly,[19] the "lumpiness" of assembly, and the relatively greater protection afforded assembly as opposed to parts by the Auto Pact rules, this latter alternative could be expected to dominate. Canada would become an assembler of finished vehicles and continue as a net importer of automotive parts.

In 1975, Canada reintroduced a duty-remission scheme aimed at closing the gap in parts trade. The reintroduction of specific duty-remission schemes aimed at parts exports signaled one major flaw of the Auto Pact: its bias toward assembly. Since 1983, the Canadian federal government has signed export-based duty-remission schemes with the majority of vehicle importers. In 1985, these duty-remission schemes were extended to include parts exported to the United States. These schemes also offer enhanced credits if "significant" investment is made in Canada. This aggressive federal government policy, plus the active courting of automotive investments by Canadian provincial governments, has led to concern in the United States and some U.S. interest in a renegotiation of the Auto Pact. The Canada–U.S. Free Trade Agreement eliminates the use of Canadian duty-remission schemes by 1996.

8.4   Trade restrictions and the use of a cost-function model

The cost-function model estimated in Chapter 5 explicitly assumes cost-minimizing behavior, and does not allow for domestic-content provisions

---

[19] See Bain (1966) and White (1971).

or any policies which inhibit the degree to which manufacturers could engage in cost minimization. The policies in North America that affect trade, production, and possibly the costs of production are tariffs, the Auto Pact, and the Voluntary Restraints Agreement (VRA).[20]

Trade restrictions, when significant, influence productivity growth and productivity comparisons; such restrictions can also work through the cost function. Trade restrictions do not necessarily imply that our cost function is misspecified. From an abstract, theoretical point of view, it is of course desirable to include all possible restrictions, including trade restrictions, in the analysis. In general, this is not practical, so we must decide which restrictions (if any) are sufficiently important to be included.

The existence of tariffs does not create a particular problem. While it is true that tariffs will distort the chosen mix (intermediate products versus labor and capital) of inputs to the production process, this distortion will be fully taken into account as the producing unit reacts to differences in factor prices. Tariffs will certainly affect costs and hence the cost function, but will not distort the estimation of production possibilities or lead to misspecification of the cost function.

A VRA affects the distribution of sales between domestic producers and importers, but the VRA does not affect the method of production. A VRA, while important then in explaining production growth, does not distort the estimated cost function.

The existence of domestic-content provisions potentially creates more of a problem from a theoretical point of view. This then is the only restriction analyzed here. In practice, domestic-content provisions do not create a problem for this study, as they did not result in binding constraints for the vast majority of the observations in the sample.

There were no domestic-content provisions in Japan, Germany, or the United States during the period under consideration. Canada did impose domestic-content constraints, with the Auto Pact stipulating various domestic-content requirements for manufacturers. For Canada in the years 1961–4, we do not know whether the Auto Pact's domestic-content provisions were binding,[21] but deleting these observations from the sample

---

[20] This fact was pointed out to us by an anonymous reader.

[21] Prior to 1965, the Canadian domestic-content requirement consisted of the following. Duty-free entry of some types of original equipment parts (but not vehicles) was permitted, so long as the manufacturer maintained the Canadian value added at a level at least 60% of the factory cost of producing automobiles in Canada. The only year for which we have been able to obtain data to evaluate this potential constraint is 1959; in that year, Canadian value added was 65% of the factory cost. See Bladen (1961, p. 108).

and reestimating the entire model did not change the parameter estimates to any significant extent.[22]

Domestic-content provisions were thus nonbinding for the 1965–84 period for all countries, as we now demonstrate. The minimum requirement that there be 50% North American content for duty-free entry into the United States has never even approached being a constraint for the Big Four. As of 1984, only about 5% of original equipment parts consumed in North America came from offshore.[23]

Even if binding, the content requirement of part 2(a) of the Auto Pact (net sales value floor in Canada) will not result in misspecification or lead to biased parameter estimates, since it affects only the quantity of output produced in Canada, a predetermined variable in a cost-function framework. In addition, firms that find the constraint binding in any year can transfer excess output produced from another year to eliminate the constraint (see Perry 1982). Finally, as shown in table 2.2 of the Federal Task Force Report (1983), this particular domestic requirement was not a binding constraint during the period for which data is available (1970–82).

None of the particular sections of the Canadian content provisions have been binding. The content requirement of part 2(b) (base year minimum) could potentially bias parameter estimates if the constraint were binding. However, table A.6 of the Federal Task Force Report (1983) demonstrates that this constraint has never been binding. It has become irrelevant because of the inflation that occurred during the 1970s.

The content requirement of part 2(c) (value added in Canada to be at least 60% of the growth and the value of cars sold) could also potentially bias parameter estimates if the constraint were binding. However, the industry outperformed the floor constraint on Canadian value added in all years since 1965 except 1980.[24] One year's exception out of 20 years' experience could not be expected to influence behavior, especially given the fact that this content requirement was a moral obligation only (it was not contained in the legal document that constituted the Auto Pact). As Perry notes, "the Federal Government has no apparent means of enforcing CVA [Canadian Value Added] standards established by the letters of

---

[22] A formal statistical test was performed on the hypothesis that the parameters are the same in both the restricted and unrestricted samples. This hypothesis could not be rejected at the 5% level, and hence any numerical difference in parameter estimates is due to the randomness introduced by selecting a different sample.

[23] See Federal Task Force (1983).

[24] See Federal Task Force (1983), figure 2-3 (p. 29) and table A-8.

undertaking. These standards are not legally binding on the producers" (Perry 1982, p. 71).

The content requirement in 2(d) (increase value added by $260 million) also was satisfied with a large margin to spare. It could not have been viewed as a binding constraint during the 1965–8 period.

In summary, since 1965 there were no trade restrictions for the United States, Japan, Germany, and Canada that would cause our model to be misspecified or lead to biased parameter estimates. The main effect of the Canada–U.S. Auto Pact was to reallocate production capacity (output) and the mix of vehicles versus parts production between Canada and the United States, and these effects on output are *exogenous* to the cost-function model. For Canada during 1961–4, there may have been a binding domestic-content restraint. However, this possibility is of no empirical importance since deleting the potentially offending observations results in observationally equivalent parameter estimates.

What is most interesting in this discussion is that the industry constantly outperformed all minimum or floor constraints contained in the Auto Pact. We utilize this important fact in our discussions of the pact's effects.

8.5   Unit-cost differentials between Canada and the United States, 1963–84

In this section we present empirical results on the levels of and changes in unit-cost differentials between Canada and the United States. The cost function on which the results depend is given in Chapter 3 as equations (3.22)–(3.34). (The basic parameter results were reported in Appendix 5.A.)

Tables 8.2–8.5 provide an analysis of these cost differentials. Table 8.2 presents the unit production cost differentials for some of the years from 1963 to 1984; the specific years included before 1978 are representative of the time periods of interest to our analysis. As in Chapter 6, the contribution of each source is measured as the difference in total unit production costs that would result if the *only* source of difference between the two countries were that particular source. In this calculation all other sources are held at their geometric mean levels between the two countries. For example, the number −6.3 under "Price of labor" indicates that if the only difference between Canada and the United States were the price of labor, then in 1963 unit production costs would have been 6.3% lower in Canada than in the United States (where production costs in both countries are measured in Canadian dollars).

Table 8.2. *Unit-cost difference and its sources (%): Canada–United States*

Year	Unit production cost difference[a]	Sources of difference							
		Price of labor	Price of capital	Price of materials	Cost efficiency	Scale economies	Capacity utilization	Country-specific efficiency	Residual
1963	2.8	-6.3	-9.1	-1.4	20.0	4.9	2.1	12.1	2.1
1972	5.9	-5.2	0.0	-2.9	18.3	1.0	1.3	15.6	-2.7
1978	3.3	-6.8	0.3	-10.9	20.9	1.1	1.4	17.9	2.5
1979	-3.1	-7.2	-0.9	-13.5	22.8	0.6	2.2	19.5	-0.8
1980	-3.7	-8.9	-0.9	-11.3	20.1	-0.7	-0.6	21.8	0.0
1981	2.9	-8.1	3.0	-11.4	22.5	-0.4	1.2	21.5	0.0
1982	-0.2	-7.6	0.8	-10.8	19.8	-1.1	-0.6	21.8	0.4
1983	1.0	-7.0	-0.1	-11.7	21.8	-0.4	2.3	19.5	1.1
1984	2.3	-6.4	1.5	-12.7	20.8	1.1	1.1	18.1	2.1

[a] [(Canada/U.S.) − 1] × 100.

Somewhat surprisingly, our data indicate that in the years preceding the Auto Pact there was little significant unit production cost differential between Canada and the United States, the greatest difference (2.8%) occurring in 1963. In this period input prices were, on average, lower in Canada than in the United States, but production efficiency was also lower in Canada.

The sixth column of Table 8.2 aggregates all of the nonprice effects together as the cost-efficiency difference. In 1963, holding factor prices at their geometric mean level between the two countries, Canadian unit production costs would have been 20% higher than the United States, because of lower Canadian cost efficiency. It is undoubtedly this term that the Auto Pact was aimed at affecting.

The next column of Table 8.2 shows the effects of economies of scale. Scale differences alone account for 4.9% higher unit production costs in Canada than in the United States (had all other variables been held at their mean levels). Wonnacott and Wonnacott (1967) estimated that inefficient scale increased costs in Canada by 13%. Our calculations based on a cost-function format show this effect to have been less than that estimated by the Wonnacotts. Our results underestimate the true effects of scale because we do not account for the far larger number of models produced in each Canadian plant.

Besides the disadvantage in scale, the other major source of cost inefficiency in Canada in this earlier period is country-specific efficiency. Taking this effect alone (holding all other variables at their mean levels), unit production costs would have been 12.1% higher in Canada than the United States. It is possible that this variable encompasses the short production runs and other embodiments of suboptimal production not measured in aggregate output per plant.

These inefficiencies in Canada (scale and country-specific effects), combined with a slightly poorer capacity utilization in Canada, would have led to substantially higher unit production costs in Canada than in the United States in the pre–Auto Pact period were it not for the favorable impact of lower factor prices in Canada.

Between 1965 and the early 1970s, Canadian auto producers rationalized their assembly production; the scale of aggregate output in Canada also increased. By 1972, the scale disadvantage to Canada had fallen by 80% from its 1963 level (from 4.9% in row 1 to 1.0% in row 2). This reduction in the scale disadvantage was due to the faster growth in Canadian production per plant relative to U.S. production in the post-1965 period. Was this faster growth due to the Auto Pact? In Section 8.10 we examine a counterfactual case – holding auto trade between Canada and the United States at its 1962–4 level, and allowing the domestic Canadian market to expand at the actual rate experienced over the 1966–84 period – in order to determine whether the Pact, per se, increased scale economies.

We expected that unit production costs between 1963 and 1972 would have fallen substantially in Canada as compared to the United States, because of the narrowing of the scale disadvantage and the rationalization of the Canadian industry. In fact, *relative Canadian unit production costs rose by 3.1 percentage points* over this period (a 5.9% unit cost disadvantage in 1972 less the 2.8% disadvantage in 1963). How do we explain this surprising result? First, an important factor leading to these increased relative unit production costs for Canada is the deterioration in Canada's very favorable factor-price regime of 1962–4. The major component of this deterioration was the price of capital. In 1963, differences in the cost of capital in the two countries alone yielded 9.1% lower production costs in Canada than in the United States. By 1972, this advantage to Canada disappeared.

Second, and most important, Canada's relative country-specific efficiency (CSE), already at a disadvantage with respect to the United States during 1962–4, continued to deteriorate over the period 1963–72. Recall that the scale effect captures the reduction in unit costs resulting from the increase in aggregate output per plant. If the rationalization of Canadian automobile production following the Auto Pact reduced unit production costs in Canada, then the CSE term should show an improvement for Canada over the 1963–72 period. It does not. Of course, rationalization in the auto industry could have improved CSE in Canada as compared to what might have occurred; in the absence of the Auto Pact the CSE term might have changed even more to Canada's disadvantage.

Between 1972 and the late 1970s, other substantial changes occurred in the relative unit production costs in the two countries. While unit production costs in 1972 were 5.9% higher in Canada than in the United States, by 1979 they were 3.1% *lower* in Canada; and in 1980, 3.7% lower. This reversal in the relative unit production costs between the two countries occurred because of a substantial relative improvement in the prices of labor and materials in Canada's favor, and because of a modest continued relative improvement in the scale of Canadian automobile production.[25] Note, however, that Canadian country-specific efficiency continued

---

[25] This substantial relative improvement in the price of materials is somewhat puzzling. In Table 8.3 we distinguish between movements in the value of the Canadian dollar versus changes in factor prices in each country; the depreciation of the Canadian dollar explains

to decline in the 1970s, reaching its trough in 1980. If the only difference between the costs of automobile production in the two countries was the CSE, then Canadian unit production costs in 1980 would have been 21.8% higher than costs in the United States. This deterioration in CSE occurs *despite* the rationalization of the Canadian auto industry.

In the early 1980s, unit production costs were almost identical in the two countries. This identity masks two important diverging forces: the lower factor prices in Canada and the relative inefficiencies of Canadian production. These two diverging forces have been in operation since the early 1960s, the period before the Auto Pact was in force.

To summarize Table 8.2: In the 21 years between 1963 and 1984, unit production costs fell slightly in Canada relative to the United States; in the latter part of this period, Canadian unit production costs were approximately equal to those in the United States. This overall relative decline in Canadian unit production costs was itself the result of several conflicting movements. First was the significant improvement in the scale of Canadian automobile production, a result that some would attribute to the Auto Pact of 1965. Second, Canadian country-specific efficiency declined relative to the United States. Removing scale effects, the efficiency level of Canadian auto production *declined* relative to U.S. production in the period following the Auto Pact. Third, relative price changes between the United States and Canada occurred over the 21-year period, some to Canada's advantage and some to the advantage of the United States. Relative changes in capacity utilization also worked to lower Canadian unit production costs relative to those in the United States.

8.6   Depreciation of the Canadian dollar

In Table 8.3, we reproduce the results of Table 8.2 except that exchange-rate movements beyond changes in purchasing power parity (PPP) are distinguished from factor-price movements in each country. (Calculations of PPP are given in Table 8.6.) In Table 8.2, factor-price movements and exchange-rate movements were not disaggregated. For example, if the

most of the factor-price effect. However, since materials are largely semifinished components, there is a possibility that if net imports into Canada from the United States are an important component of materials costs, transfer-price changes could account for the observed changes in relative materials costs. With higher tax rates in Canada than the United States, auto firms could raise the transfer price of materials into Canadian assembly, thus transferring profits to the lower tax regime – the United States. This difference in tax rates should have led to relative increases in Canadian materials costs, but the opposite actually occurred.

Table 8.3. *Unit-cost difference and its sources (%), including exchange-rate fluctuations from purchasing power parity: Canada–United States*

Year	Unit production cost difference[a]	Sources of difference							
		Price of labor	Price of capital	Price of materials	Cost efficiency	Scale economies	Capacity utilization	Country-specific efficiency	Exchange-rate fluctuation
1963	2.8	-4.8	-7.8	4.3	20.0	4.9	2.1	12.1	-8.2
1972	5.9	-5.9	-0.6	-5.4	18.3	1.0	1.3	15.6	3.9
1978	3.3	-6.3	0.7	-9.2	20.9	1.1	1.4	17.9	-2.7
1979	-3.1	-6.6	-0.3	-11.5	22.8	0.6	2.2	19.5	-3.5
1980	-3.7	-8.1	0.0	-8.9	20.1	-0.7	-0.6	21.8	-4.2
1981	2.9	-7.1	4.3	-8.2	22.5	-0.4	1.2	21.5	-5.8
1982	-0.2	-6.6	2.2	-7.5	19.8	-1.1	-0.6	21.8	-6.0
1983	1.0	-6.5	0.5	-9.7	21.8	-0.4	2.3	19.5	-3.4
1984	2.3	-5.4	2.5	-9.1	20.8	1.1	1.1	18.1	-5.8

[a] $[(\text{Canada}/\text{U.S.}) - 1] \times 100$.

wage rate were fixed in both countries over a two-year period but the Canadian dollar appreciated by 5% in that period, then it would appear that the Canadian wage rate rose by 5% relative to U.S. wages. In Table 8.3, changes in nominal wage rates are distinguished from relative wage rate changes resulting from changes in exchange rates. Table 8.3 shows that the lower price of labor in Canada would by itself have created a 4.8–8.1% Canadian cost advantage over the United States for the 1963–84 period. This advantage rose monotonically to its peak in 1980 and then fell monotonically. The price of capital services rose considerably in Canada relative to the United States, so that the Canadian advantage in capital costs fell sharply by 1972. In the 1980s, Canada was, on average, at a small disadvantage with respect to capital costs. The price of materials changed substantially in favor of Canada over the period, from a 4.3% disadvantage (in terms of unit production costs) in 1963 to a 9.1% advantage in 1984.[26]

Movements in exchange rates relative to PPP accounted for much of the worsening of Canadian unit production costs over the 1963–72 period, but only part of the improvement in Canadian relative unit production costs over the 1972–84 period. In 1963, the divergence of the actual exchange rate from its equilibrium value would have meant that, ceteris paribus, unit production costs were 8.2% lower in Canada than in the United States; by 1972 this advantage to Canada had become a 3.9% disadvantage, a movement in nine years of 12.1 percentage points in favor of the United States. Exchange-rate fluctuations around PPP account for an *improvement* in the relative costs of production in Canada as compared to the United States. The devaluation of the Canadian dollar below PPP in 1984 resulted in 5.8% lower unit costs of production in Canada.

[26] If net imports of materials into Canada from the United States form an important component of material costs, then the exchange-rate effect of a devaluation of the Canadian dollar could be overestimated and the materials price effect underestimated. This would occur because, while Canadian dollar devaluation makes inputs into U.S. production purchased in the United States more expensive when measured in Canadian dollars, inputs (presumably materials) into Canadian production purchased in the United States also become more expensive in Canadian dollars. Hence, some of the apparent factor-price advantage to Canadian producers from devaluation would be canceled out. Similarly, the corresponding appreciation of the U.S. dollar would not lead to an increase in materials prices (in Canadian dollars) for those materials imported from Canada. The evidence from Table 8.3 is that this complication is probably not of importance empirically. The Canadian advantage due to lower materials prices increased considerably during 1977–80, the period of substantial devaluation of the Canadian dollar. This would not have occurred had imports from the United States played a significant role in determining the materials price index.

8.7   Cost-efficiency differences

Table 8.3 includes the cost-efficiency differences (CED) between the two countries, when factor prices are held at their geometric mean levels (column 6). Remember that CED measures technical efficiency. In 1963, if factor prices and exchange rates had not differed between the two countries (factor prices at means, exchange rates at PPP), unit production costs would have been 20% higher in Canada than in the United States. Over the nine-year period 1963–72 the Canadian CED disadvantage fell by 1.7 percentage points, but over the period 1972–84 the Canadian CED disadvantage increased by 2.5 percentage points. This is a crucial point. In Table 8.3, unit production costs are shown to be lower in Canada than in the United States during 1979 and 1980. However, cost-efficiency differences (technological rather than factor-price differentials) in production show substantial and continued advantages to the United States. The improvements in Canadian CED relative to the United States occurred through improvements in aggregate output; these improvements were, however, more than offset by a relative decline in Canadian country-specific efficiency. These results indicate that factor-price advantages, including the devaluation of the Canadian dollar, underlie Canada's slight advantage over the United States in unit production costs in the 1980s.

8.8   Equilibrium estimates

Table 8.4 presents the equilibrium unit-cost differentials and their sources, holding capacity utilization (not exchange rates) at their normal levels. This data indicates some surprising results. In the early 1960s (see row 1, 1963), prior to the Auto Pact, equilibrium unit costs were somewhat lower in Canada than the United States, with factor-price advantages to Canada actually offsetting its lower technical efficiency. In the early to mid-1970s, Canada's equilibrium unit-cost advantage was reversed. Since 1978, production costs (by this equilibrium concept) have been lower in Canada than in the United States.

In Table 8.5, in addition to holding capacity utilization at its normal level, we hold the relative exchange rates at their equilibrium PPP levels (see Table 8.6). In these calculations, unit production costs for 1963 (calculated using the estimated cost function) are 7.4% higher in Canada than in the United States. Over the nine-year period 1963–72, there is a substantial reduction in this measure of long-run equilibrium Canadian

Table 8.4. *Unit-cost difference and its sources (%): Canada–United States (equilibrium – not adjusting for exchange-rate fluctuations)*

Year	Unit production cost difference[a]	Sources of difference					Country-specific efficiency	Cost efficiency
		Price of labor	Price of capital	Price of materials	Scale economies			
1963	−1.4	−6.2	−9.0	−1.5	4.9	11.7	17.1
1972	7.0	−5.1	0.0	−3.0	1.0	15.0	16.1
1978	−1.2	−6.6	0.3	−11.0	1.1	17.3	18.5
1979	−5.9	−6.9	−0.8	−13.9	0.6	17.7	18.4
1980	−6.7	−8.3	−0.7	−12.4	−0.7	17.9	17.0
1981	−3.3	−7.6	2.2	−12.6	−0.4	17.6	17.2
1982	−4.9	−7.2	0.5	−12.2	−1.1	17.4	16.1
1983	−4.5	−6.7	−0.1	−12.3	−0.4	17.1	16.7
1984	−2.0	−6.2	1.4	−12.9	1.1	17.0	18.4

[a] [(Canada/U.S.) − 1] × 100.

Table 8.5. *Unit-cost difference and its sources (%): Canada–United States (equilibrium – adjusting for exchange-rate fluctuations)*

Year	Unit production cost difference[a]	Sources of difference				Country-specific efficiency	Cost efficiency
		Price of labor	Price of capital	Price of materials	Scale economies		
1963	7.4	−4.8	−7.7	4.3	4.9	11.7	17.1
1972	2.9	−5.8	−0.5	−5.4	1.0	15.0	16.1
1978	1.5	−6.2	0.7	−9.3	1.1	17.3	18.5
1979	−2.5	−6.4	−0.2	−11.8	0.6	17.7	18.4
1980	−2.6	−7.7	0.0	−9.9	−0.7	17.9	17.0
1981	2.7	−6.6	3.2	−9.0	−0.4	17.6	17.2
1982	1.1	−6.2	1.5	−8.5	−1.1	17.4	16.1
1983	−1.2	−6.1	0.4	−10.2	−0.4	17.1	16.7
1984	4.1	−5.3	2.3	−9.3	1.1	17.0	18.4

[a] [(Canada/U.S.)−1]×100.

Table 8.6. *Purchasing power parity (PPP)*

Year	PPP (Can.$/U.S.$) Beginning of year	Inflation rate I during year (%) U.S.	Canada	PPP (Can.$/U.S.$) End of year	Midyear
1960				0.94	
1961	0.94	0.0	1.9	0.96	0.95
1962	0.96	0.0	2.9	0.99	0.98
1963	0.99	1.0	0.9	0.99	0.98
1964	0.99	0.0	0.0	0.99	0.99
1965	0.99	3.0	4.6	1.01	1.00
1966	1.01	1.9	0.9	1.00	1.01
1967	1.00	0.9	2.6	1.02	1.01
1968	1.02	2.8	4.6	1.04	1.03
1969	1.04	5.5	3.5	1.02	1.03
1970	1.02	2.0	-0.1	0.99	1.01
1971	0.99	4.1	4.8	1.00	1.00
1972	1.00	7.0	12.3	1.05	1.03
1973	1.05	20.9	27.2	1.10	1.08
1974	1.10	17.2	13.0	1.06	1.08
1975	1.06	4.4	3.7	1.05	1.06
1976	1.05	4.8	6.3	1.07	1.06
1977	1.07	6.3	8.7	1.09	1.08
1978	1.09	10.4	13.7	1.12	1.11
1979	1.12	15.4	16.5	1.13	1.13
1980	1.13	11.3	9.5	1.11	1.12
1981	1.11	5.2	7.8	1.14	1.13
1982	1.14	0.1	4.0	1.18	1.16
1983	1.18	2.7	4.1	1.20	1.19
1984	1.20	0.4	3.6	1.24	1.22

Note: $PPP_E = PPP_B \cdot [(1+I^C)/(1+I^U)]$ and $PPP_B = PPP_E \cdot [(1+I^U)/(1+I^C)]$, where $PPP_B = PPP$ at beginning of year; $PPP_E = PPP$ at end of year; $I^C =$ one-year rate of inflation in Canada; and $I^U =$ one-year rate of inflation in the United States.

unit production costs relative to those in the United States. This improvement is due to relative improvements in the Canadian price of materials and to scale economies associated with larger aggregate output per plant.

8.9 Output-price and marginal-cost differences

The second column of Table 8.7 provides estimates of the output-price differences between wholesale auto prices in Canada and those in the United

Table 8.7. *Output-price and unit-cost differences*[a]

Year	Output-price difference	Unit-cost difference	Short-run marginal cost difference	Long-run marginal cost difference	Average variable cost difference
1963	5.8	2.8	−11.9	−4.7	10.4
1972	7.2	5.9	−1.3	4.6	11.3
1978	−0.9	3.3	−14.9	−8.6	2.3
1979	−3.8	−3.1	−20.0	−12.9	−0.2
1980	−2.4	−3.7	−19.8	−14.8	−0.7
1981	−7.0	2.9	−25.5	−12.9	−2.8
1982	−9.2	−0.2	−22.2	−13.4	−2.2
1983	−5.8	1.0	−19.6	−11.8	−0.8
1984	−7.4	2.3	−16.3	−11.0	−2.5

[a] $[(\text{Canada}/\text{U.S.}) - 1] \times 100$.

States. In 1963, wholesale prices in Canada were 5.8% above those in the United States (in Canadian dollars). In that same year, unit costs were only 2.8% higher in Canada than in the United States (in a common currency unit, column 3). However, taking the exchange rate at its PPP level (Table 8.5), costs were 7.4% higher in Canada. Between 1963 and 1972, the unit-cost difference between Canada and the United States rose to 5.9%; the difference between wholesale prices in the two countries also rose, but the price–cost difference narrowed. Between 1972 and 1978, wholesale prices as well as unit production costs fell in Canada relative to the United States, the former falling more sharply than the latter. In 1979 and 1980, the differential between Canadian and U.S. wholesale prices was similar to the differential in unit production costs. During the 1980s Canadian relative output prices were significantly lower than relative unit costs. This might be attributed to lags in adjusting prices to costs, especially given sharp and unpredicted changes in currency rates and capacity utilization.

One feature of Table 8.7 is that the price–cost margin fell in Canada relative to that in the United States, post–Auto Pact. The relative Canadian price decrease may have been an implicit condition that the auto firms accepted for the Auto Pact benefits. Another possible explanation could be the entry and expansion of British and European importers into Canada.

Also shown in Table 8.7 are differences between short-run and long-run marginal costs. The long-run marginal costs are calculated under the assumption of full utilization of capacity. In 1963, when wholesale prices were 5.8% higher in Canada, short-run marginal costs were 11.9% *lower* in Canada due to relative underutilization of capacity. Long-run marginal costs in 1963 were 4.7% lower in Canada than in the United States. In our model, underutilization of capacity raises unit (average) costs and lowers marginal costs in the short run. From 1963 to 1972, the differences between both relative short-run and long-run marginal costs decreased, moving in the same direction as the change in relative output prices. Between 1972 and 1978, the difference between Canadian and U.S. wholesale prices narrowed significantly, whereas the differences between relative short-run and long-run marginal costs widened. Over the 1980s, Canadian wholesale prices continued to fall relative to U.S. wholesale prices; relative marginal costs also fell. On average, between 1982 and 1984, Canadian wholesale prices were 7.5% below U.S. wholesale prices. In this same three-year period, this differential in wholesale prices was substantially less than the differential between both short-run and long-run marginal costs.

As can be observed from Table 8.7, swings in marginal costs were much more pronounced than swings in prices. This fact suggests that automobile firms were probably using pricing rules that involved a markup over average variable cost. The last column in Table 8.7 is consistent with this hypothesis, since average variable cost differences are much more similar to price differences than are marginal-cost differences. Pricing rules appear to be only partially adjusted in the face of changing market conditions (as reflected in variations in short-run marginal costs), which implies that these firms have sufficient market power to sustain this behavior, even when confronted by low levels of capacity utilization and hence low levels of short-run marginal cost.

8.10   A counterfactual example: cost characteristics of Canadian automobile production in the absence of the Auto Pact

In the preceding sections we have seen that, following the Auto Pact of 1965, production of motor vehicles in Canada grew more quickly than output in the United States, leading to increased efficiency and reduced unit production costs in Canada. But the output of the Canadian auto industry may as well have grown quickly without the Auto Pact, given the fast growth of income and population and the changing demographics of Canada in the post-1965 period. In this section we examine a counterfactual case: a world without the Auto Pact.

In order to examine a hypothetical world that does not include the Auto Pact – the *NAP scenario* – we made the following calculations. First, we noted that 28% of Canadian auto output (parts and finished cars) was imported from the United States in the 1962–4 period, while only 2% of Canadian output was exported to the United States. In the years 1966 to 1984, we assume in the hypothetical NAP world that net imports from the United States to Canada would remain at the levels actually achieved in the 1962–4 period. We also assume that exports from Canada to the United States above these levels would not have occurred (we therefore deduct the value of these exports from the value of domestic Canadian production),[27] and that imports from the United States to Canada above the 1962–4 value could have been produced in Canada (we therefore add these imports to the value of domestic Canadian production).[28] In this hypothetical world, Canadian auto firms produce for the domestic market, rather than being integrated into the North American market.

Output falls sharply in this NAP world, to 52% of actual values by 1984. Given this substantial decrease in total output, we must make some assumption as to the number of plants and their average size in a NAP world. A lower output combined with high tariffs on finished vehicles would have increased the number of models produced in Canada. In order to estimate an upper bound on the impact of the Auto Pact, we assume that the number of plants in the NAP world would have been the same as the actual number, and their average size therefore only 52% of their actual size.[29]

We incorporated one other effect in making these hypothetical calculations. We have seen that the differential between wholesale prices in Canada and those in the United States narrowed after the introduction of the Auto Pact. We hypothesized that in the absence of the Auto Pact, Canadian wholesale prices would have retained their 1963–5 ratio to U.S. wholesale prices (in Canadian dollars). This calculation raises the wholesale price in Canada in the post-1965 period by 5% in the absence of the Auto Pact. Assuming a unitary elasticity of demand, we reduced Canadian output correspondingly by 5%.

[27] We also deducted from the value of Canadian output the materials inputs that would have been used to produce these finished car exports. The ratio of materials inputs to assembly output was held at its average 1963–5 value.

[28] Offsetting changes were made to the value of U.S. production, to ensure that total output matched actual values.

[29] We also assumed that capacity utilization and product mix would have remained the same in the NAP world as actually occurred.

Table 8.8. *Canadian relative unit-cost reductions due to the Auto Pact and their sources (motor vehicle industry)*

Years	Relative production cost reduction (%)^a	Sources of reduction	
		Scale economies	Country-specific efficiency
1970–72	7.6	6.1	1.5
1977–79	4.5	3.5	1.0
1979	3.0	2.3	0.8
1980	3.8	3.0	0.7
1981	4.7	3.6	1.0
1982	9.8	7.5	2.2
1983	8.3	6.4	1.8
1984	9.9	7.4	2.2

^{a} [(Canada/U.S.) -1] $\times 100$.

Using this hypothetical data, we recalculated unit production cost differences and their sources from equation (3.14), assuming all other exogenous variables were unaffected by the introduction of the Auto Pact. Table 8.8 presents the differences between this hypothetical NAP world and actual experience.

For the period 1970–2, we calculate that *the Auto Pact reduced unit production costs in Canada by 7.6%* below their (hypothetical) values in the pact's absence.[30] This improvement in unit production costs comes about through significant improvements in scale. If all that differed between the United States and Canada were scale (all other variables held at their mean levels), then the scale improvement due to the Auto Pact reduced unit production costs in the 1970–2 period by 6.1%. These values are somewhat lower than expected. The data suggests that some of the improvements in scale that actually occurred over the periods 1962–4 to

[30] Prior to the Auto Pact, some rationalization could have occurred because parts were effectively importable if a 60% domestic content was met. One might then assume that at least 40% of the costs of producing a car in Canada was at minimum level. The 1965 Auto Pact, if it lowered unit production costs in Canada by 7.6% relative to U.S. production costs, then represented a 12.7% reduction (7.6%/60%) in the Canadian costs of production.

1970–2 would have occurred anyway through growth of the domestic Canadian market. The results also suggest that in the absence of the Auto Pact, country-specific efficiency would have been lower (by 1.5%) in Canada than that actually experienced. Again, this implies a smaller improvement due to the Auto Pact than most observers have suggested. The bottom line is that, according to our hypothetical analysis, unit production costs fell 7.6% because of the Auto Pact.

From the periods 1970–2 to 1977–9, growth in the Canadian market for motor vehicles was greater in our NAP world than that actually experienced in the United States. As a result, the improvement attributed to the Auto Pact diminishes. We estimate that in the pact's absence, unit production costs would have been only 4.5% higher in Canada in 1977–9 than actual unit costs. The scale effect in the NAP case continues to show an advantage when compared to actual results (3.5% of unit production costs). Country-specific efficiency is 1% higher in Canada in the Auto Pact case for 1977–9. Again, this scant advantage of the Auto Pact can be attributed to rapid growth of the Canadian market over the periods 1970–2 to 1977–9.

Our hypothetical case demonstrates that the Auto Pact was but one of a number of forces impinging on the Canadian auto industry. The pact had a significant effect by 1970–2, reducing unit production costs in Canada by 7.6%; in the later part of the 1970s, cost-reducing effects of the pact are lower. The Auto Pact's effect becomes more significant in the 1980s, as actual Canadian exports to the United States increase.

It is in the 1982–4 period that the Auto Pact has its most significant impact on Canadian unit production costs, reducing them on average by 9.3% relative to our hypothetical world. Again, scale effects due to the Auto Pact account for the bulk (76%) of the unit-cost reduction in favor of Canada, with some improvement in CSE due to the pact as well. The reason that the Auto Pact is most significant in the early 1980s, rather than in the 1970s, is the reduction in Canadian domestic sales in the 1980s and thus the increased importance of exports.

We estimate that the impact of the Auto Pact was less than commonly believed for two reasons. First, aggregate sales in the domestic Canadian market increased substantially, leading to the potential of scale economies for domestic producers. Much of the output expansion that actually occurred over the periods 1963–4 to 1970–2 would have occurred anyway through the growth of the domestic Canadian market. Second, the data suggests that, after accounting for scale, the technical efficiency of Canadian auto production increased only marginally relative to that experienced in the United States (2.2 percentage points by 1984, or 15% of the actual CSE gap in 1984); the Auto Pact did not improve Canadian CSE enormously over what it would otherwise have been. Still, the Auto Pact may have had a more significant positive effect than we have measured, as CSE may have deteriorated even more sharply in the pact's absence.

8.11   The Auto Pact revisited

What do all these rather surprising results (at least in terms of conventional wisdom) signify? First, a brief recapitulation. In 1963, before the Canada–U.S. Auto Pact, actual unit production costs (in a common currency) were somewhat higher (2.8%, Table 8.2) in Canada than in the United States. A careful observer would have noted, first, that costs at PPP were 7.4% higher in Canada (Table 8.5), and second, that cost-efficiency differences showed a substantial 20% disadvantage to Canada. Plant scale economies alone accounted for 5% higher unit costs in Canada than in the United States; country-specific efficiency was significantly lower (explaining a 12% difference in unit production costs) in Canada. The increase in Canadian aggregate and per-plant output during the periods 1962–4 to 1977–9 was substantial and had an impact in reducing unit production costs. All this improvement in scale, however, need not have resulted from the Auto Pact per se.

By 1979, then, one might well have expected an overwhelming Canadian cost advantage in automobile production, given the possible efficiency gains due to the Auto Pact, lower Canadian wage rates, and the depreciation of the Canadian dollar. We estimate that a cost advantage to Canada did exist in 1979. However, this advantage masked a significant cost-efficiency disadvantage to Canada, and furthermore Canadian CSE had deteriorated vis-à-vis the United States, even though the assembly of cars was rationalized in Canada in the 1966–72 period. We estimate that if technical efficiency *had* been equal in the two countries, Canadian unit costs in 1979 would have been 20% less than U.S. unit costs, owing to lower factor prices.

Over the periods 1962–4 to 1977–9, changes in Canada–U.S. wholesale prices directionally matched changes in relative cost, with the price-cost ratio difference narrowing over the period and the price–cost margin falling in Canada. The wholesale price was, however, only 4% lower in Canada in 1979. In addition, under the Auto Pact Canada during 1979 had a net trade deficit with the United States of $2.7 billion in automobile products.

Table 8.9. *Annual growth rates in the automobile industry (%)*

Years	Output		Total factor productivity		Labor productivity	
	U.S.	Canada	U.S.	Canada	U.S.	Canada
1962–65	13.2	20.7	1.9	2.1	2.1	5.2
1966–72	1.4	10.8	1.1	2.8	2.5	7.2
1966–79	2.1	7.6	1.3	1.6	2.4	5.3
1966–84	1.3	6.5	0.9	1.1	2.2	4.1
1972–79	2.8	5.0	1.6	0.7	2.3	3.6
1980–84	−0.8	3.5	0	−0.2	1.6	1.3

We have examined the impact of the Auto Pact on unit costs of production and technical efficiency in Canada. We attributed to the pact those scale effects in excess of the growth in the domestic market, which indicated that the Auto Pact had reduced unit production costs by 7.6 percentage points by 1970–2, primarily through improvements in scale in Canada. But an improvement of about 15 percentage points would have been needed to reach technical-efficiency parity with the United States, according to Table 8.2.

Our results are actually not surprising, when one considers changes in growth rates and in total factor productivity (TFP) for the two countries. This data is shown in Table 8.9. These figures are not based on any hypothetical world or on an econometric cost function; rather, they are based on the actual experience of the two countries' auto industries. Over any time period since 1965, output in Canada has grown far faster than output in the United States. However, corresponding changes in TFP growth do not show such significant advantages to Canada. From 1966 to 1972, aggregate output grew 7.7 times faster in Canada than in the United States, while TFP growth in Canada was only 2.5 times that of the United States. From 1966 to 1984, TFP also grew faster in Canada than in the United States, but not appreciably so. In fact, TFP growth in Canada since 1972 has been below that in the United States. Except for the most recent period (post-1979), growth in labor productivity in Canada has at least doubled that in the United States. The superior performance of Canadian labor productivity as compared to Canadian TFP is due primarily to the substitution of capital and materials inputs for labor.

Table 8.10. *Total factor productivity growth rates (actual data)*

Years	Including scale effects		Excluding scale effects	
	U.S.	Canada	U.S.	Canada
1962–65	1.11	1.64	0	0.64
1966–70	−0.68	2.18	−1.01	0.30
1971–75	2.08	1.68	1.86	0.14
1976–79	2.34	1.20	2.12	1.44
1980–84	2.34	1.98	1.85	1.63

In Table 8.10 we display two additional series on TFP growth; the second excludes from TFP calculations any beneficial effects of improvements in scale. Including scale effects, we see that TFP grew at a higher annual rate in Canada than the United States prior to 1970 but at a higher rate in the United States after 1970. The period of rationalization following the Auto Pact (1966–70) did see substantial improvement in Canadian TFP growth relative to that in the United States. Excluding scale effects, Canadian TFP growth would have been substantially worse than in the United States in the post-1970 period. This data underlines our basic finding: the Auto Pact did not improve the efficiency of Canadian auto production to the extent that is commonly thought. Neither total factor productivity nor relative unit production costs in Canada show a substantial improvement after 1970.

The values in Table 8.8 use actual data rather than estimated values from the regression. Using estimated values alters some conclusions; the numbers in Table 8.10 would be altered as shown in Table 8.11. These estimated values sugggest that the U.S. industry outperformed the Canadian industry in the 1962–5 period and that the Canadian industry outperformed the U.S. industry in the 1980–84 period. (Canadian TFP growth for 1980–84 is estimated at 3.4% per year, instead of the actual value 1.98% per year.)

Our estimated results may underestimate the cost-reducing impact of the Auto Pact if the Canadian automobile industry outperformed the rest of the Canadian manufacturing sector. Sharpe (1983) examines total factor productivity growth rates at the two-digit SIC level in Canada and the United States. The results for total manufacturing and transportation

Table 8.11. *Total factor productivity growth rates (data estimated from regression)*

Years	Including scale effects		Excluding scale effects	
	U.S.	Canada	U.S.	Canada
1962–65	1.8	0.6	0.7	−0.3
1966–70	−0.3	1.4	−0.6	−0.5
1971–75	1.1	1.9	0.9	0.4
1976–79	2.2	0.4	2.0	0.7
1980–84	3.2	3.4	2.8	3.0

Table 8.12. *Annual total factor productivity growth rate (value-added basis)*

	1961–73		1973–79	
	U.S.	Canada	U.S.	Canada
Total manufacturing	3.1	1.4	0.8	0.8
Transportation equipment	2.9	2.4	0.3	0.7

equipment – largely automobiles, but also including railway rolling stock and ship and aircraft equipment (Canada had little aircraft production) – are presented in Table 8.12.

For the 1961–73 period (Sharpe does not break out the 1965–73 period), the Canadian transportation equipment sector outperformed the Canadian manufacturing sector, and by a margin exceeding that of the U.S. transportation equipment sector relative to U.S. manufacturing. In the United States during this period, the growth rate of TFP was slightly lower for transportation equipment than for total manufacturing. Had this relationship existed in Canada, total factor productivity in transportation equipment would have grown at an annual rate of 1.4%; instead it grew 1.0% faster each year, at 2.4%. Similarly, in the period 1973–9, the Canadian transportation equipment sector outperformed its U.S. counterpart, with total factor productivity growing at nearly the same rate as it did for all manufacturing; in the United States, TFP grew at only half the rate of total manufacturing. This, then, is limited evidence that (at least from 1961 to 1973) the Canadian transportation equipment sector performed well compared to total manufacturing and the comparable U.S. sector. This performance was not, however, exceptional.[31]

Berndt and Fuss (1986) estimate that TFP in U.S. total manufacturing grew (on a gross-output basis) at a rate of 0.6% per annum over the 1965–73 period. For Canada, the corresponding rate has also been estimated as 0.6% (Denny and Fuss 1980). The similarity in relative Canada–U.S. TFP growth rates in total manufacturing during 1965–73 suggests that the Canadian CSE for manufacturing in general did not deteriorate significantly more so than for automotive production. The much more rapid output growth rate in automobile production (12.8% versus 4.7% in total manufacturing during 1966–72) meant that economies of scale were exploited to a greater extent in automobile manufacturing. These economies, which were only partially attributable to the Auto Pact, account for narrowing of the efficiency gap in automobile manufacturing; no such narrowing occurred in total manufacturing.[32]

Most previous analysts of the Auto Pact (Beigie 1970, Wilton 1976) have been misled by equating labor productivity (LP) gains with efficiency gains. Labor productivity grew much more rapidly in Canada than in the United States, both immediately after the Auto Pact agreement (1966–72) and during the longer period 1966–79 (see Table 8.9). In fact, from Table 8.13 we can see that a Canadian LP disadvantage of 46.2% in 1966 had been reduced by over 60% by 1972, and had been almost entirely eliminated by 1979. But LP gains are not synonymous with efficiency (TFP) gains. The growth in LP is equal to the growth in TFP plus a factor-substitution effect (due to changes in relative input prices), plus a bias effect (see Appendix 8.A). This bias effect measures the differential impact on labor demand (relative to other factors of production) of events that can yield efficiency gains through TFP growth (e.g., scale expansion, technical change, and increases in capacity utilization), but is not itself a measure of efficiency gains.

Table 8.14 demonstrates that only 34% of the growth in Canadian LP during 1966–84 is due to efficiency gains (TFP growth). The remainder is

[31] In contrast, annual TFP growth in the Japanese auto industry averaged 3.8% in the period 1970–80. See Chapter 6.

[32] The thrust of this section is supported by Baldwin and Gorecki's (1986) Canada–U.S. value-added TFP level comparisons, which utilize disaggregated Canadian data for individual establishments. They find that for the 2-digit transportation equipment industry (consisting of eight four-digit subindustries), the Canadian industry was only 72% as efficient as its U.S. counterpart in 1970, and only 67% as efficient in 1979.

Table 8.13. *Labor productivity*
(real output/hour worked)

Year	Canada	U.S.	% U.S. advantage[a]
1966	22.1	32.3	46.2
1972	32.3	38.0	17.6
1979	42.2	43.2	2.4
1984	44.1	45.7	3.6

[a] $[(\text{Canada}/\text{U.S.}) - 1] \times 100$.

Table 8.14. *Labor productivity growth and its sources,*
Canadian automobile industry

Years	Labor productivity growth rate (%)	% contribution due to		
		Total factor productivity growth	Bias	Factor substitution
1962–65	5.2	27.6	36.9	35.4
1966–72	7.2	33.2	46.3	20.5
1966–79	5.3	32.0	46.7	21.3
1966–84	4.1	34.4	49.8	15.9
1972–79	3.6	25.1	49.3	25.5
1980–84	1.3	45.6	54.8	−0.4

due to substitution away from labor (primarily toward materials) in response to a higher wage rate relative to other factor prices, as well as to
the net labor-saving bias of increases in scale and technical change. That
LP grew more rapidly than TFP is also evidenced when value-added measures of productivity are employed. Table 8.15 shows results obtained on
a value-added basis by Sharpe (1983).

8.12   Conclusions

The major finding of this chapter is that the Canada–U.S. Auto Pact's
selective trade liberalization provisions did not improve – to the extent

Table 8.15. *Productivity growth rates (value-added basis)*

Industry	Productivity measure	1961–73 average % growth		1973–9 average % growth	
		U.S.	Canada	U.S.	Canada
Transportation	LP	3.6	6.4	1.0	3.3
equipment	TFP	2.9	2.4	0.3	0.7
Motor vehicles	LP	4.3	8.5	1.6	1.5
and equipment	TFP	n.c.	n.c.	n.c.	n.c.

Note: n.c. means "not calculated."

previously thought – the efficiency of Canadian automobile production relative to U.S. production. This finding is consistent with Cox and Harris's (1985, p. 131) computational results that, as of 1976, the transportation equipment industry in Canada would be the big winner from unilateral or multilateral free trade, primarily because "the possibility of substantial rationalization exists." Nevertheless, our empirical results are surprising because profit-maximizing firms that pursue cost-minimizing strategies should rationalize if permitted to do so and the Auto Pact provided the needed mechanism.

There exist several possible explanations for our result. First, scale effects and specialization disadvantages in small economies may be less than previously thought. Our estimated "actual" scale elasticity for Canadian auto production for 1968 is 1.18, somewhat below the estimate of 1.25 used by Cox and Harris.[33] Our results do include a closing of the scale gap by the mid-1970s. What does not occur is the closing of the non-scale efficiency gap. But if unexploited economies of rationalization are not present, how does one explain the persistent 20% Canadian efficiency disadvantage?

---

[33] Cox and Harris used an estimate that was approximately halfway between the econometric estimate for 1968 calculated by Fuss and Gupta (1981) and the engineering estimate contained in Gorecki (1978). As noted by Cox and Harris (1985), the econometric estimates are consistently below engineering estimates. However, since the engineering estimates assume a single product line, they include any theoretical cost savings from specialization. Had we applied Cox and Harris's scale elasticity estimate of 1.25 to our aggregate output growth, we would have obtained a larger efficiency gain attributable to scale economies under the Auto Pact but a correspondingly smaller gain attributable to CSE (i.e., specialization), since the sum of the two – relative TFP growth – would remain unchanged.

Second, the Canadian domestic-content provisions of the Auto Pact may have prevented a high degree of rationalization. This explanation appears unlikely, as manufacturers have consistently exceeded the content requirements by wide margins.

Finally, and perhaps most likely, the oligopolistic structure of the automobile industry in Canada during the period 1966–72 probably meant that competitive pressures for cost-reducing rationalization were minimal,[34] and the Auto Pact did nothing to increase them. If the automobile industry in Canada is typical of oligopolistic industries in small economies with unexploited opportunities for rationalization, a halfway measure such as the selective trade liberalization policy represented by the Auto Pact is unlikely to lead to parity in efficiency. The existence of the opportunity to rationalize appears inadequate compared to the competitive pressures that can be unleashed by unrestricted trade liberalization.[35]

These results are consistent with Harry Johnson's 1963 analysis that the Bladen Plan represented increased effective protection for assembly in Canada and for independent Canadian parts producers. Three effects should have resulted from the Auto Pact. First, there should have been cost reductions due to rationalization if assembling fewer models in larger volumes leads in fact to significant cost savings. Second, the increased volume in production should itself have led to cost savings if there are economies of scale with respect to increases in output. The third effect should have been an increase in the proportion of production due to assembly, given the bias toward assembly inherent in the pact.

What are the effects that we actually see? First, we do see a reduction in relative unit production costs in Canada (7% relative to the United States by 1972), due primarily to exploitation of economics of scale. This, however, does not close the efficiency gap that existed in the years prior

---

[34] After the oil crisis of 1973, the switch in consumer preferences toward small, energy-efficient automobiles led to increased competitive pressures from European and Japanese producers. The Voluntary Restraint Agreements among Japan, Canada, and the United States have since 1981 substantially reduced the competitive threat of Japanese imports.

[35] We are not suggesting that the selective trade liberalization of the Auto Pact provided no significant benefits to Canada, but rather that an increase in efficiency to U.S. levels was not among the benefits. The elimination of tariffs for North American producers led to a very large increase in intraindustry trade across the U.S.–Canada border, as producers exploited intraindustry cost advantages. In addition, Canada has been a clear winner in terms of the distribution of production. We estimated that the Auto Pact led to a 52% increase in Canadian production capacity by 1970 over what it would otherwise have been, although this advantage declined to 24% by 1975. In the United States, production capacity was 4% less in 1970 than it would have been without the Auto Pact; this disadvantage declined to 2% by 1975.

to the Auto Pact. In addition, the hypothetical no–Auto Pact scenario has demonstrated that much of this gain from increased scale could have occurred from the growth of the Canadian domestic market itself (except for the turnaround following 1982). What of rationalization? Here is the basic conundrum. If the main effect of the Auto Pact was to rationalize assembly and parts production, and all agree that such rationalization occurred (especially in assembly), then there should have been a very substantial increase in Canadian total factor productivity relative to the United States. This is not observed in the data that we have used.

Finally, and somewhat surprisingly, the pact's inherent bias toward assembly is not evident in the data (see Table 8.16). The share of assembly output remained virtually unchanged in the post–Auto Pact period.

B   COST AND PRODUCTIVITY COMPARISONS:
CANADA–JAPAN AND CANADA–GERMANY

In Chapter 7 we analyzed the results of comparing costs and productivity in the United States, Japan, and Germany. In this chapter we have compared Canada and the United States. By extension, a comparison between Canada and the two non–North American producers is implicit: Canada was less efficient than the United States and therefore far less efficient than Germany or Japan. We provide several tables to highlight the results, examining actual unit-cost comparisons and long-run equilibria (with exchange rates and capacity utilization each at their normal levels).

We begin with Tables 8.17 and 8.18, which provide actual unit-cost comparisons and their sources of differences. In Table 8.17, we note that the Canadian unit-cost disadvantage compared to Japan was nearly the same in 1970 and 1982–1984. Again, this similarity masks different underlying reasons for higher Canadian production costs. In 1970, the source of the Canadian disadvantage was mainly factor prices, but in 1984 the source was almost entirely an efficiency disadvantage. In 1970, holding factor prices at their geometric means between the two countries, cost efficiency differences would have meant 11.3% higher unit costs in Canada; by 1984, this efficiency disadvantage was 32.6%. Within the cost-efficiency aggregate, Canada has lost a portion of its advantage in scale. The major source of the Japanese advantage over Canada lies in country-specific efficiency. Between 1970 and 1974 there was a sharp deterioration in Canadian CSE relative to Japan; between 1974 and 1980 a steady erosion in Canadian relative CSE occurred also.

Table 8.16. *Share of assembly output in Canadian automotive industry*

1961	70.1
1962	71.0
1963	71.6
1964	71.3
1965	73.0
1966	71.4
1967	74.0
1968	73.3
1969	73.8
1970	73.1
1971	72.2
1972	71.9
1973	71.3
1974	75.3
1975	78.1
1976	74.0
1977	71.9
1978	72.2
1979	76.3
1980	78.8
1981	75.5
1982	75.1
1983	72.6
1984	70.6

Source: Statistics Canada, *Motor Vehicle Manufacturers* (to 1980); Statistics Canada, *Motor Vehicle Industry* (1981–4).

Table 8.18 provides the same data as in Table 8.17, but for a Canada–Germany comparison. Note that, in 1970, Canadian unit costs were 44.3% higher than German unit costs. In contrast to the situation with Japan, Canada's cost disadvantage with Germany in 1970 was primarily a result of lower Canadian efficiency, due to lower CSE. The results for 1963 are similar.

In 1980, Canada had 33.2% *higher* unit costs than Japan but 7.4% *lower* unit costs than Germany. The Canadian advantage over Germany

Table 8.17. *Unit-cost difference and its sources (%): Japan–Canada*

Year	Unit production cost difference[a]	Sources of difference							
		Price of labor	Price of capital	Price of materials	Cost efficiency	Scale economies	Capacity utilization	Country-specific efficiency	Residual
1970	-41.5	-14.1	-6.6	-1.9	-11.3	8.7	-6.4	-12.8	-1.5
1974	-19.8	-8.7	-4.5	26.2	-15.6	8.3	-1.9	-20.6	-0.1
1975	-27.2	-7.0	-5.9	20.8	-19.9	8.5	-4.6	-22.6	1.5
1978	-10.4	-3.3	-1.6	34.3	-25.9	3.3	-2.1	-26.7	-0.6
1979	-17.7	-4.0	-1.7	26.4	-30.4	2.8	-4.6	-29.1	4.0
1980	-33.2	-4.8	-3.3	26.0	-37.3	3.4	-11.5	-31.5	0.1
1982	-44.0	-4.7	-6.2	16.4	-37.0	3.1	-13.8	-29.2	-0.2
1984	-37.4	-3.6	-5.9	18.7	-32.6	2.3	-1.9	-32.9	1.3

[a] [(Japan/Canada) − 1] × 100.

Table 8.18. *Unit-cost difference and its sources (%): Germany–Canada*

Year	Unit production cost difference[a]	Sources of difference							
		Price of labor	Price of capital	Price of materials	Cost efficiency	Scale economies	Capacity utilization	Country-specific efficiency	Residual
1963	-45.8	-14.5	-5.1	3.3	-35.6	-1.6	-0.7	-34.1	0.4
1970	-44.3	-13.3	-9.3	3.1	-33.7	1.0	-6.1	-30.1	3.9
1974	-5.1	-2.0	-2.2	27.1	-25.3	2.9	0.5	-27.8	4.3
1975	-7.7	0.2	-3.6	27.7	-26.0	4.5	-3.2	-26.7	1.3
1978	2.9	5.5	1.7	35.1	-26.9	1.8	-2.1	-26.6	-3.0
1979	17.6	11.4	4.7	41.1	-28.5	3.2	-5.6	-26.7	0
1980	7.4	13.2	4.7	34.9	-33.6	3.8	-11.9	-27.4	1.3

[a] [(Germany/Canada) −1] × 100.

in 1980 was due to a large advantage in factor prices, offsetting a continued substantial Canadian disadvantage in technical efficiency. Note that the German CSE advantage over Canada fell somewhat between 1963 and 1974 (from 34.1% to 27.8%), but has remained nearly constant since then.

In Tables 8.19 and 8.20 we provide the long-term equilibrium results for Canada, Japan, and Germany since 1978, holding exchange rates at their FEER levels and capacity utilization at normal levels. In 1980, actual Canadian unit costs were 33.2% above those in Japan (Table 8.17) but 7.4% below those in Germany (Table 8.18). In the long-run equilibrium case, Canadian unit costs were 21.7% above Japanese costs and 15.5% below German costs in 1980. The Canadian long-run efficiency disadvantage in 1980 was slightly greater with respect to Japan than Germany. In 1980, Canadian motor vehicle producers had factor-price advantages over both German and Japanese producers, but these advantages were much more substantial relative to Germany than to Japan. In 1984, long-run equilibrium calculations show Canadian producers with 28.5% higher unit costs than Japanese producers, with factor-price advantages offsetting a small portion of the Canadian long-run efficiency disadvantage.

Appendix 8.A: Decomposition of labor productivity growth

The demand for labor is given by the function

$$L = L(\mathbf{w}, Q, \mathbf{T}), \tag{8.A.1}$$

where $\mathbf{w}, Q, \mathbf{T}$ are (respectively) input prices, capacity output, and technological characteristics, as defined in Chapter 3. Applying the quadratic lemma to (8.A.1) yields:

$$\Delta \log L = \frac{1}{2} \sum_i \left(\frac{\partial \log L_t}{\partial \log w_{it}} + \frac{\partial \log L_{t-1}}{\partial \log w_{i,t-1}} \right) \cdot \Delta \log w_i$$

$$+ \frac{1}{2} \left(\frac{\partial \log L_t}{\partial \log Q_t} + \frac{\partial \log L_{t-1}}{\partial \log Q_{t-1}} \right) \cdot \Delta \log Q$$

$$+ \frac{1}{2} \sum_l \left(\frac{\partial \log L_t}{\partial \log T_{lt}} + \frac{\partial \log L_{t-1}}{\partial \log T_{l,t-1}} \right) \cdot \Delta \log T_l. \tag{8.A.2}$$

Labor productivity growth is discretely approximated by

$$\Delta \log \mathrm{LP} = \Delta \log q - \Delta \log L, \tag{8.A.3}$$

Table 8.19. *Unit-cost difference and its sources (%): Japan–Canada (equilibrium – adjusting for exchange-rate fluctuations)*

| Year | Unit production cost difference[a] | Sources of difference | | | | | | |
		Price of labor	Price of capital	Price of materials	Scale economies	Country-specific efficiency	Cost efficiency
1978	−13.4	−5.1	−2.6	23.6	3.2	−26.6	−24.2
1979	−16.1	−4.7	−1.6	21.9	2.8	−28.7	−26.7
1980	−21.7	−5.7	−2.7	19.2	3.4	−30.8	−28.4
1982	−24.6	−5.4	−3.5	11.1	3.2	−27.9	−25.7
1984	−28.5	−4.5	−3.8	12.5	2.4	−32.4	−30.8

[a] [(Japan/Canada) −1] × 100.

Table 8.20. *Unit-cost difference and its sources (%): Germany–Canada (equilibrium – adjusting for exchange-rate fluctuations)*

Year	Unit production cost difference[a]	Sources of difference					
		Price of labor	Price of capital	Price of materials	Scale economies	Country-specific efficiency	Cost efficiency
1978	3.3	4.3	0.9	31.2	1.8	−26.6	−25.2
1979	13.3	8.7	2.9	33.5	3.2	−26.5	−24.1
1980	15.5	11.3	3.2	32.4	3.8	−26.9	−24.1

[a] [(Germany/Canada)−1]×100.

where $q = Q \cdot T_1$ is actual output (T_1 = capacity utilization rate). Combining (8.A.2) and (8.A.3) yields

$$\Delta LP = -\frac{1}{2} \cdot \sum_i (ELw_{i,t-1} + ELw_{i,t-1}) \cdot \Delta \log w_i$$

$$+ [1 - \tfrac{1}{2} \cdot (ELQ_t + ELQ_{t-1})] \cdot \Delta \log Q$$

$$+ [1 - \tfrac{1}{2} \cdot (ELT_{1,t} + ELT_{1,t-1})] \cdot \Delta \log T_1$$

$$- \sum_{l \neq 1} (ELT_{l,t} + ELT_{l,t-1}) \cdot \Delta \log T_l, \qquad (8.A.4)$$

where

ELw_i = price elasticity of labor with respect to input i;
ELQ = elasticity of labor with respect to capacity output;
ELT_l = elasticity of labor with respect to technological characteristic l.

Equation (8.A.4) can be rewritten as

ΔLP

$$= \left[-\frac{1}{2} \sum_i (ELw_{i,t} + ELw_{i,t-1}) \cdot \Delta \log w_i \right]$$

$$+ \left[1 - \frac{1}{2} \cdot (ECQ_t + ECQ_{t-1}) \cdot \Delta \log Q \right.$$

$$+ \left(1 - \frac{1}{2} \cdot (ECT_{1,t} + ECT_{1,t-1}) \right) \cdot \Delta \log T_1$$

$$\left. - \frac{1}{2} \sum_{l \neq 1} (ECT_{l,t} + ECT_{l,t-1}) \cdot \Delta \log T_l \right]$$

$$+ \left[\left\{ \frac{1}{2} \cdot (ECQ_t + ECQ_{t-1}) - \frac{1}{2} \cdot (ELQ_t + ECQ_{t-1}) \right\} \cdot \Delta \log Q \right.$$

$$\left. + \left\{ \frac{1}{2} \cdot \sum_l (ECT_{l,t} + ECT_{l,t-1}) - \frac{1}{2} \cdot \sum_l (ELT_{l,t} + ELT_{l,t-1}) \right\} \Delta \log T_l \right],$$

$$(8.A.5)$$

where

ECQ = elasticity of cost with respect to capacity output;
ECQ_l = elasticity of cost with respect to technological characteristic l.

The term inside the first set of large square brackets is the factor substitution effect. The term inside the second set is the expression for the discrete approximation to total factor productivity growth. Finally, the term inside the third set is the bias effect.

CHAPTER 9

Summary and conclusions

In the introduction to this volume we demonstrated how "relative competitiveness" depends on a host of factors such as input prices and exchange rates, as well as on aspects of technical efficiency like economies of scale and country-specific efficiency. We also discussed how trade flows between countries can be influenced by basic relative competitiveness and by policies such as exchange rates, taxes, subsidies, and direct interventions in tariffs, quotas, and Voluntary Restraint Agreements (VRAs). A key issue raised in the first two chapters is the distinction between short-run temporary dislocations and longer-run fundamental movements. In particular, capacity utilization was singled out as a crucial factor affecting short-run movements in unit cost and productivity in an industry with the capital intensity of automobile production. We also showed how temporary disequilibria in foreign-exchange markets could muddy the analysis of long-run fundamental changes in relative competitiveness.

Chapter 2 provided a historical summary of the absolute and relative movements in automobile production: the values of output and input (and input prices) since the early 1960s. In 1961, the United States produced 5.5 million passenger vehicles, 2.4 times as many automobiles as the combined outputs of Japan, Germany, and Canada. In 1961, the Japanese produced 250,000 motor cars, or approximately 5% of the number produced in the United States, 15% of the number produced in Germany, and 60% of the number produced in Canada. In 1961 only the German auto industry was a significant exporter, with half of its output being shipped to the United States, Canada, and other European countries. By 1984, in contrast, automobile production in the United States was only 10% greater than in Japan, where auto production was now twice as great as in Germany and seven times as great as Canadian production. Japan and Germany were major exporters; Japan's export success was so great that the United States and Canada negotiated "voluntary" export restraints in 1981. Compared to North America, Japan (and Germany to a much lower degree) had enormous increases in output over the 1961–84 period.

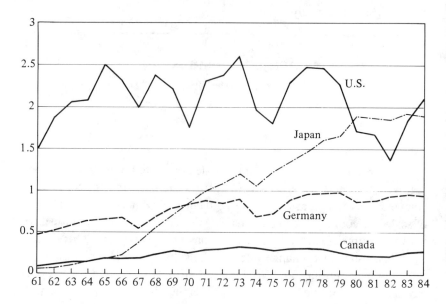

Figure 9.1. Index of automobile production (Japan 1971 = 1.0).

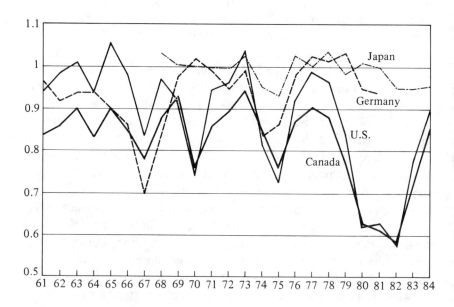

Figure 9.2. Index of capacity utilization (normalized by Japanese average).

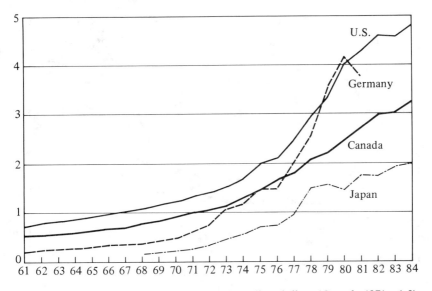

Figure 9.3. Labor price index, Canadian dollars (Canada 1971 = 1.0).

Besides the remarkable upward trend in motor vehicle production, fluctuations about the trend were far less in Japan than in North America. Figure 9.1 plots the trend in number of automobiles produced, and Figure 9.2 plots the utilization rate of capacity. Note the steady growth rate in Japan (and in Germany but lower) as compared to the evident fluctuations around a near trendless path for the North American auto producers.

Figure 9.3 plots the data for the price of labor, Figure 9.4 plots total average weighted input price; both series are given in Canadian dollars (the weights are the factor shares in total costs). Over the 1961–80 period, wage rates increased the most in Germany and the least in Canada; note that this includes movements in exchange rates. Japanese wage rates also rose appreciably. The aggregate input price index increased most in Germany and Japan (until 1980). Remember that in 1961 the actual level of input prices was far lower in Japan and Germany than in the United States and Canada. Thus any North American cost disadvantage in 1961 could be attributed to factor prices, if production outside North America were less efficient than production in North America. In 1961, however, German car producers were more efficient than North American producers.

The level of total factor productivity (TFP) in any one year is measured as real output per unit of aggregate real input, or, conversely, as cost

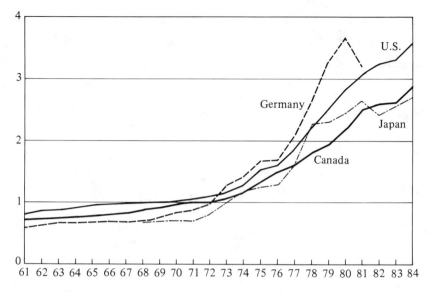

Figure 9.4. Aggregate input price index, Canadian dollars (Canada 1971 = 1.0).

efficiency (CE) – the real costs per unit of output. Lower costs outside North America could be (and were) accompanied by lower TFP. At any moment in time there is no necessary relationship between the differential in production costs between two countries and the differential in TFP.

We stated in Section 1.2 that the fundamental question for TFP or CE calculations is the following: If all four countries had the same factor prices, who would have a comparative advantage in automobile production? The question is not new. While many other authors have examined this question, what distinguishes our work is the use of an objective, precise methodology (dependent, of course, on the data available). Others who have used accounting methodologies – annual reports or firm-specific data – have been forced to make arbitrary adjustments for the mix of cars produced, the average weight of a car, or the levels of vertical integration. Where we had to make adjustments (e.g., with respect to product mix), we used formal methods rather than ad hoc adjustments.

The answers to our "fundamental question" that were available in the literature showed a large comparative advantage to the United States in the 1960s, a declining advantage in the 1970s, and an enormous comparative advantage to the Japanese in the 1980s. However, the methodologies

Table 9.1. *Average annual rates of growth, 1970–84*

	U.S.	Japan	Germany[a]	Canada
TFP growth	1.3	3.0	1.3	1.3
Unit cost increases				
In own currency	6.2	2.4	6.8	6.5
In Canadian dollars	7.9	7.0	15.6	6.5
Sources of increase (in own currency)				
Factor prices	7.5	5.5	8.0	8.0
Scale economies	−0.3	−0.4	−0.3	−0.7
Technical change	−0.8	−2.7	−1.1	−0.3
Capacity utilization	−0.3	0	0.1	−0.3

[a] 1970–80 only.

applied call these findings somewhat into question. When we made our own adjustments to the accounting methodologies employed by others, we arrived at the following decomposition of the percentage cost advantage of Mazda over Ford in 1981 (see Table 2.35):

Labor productivity	23%
Labor price	42%
Undervalued yen	16%

We then turned to a theoretical cost-minimization model and its econometric formulation. The results of the econometric estimation of the theoretical model were presented in Chapters 6, 7, and 8. Table 9.1 summarizes the comparisons of TFP and unit-cost growth rates in the four countries as well as the sources of unit cost increases. Table 9.2 summarizes level comparisons of cost advantage and their underlying sources, including data on "comparative advantage" (i.e., cost efficiency) – our answer to the fundamental question.

In the first part of Table 9.1 the basic data are presented; no econometric model is used. Annual growth rates of TFP in Japan were 2.5 times those of the North American and German auto sectors over the 1970–84 period (German data through 1981 only). Correspondingly, unit-cost increases in Japan were 40% of the cost increases in the other three countries. Average factor-price increases grew at high rates in all four countries, ranging from an annual 5.5% rate of increase in Japan to 8.0% in

Table 9.2. *Unit-cost differences and their sources*

	1970	1975	1978	1980	1984
(a) Total difference					
Japan/U.S.	−34.1	−21.2	−6.3	−35.1	−35.4
Germany/U.S.	−37.1	−0.5	6.9	3.0	n.a.
Canada/U.S.	11.0	6.6	3.3	−3.7	2.3
(b) Price of labor					
Japan/U.S.	−23.0	−16.7	−10.8	−15.2	−13.0
Germany/U.S.	−19.9	−7.5	−3.6	0.8	n.a.
Canada/U.S.	−4.9	−5.7	−6.8	−8.9	−6.4
(c) Total CED					
Japan/U.S.	9.7	−4.9	−8.1	−22.1	−17.2
Germany/U.S.	−17.0	−12.6	−9.4	−18.4	n.a.
Canada/U.S.	19.5	14.3	20.9	20.1	20.8
(d) Long-run equilibrium CED					
Japan/U.S.	n.a.	n.a.	−7.7	−13.7	−16.7
Germany/U.S.	n.a.	n.a.	−9.1	−9.5	n.a.
Canada/U.S.	18.1	13.6	18.5	17.0	18.4

Note: n.a. means "not available."

Germany and Canada.[1] Japan had the lowest annual rate of factor-price increase (denominated in domestic currencies), combined with the highest rate of technical change. As a result, unit-cost increases were far lower in Japan than in the other three countries. In a common currency, unit-cost increases in Japan were close to those in North America (German cost increases at nearly a 16% annual rate!), demonstrating the large appreciation of the yen (and mark) relative to the U.S. and Canadian dollars.

The impact of technical change is evident in Table 9.1: Technical change reduced unit costs by 2.7% per year on average in Japan, only 1.1% per year in Germany, 0.8% in the United States, and 0.3% in Canada. Increases in the aggregate size of output per plant, economies of scale, contributed 0.3–0.4% per year to unit-cost reductions except in Canada (the smallest auto sector), where the impact of scale economies, on average, far outweighed the impact of technical change in reducing costs.

---

[1] This result is not at variance with the data shown in Figures 3 and 4 since these figures include movements in both factor prices and exchange rates relative to the Canadian dollar.

Another overall view of unit-cost comparisons is given in Table 9.2. Here we summarize the results of Chapters 7 and 8, where differences in the levels of unit costs were calculated and sources of the differences detailed, from results of the estimation of the econometric model. Rows under headings (*a*), (*b*), and (*c*) are the actual short-run differentials, showing (respectively) the total difference, the difference due to the price of labor alone, and the total cost-efficiency difference. These results are similar to the results given in Tables 7.1, 7.5, and 8.2, and include product-mix differences between countries. Rows under heading (*d*) are the long-run equilibrium results assuming that capacity utilization was normal and exchange rates were at their fundamental equilibrium value; these results are consistent with those in Tables 7.4, 7.8, and 8.5.

In 1970, actual unit costs of production for an average car were lowest in Germany and highest in Canada (rows *a*). German unit production costs were 48% below those in Canada, 34% below those in the United States, and 3% below those in Japan. Japanese unit costs of production were 34% below those incurred in the United States. In 1970, differences in labor costs alone explained more than 50% of the German and Japanese cost advantages over the American products. Canadian producers, however, had lower labor costs than in the United States, so higher Canadian production costs did not stem from higher labor costs. Examining cost efficiency alone (i.e., maintaining all factor prices at their geometric mean in any two-way comparison) shows that German auto producers had a real technical cost advantage over producers in the other three countries – by 37% over Canadian firms, 27% over Japanese manufacturers, and 17% over U.S. firms. In 1970, then, the U.S. auto industry (as distinct from the Canadian auto sector) was in second place in the CED tournament to the German auto sector, but with a substantial 10% advantage over Japanese producers.[2]

Anyone predicting the auto industry's future based on 1970 data would have been incorrect; in five years, massive changes occurred. By 1975, unit costs of production were identical in the United States and Germany, the United States having closed a 37% cost gap in five years! Japanese car producers also made enormous progress in this five-year period, so that by 1975 their unit costs were 21% below Germany and still below the United States (however, their cost advantage over the United States fell by one-third during this period). The Canadians continued to lag.

Taking simple trends over the 1970–5 period might have forecast a continued American closing of the cost gap. However, abstracting from

[2] We cannot calculate long-run CED values for 1970 and 1975 because fundamental equilibrium exchange rate data is not available.

factor price changes, an examination of real technical-efficiency changes tells a totally different and crucial story (as first revealed by Toder et al. 1978). Whereas in 1970 the U.S. producers were 10% technically more efficient than the Japanese in producing an average car, by 1975 the Japanese were 5% more efficient – an enormous reversal in five years. In 1975, the German car industry was still the most efficient, followed by Japan, the United States, and Canada. Thus, the large change in unit costs of production in favor of the United States over the period 1970–5 masked two contradictory trends: improvements in factor prices favoring the United States (see rows *b*) and deterioration in the U.S. producers' relative efficiency.

Between 1975 and 1978, the trends in unit costs evident over the 1970–5 period continued. In 1978, unit production costs were lower in the United States and Canada than in Germany; North American unit costs were closest to those in Japan (6% higher in the United States, 10% higher in Canada). Yet only two years later, in 1980, Japanese unit costs were 35% below those in the United States, Canadian unit costs were 4% below those in the United States, and Germany was the highest-cost producer. The year 1978 was thus a watershed in the auto industry.

Between 1975 and 1978 the American disadvantage in technical efficiency (compared to Japanese producers) continued to climb. Between 1978 and 1980, U.S. producers saw the gap in short-run technical efficiency between them and the Japanese increase by a factor of 2.5; during this same period, the American disadvantage in short-run cost efficiency differences (CED) relative to German car producers doubled.

The reasons why the trends in unit costs over the 1978–80 period could not be sustained are shown in rows (*c*) of Table 9.2. One of the main advantages of the methodology used in this book is that one is able to decompose this astonishing three-year decline in the relative technical efficiency of North American car producers into short-term and long-term sources. Between 1978 and 1980, the entire change in relative efficiency between U.S. and German auto producers was due to short-run declines in capacity utilization in the U.S. auto industry that were not experienced in the German industry. In fact, long-run CED moved much to the U.S. advantage, as compared to Germany, in the 1978–80 period. While U.S. technical efficiency in this period continued to erode substantially relative to Japan, 60% of the apparent gain by Japan was due to short-run phenomena (massive 1980 underemployment of U.S. fixed assets) not experienced in Japan. Note that from 1978 to 1980 the improvement in U.S. factor prices relative to Japan noted over the period 1970–8 was reversed, owing largely to relative exchange-rate movements. One would not want to make policy decisions based on short-run data.

From 1980 to 1984 there was no significant change in the relative unit costs of production between the United States and Japan (rows *a*). Although the measured technical efficiency of U.S. producers increased relative to the Japanese over this period (rows *c*), this increase was illusory. The relative technical improvement for U.S. producers was entirely due to the increased capacity utilization of 1984 over 1980. Between 1980 and 1984, the Japanese auto industry continued to build a substantial advantage in long-term technical efficiency, to a level of 17% in 1984.

Combining the evidence from Tables 9.1 and 9.2 leads to the following conclusions. In 1970, the United States was the second highest-cost producer of automobiles of the four countries (remember this is for an average, comparable car, after correcting for differences in size and weight). However, the United States was the second-most efficient producer of cars (after Germany), having a near 10% technical-efficiency advantage over Japanese auto producers and 20% over Canadian plants (which were owned by U.S. manufacturers). In 1970, then, the American cost disadvantage, compared to Japan and Canada, was totally a function of factor prices. Compared to German producers, the U.S. cost disadvantage was half factor prices, half less efficient production.

American factor-price disadvantages relative to Japan, Germany, and Canada were well known, and were hardly confined to the auto sector. However, unless it can be shown that factor-price disadvantages are a form of dividing monopoly profits, or due to imperfections in factor markets, there is no need for a public policy response. Indeed, public policy would likely be inefficient. Generally higher factor prices in the United States would be reflected in exchange rates; there is no need to intervene in one specific industry. Thus, trade patterns in 1970 could be explained by comparative costs. Policy questions would then have concentrated on CED: Why was Japanese industry less efficient than the U.S. and German industries? Why was Canadian industry, five years after the Auto Pact, the least efficient of the four countries? Why was the U.S. auto sector less efficient than German auto producers?

The decade of the 1970s saw a quite amazing relative shift between the United States, Germany, and Japan in CED and TFP. Canada continued to lag. Over this decade, average TFP growth was 1.7% per year higher in Japan than in the other three countries. A 1.7% annual greater TFP growth over 10 years translates into a total (compounded) advantage of 18.4%. This TFP growth was due to greater technical change per year in

Japan (2.7% per year versus 0.8% in the United States, 1.1% in Germany, and 0.3% in Canada) as well as higher capacity utilization in Japan. Not only was TFP highest in Japan, but the average weighted factor price in Japan grew the slowest of the four countries (as measured in a country's own currency). As a result, the Japanese maintained their unit-cost advantage over the United States, even with an appreciating yen.

The Japanese auto producers, who had a slight (3%) unit-cost advantage compared to German producers in 1970, overwhelmed German manufacturers by 1975, and in 1980 had a 38% unit-cost advantage. The strong deutsche mark did not assist this one German manufacturing sector vis-à-vis Japanese producers. The very large change in the relative costs of car production in Germany as compared to Japan was fueled by sharply rising factor prices in Germany and a reversal of the 1970 German CED advantage. In 1970 German auto producers had an 8% higher technical efficiency than Japan but by 1980 this had turned to a 4% disadvantage.

But surely the main story, and the story known and repeated, is one of enormous growth of the Japanese auto industry, driven by far greater technical-efficiency improvements than in its competitors. In 1970 the Japanese had a 10% technical disadvantage compared to the United States, yet in 1984 they held a 17% advantage. This reversal of Japan's CED disadvantage is a consequence of Japan's higher TFP growth rate.

Although this study provides the first detailed analysis of unit costs, technical efficiency, and TFP in the auto sectors of these four countries, it cannot explain *why* the Japanese had a greater technical advance or why CED has altered so drastically in favor of the Japanese. The story needs a sequel. The advances in the Japanese management of plants and of technology – quality circles, *kanban,* the greater efficiency in engineering innovation in Japan than in the United States – would all be important. The reader likely knows already of *n* books describing the Japanese miracle! What is crucial for policy analysis in the auto sector is that the growth in Japanese TFP in the 1970s was not unique to autos, and was accompanied by (perhaps led by) Japanese production of quality goods of a style desired by consumers. Appropriate responses to the Japanese challenge would have been technological improvements in product design, quality, and production techniques. While these have occurred in the United States, the immediate response to the sharp rise of Japanese car imports was the VRA of 1981.

The 1981 Voluntary Restraint Agreement was a policy response to the 1980 depression in the U.S. auto industry, with capacity utilization falling to 54.3%, enormous losses for each U.S. firm, and Chrysler teetering on the edge of bankruptcy. As a reaction to the short-run crisis, the VRA –

by increasing the demand for North American–made cars – increased capacity utilization, thus lowering unit costs and increasing the profitability of North American car producers. Insofar as profits, cash flow, and investors' and debt-holders' expectations improved because of the VRA, that short-run policy could have assisted in the long-run restructuring of the U.S. car industry. It was crucial that the VRA be short-run; in the long run, as with any quota, the protection offered domestic producers could generate inefficiency rather than the desired restructuring. The quotas were formally in place from April 1981 to 1985 (and informally in operation after 1985). The number of Japanese cars allowed into the United States was 1.68 million in 1981, 1982, and 1983, 1.85 million in the 1984–5 model year, and 2.3 million in more recent years.

In Table 9.2, the potential impact of the VRA on long-run equilibrium CED can be examined. The long-run equilibrium CED (LRCED) maintains capacity utilization at normal rates and exchange rates at their fundamental equilibrium; this measure thus provides information on the underlying long-run technical efficiency of production. The table indicates that between 1980 and 1984 the Japanese advantage in LRCED climbed three percentage points, from 13.7% in 1980 to 16.7% in 1984 (a 22% increase to Japan's advantage). While 1984 may be too early a year in which to examine U.S. manufacturers' response, it does indicate that the U.S. producers' relative LRCED disadvantage worsened after establishment of the VRA.

The VRA is a costly form of protection. A 1983 Wharton Econometrics study estimated that in 1981–2 the quotas generated excess demand that raised the average price of a Japanese car by $920 to $960 – for 1.68 million cars.[3] This represents an additional cost to U.S. consumers of $1.5 billion. Crandall (1984) used two methods to estimate the VRA's impacts. In one analysis he estimated that the average price of a new car produced in the United States increased by $237 in 1981 and 1982, and by $829 in 1983 when demand increased substantially; a second method yields an average of $370 per small car for 1981–3. Using an average of $400 per car, Crandall estimates a $2.3 billion loss in consumer welfare on domestically produced cars in 1983.

The Canadian auto industry since 1965 experienced a large increase in output and a corresponding increase in its share of North American production. The Auto Pact of 1965 was designed to increase productivity and efficiency in Canadian auto production. We have shown that it has done so, but a substantial gap still exists between Canadian and U.S. auto production CED. While Canadian unit production costs in 1984 were close to

---

[3] See Crandall (1984).

those of the United States and an improvement over 1970, the Canadian relative disadvantage in CED was somewhat higher in 1984 than in 1970. We are not the first authors to note the gap,[4] and have few explanations to account for its persistence. We examined the impact of the Auto Pact by constructing a counterfactual world where the Canadian auto industry still operated in the pre-1961 separated market. In this world costs are higher and productivity is lower than the actual experience. We estimate that in 1984, had the Auto Pact not been in existence, unit costs would have been some 9 percentage points higher than actual, and CED 2.2 percentage points lower. The implied improvements due to the Auto Pact are substantial but do not close the gap.

Canadian authorities have reacted to this CED and the continued trade deficit (overall, a surplus with the United States) by imposing their own VRA against Japanese imports, by adopting a range of protective measures designed to increase auto parts exports, and by a policy of subsidizing investments in new plants. We take these policies as affirmation of the fact that the Auto Pact of 1965 did not succeed in all its goals. The Canada–U.S. Free Trade Agreement (effective January 1, 1989) alters some aspects of the Auto Pact, by raising the barriers against producers other than the Big Three and by gradually eliminating the Canadian use of policies to increase preferentially exports of Canadian parts at the expense of U.S. parts.

German car producers entered the decade of the 1970s with the lowest-cost and most efficient auto-producing industry of the four examined here. They left the decade as the highest-cost producers. The story is simple. In 1970 German car producers had a 17% CED advantage over U.S. producers, and in 1980 that CED advantage was nearly identical, at 18.4%. Therefore, it is clear that changes in factor prices (labor, material, capital, and exchange-rate movements) were responsible for the higher costs of German auto producers. What was once a low-cost industry exporting high volumes to North America became a high-cost industry (relative to Japanese and North American producers).

The U.S. and Canadian VRAs may have been necessary and expedient short-run policies for allowing their car industries to recover from the debacle of 1980 and 1981. However, as we have demonstrated, the source of North American producers' disadvantages cannot be ameliorated in the long run by protection. Long-run protection would increase prices and profits, lower consumer welfare, and do little by itself to redress the

---

[4] Cox and Harris (1985) estimate that substantial gains in Canadian relative performance in the auto sector were still available.

fundamental problems. These problems are twofold. First, there is the long-run technical inefficiency (at least as of 1984) of North American car producers. That disadvantage may have lapsed in the last six years with the numerous closures of older U.S. plants and substantial investment in new plants and technology (e.g., GM's Saturn project). Therefore, if we could measure the technical efficiency of the U.S. car industry in 1990, it would undoubtedly be higher than in 1984 owing to these measures as well as to the rapid and substantial growth of Japanese (and Korean) "transplants" in North America. These foreign-controlled assembly plants were induced by the VRA and fears of an even more-protected U.S. market. However, as U.S. producers continue to lurch from success to failure, calls are heard for new protection (e.g., domestic-content provisions for transplants) and for some form of industrial policy where the government would assist in continued restructuring. These calls are tied to the second fundamental problem: the inability of the Big Three consistently to produce cars that consumers wish to purchase. In our analysis, we differentiated between short-run and long-run CED by maintaining that changes in capacity utilization are short-run movements that mask fundamental long-term trends in efficiency. However, the massive problem of U.S. auto producers in 1980 and 1981 was not that consumers did not want to buy cars, but rather that consumers did not want to buy large American-made cars. We have labeled declines in capacity utilization as short-run, but they may be long-run in the sense of denoting the inability of U.S. multinationals to produce quality cars of the kind that people wish to purchase.

If we were able to measure costs and CED of production in Japan in 1990 we would probably see a similar pattern to 1984, as well as some continuation of the changes experienced in the 1980–4 period. The Japanese auto industry has experienced steady substantial growth; in the years 1970 to 1980, auto production in Japan grew from 3.179 million cars to 7.038 million cars. With a compound annual growth rate of 7% per year, new investment, increased employment, R & D, and the introduction of new methodologies is relatively easy. In 1981 and 1982, however, car production in Japan fell below 1980 levels; in 1984, production fell slightly below 1983 levels (see Table 9.3). Production grew by 8.6% between 1984 and 1985 and continued to grow throughout the 1980s (reaching 9 million cars in 1989), reversing the declines of 1980–4 but not reaching the growth rate of the 1970s. This does not tell the whole story. In 1983, all Japanese-made cars were produced in Japan. In 1989, Japanese car producers assembled 7.0% of their entire production in North America, with over 1 million autos produced there.

Table 9.3. *Motor vehicle production (thousands)*

Year	Japan		U.S.	U.S. cars	Japanese transplants			Canada	Cars		
	All vehicles	Cars	All vehicles	Domestic producers	Sold by Japanese	Total	Other	All vehicles	Domestic	Japanese	Other
1980	11,043	7,038.1	8,010	6,216.4	0	0	200.4	1,373.1	836.8	0	10.0
1981	11,180	6,974.1	7,981	6,109.4	0	0	170.7	1,198.4	733.2	0	10.3
1982	10,732	6,886.9	6,876	4,887.0	0.6	0.6	86.2	1,270.0	794.8	0	6.9
1983	11,056	7,151.9	9,513	6,958.8	55.3	55.3	98.2	1,523.3	958.4	0	10.4
1984	11,393	7,073.2	10,294	7,564.3	138.6	138.6	74.8	1,878.0	1,051.7	0	10.4
1985	12,271	7,647.0	11,671	7,842.5	192.2	247.2	96.3	1,936.5	1,081.0	0	10.0
1986	12,260	7,809.8	11,373	7,226.1	327.6	519.2	84.4	1,863.8	1,062.4	0.5	10.4
1987	12,249	7,891.1	10,975	6,395.3	489.3	633.0	66.7	1,563.9	785.7	15.7	8.5
1988	12,700	8,198.0	11,010	6,306.9	631.9	786.2	36.0	1,780.3	969.8	50.0	6.6
1989	13,026	9,052.0	11,125	5,696.0	971.8	1,134.0	0	1,935.8	889.0	106.3	11.9

Source: Crain Automotive Group, *Automotive News* (various issues).

Table 9.4. *Capacity and capacity utilization, North American auto industry, 1988 and 1992 (thousands of cars and light trucks)*

	1988	1992
American-owned capacity	13,757	12,480
Japanese transplant capacity	1,130	2,530
Other capacity[a]	250	110
Total capacity	15,137	15,120
Total production	12,920	12,920
Capacity utilization[b]	85%	85%

[a] Volkswagen, Hyundai, and Volvo.
[b] Assumes total vehicle sales are the same in 1988 and 1992, and that imports and exports are the same in both years. Assuming that transplant capacity was fully utilized in 1988 leads to a capacity utilization rate of 84% for U.S. producers.

In 1980, Japan produced the same number of cars as in all of North America (13% more than in the United States alone). In 1990, 33% more cars were produced in Japan than in the United States; 59% more excluding the U.S. production of Japanese transplants in the United States. In 1990, the Big Three produced 37% fewer cars in North America than the Japanese producers built in Japan; total North American car production in 1990 was 87% of the level assembled in Japan.

All is not well for the Japanese auto producers, however. Since 1981 auto firms in Japan have been looking more like U.S. producers: lower rates of aggregate growth in output, with some fluctuations in capacity utilization. On average, car output between 1981 and 1989 grew at slightly over 2% per year in Japan, compared to 10% per year in the 1970s. The major change in performance is due to the impact of U.S. VRAs, exchange-rate fluctuations, and increased competition from U.S. and European producers. Newspaper reports suggest financial difficulties at smaller Japanese auto manufacturers (Suburu, Suzuki, and Mitsubishi). In 1988–9 severe problems were reported at Nissan.

Tables 9.4 and 9.5 detail capacity and capacity utilization data in the North American auto assembly industry for 1988, with projections for 1992. Japanese transplant capacity is scheduled to grow to 2.53 million

Table 9.5. *Details of Japanese transplant capacity, 1988 and 1992 (thousands of cars and light trucks)*

	1988	1992
CAMI (GM–Suzuki)		
Ingersoll, ON (Canada)	0	200
Diamond-Star (Chrysler–Mitsubishi)		
Normal, IL (U.S.)	0	240
Honda		
Marysville, OH (U.S.)	360	360
East Liberty, OH (U.S.)	0	180
Alliston, ON (Canada)	50	80
Mazda		
Flat Rock, MI (U.S.)	240	240
NUMMI (GM–Toyota)		
Fremont, CA (U.S.)	240	340
Nissan		
Smyrna, TN (U.S.)	240	480
SIA (Subaru–Isuzu)		
Lafayette, IN (U.S.)	0	120
Toyota		
Georgetown, KY (U.S.)	0	240
Cambridge, ON (Canada)	0	50
Total	1,130	2,530

Note: Based on public announcements by assembler companies and estimates of the author (Womack, 1990) from announced new product plans.

cars per year by 1992, while the net capacity of U.S. firms is projected to fall by 1.2 million cars per year.

Investment data is provided in Table 9.6. In 1980, investment in plant and equipment in the North American auto industry was double that of Japan. Annual investment in North America rose by nearly 50% between 1980 and 1985. In Japan, annual investment rose by only 18% over that same five-year period. However, between 1985 and 1988 annual investment in the North American auto sector fell 18%; investment in the Japanese auto sector accelerated, exceeding $10 billion in 1988 (nearly the same as in the United States).

Table 9.6. *Plant and equipment investment in the motor vehicle industry (billions)*

Year	Japan[a] U.S.$	Yen	United States U.S.$	Canada U.S.$	Can.$	North America U.S.$
1980	4.89	1,099.8	9.02	0.83	0.97	9.85
1984	4.17	990.7	11.20	0.34	0.44	11.54
1985	5.78	1,379.7	14.63	0.74	1.01	15.37
1986	7.40	1,246.8	13.95	1.71	2.38	15.66
1987	7.13	1,031.2	11.91	1.76	2.33	13.67
1988	10.17	1,304.4	10.60	2.08	2.56	12.68
1989	9.74	1,340.2	n.a.	1.99	2.36	n.a.

Note: n.a. means "not available."
[a] Fiscal-year basis.
Sources: U.S. Department of Commerce, personal communication. Japan Motor Industrial Federation Inc., *Future of the Japanese Automotive Industry,* A Report of the Consultative Committee on the Automobile Industry (October 1989).

Data on research and development expenditures is given in Table 9.7. According to this data, U.S. motor vehicle firms in 1980 spent 160% more on research than Japanese motor vehicle firms. In 1985, U.S. motor vehicle firms spent 113% more on R & D than the Japanese, but only 22% more in 1988. In the nine years 1980–8, the U.S. motor vehicle industry spent $48.39 billion on R & D while their Japanese counterpart spent $28.12 billion. One cannot see real cause for U.S. auto industry problems in this data on R & D expenditures. Of course, it is the output of research that counts, not input costs; but no data on such output exists.

As we begin the decade of the 1990s, we expect that the Japanese advantage in unit costs and technical efficiency will diminish, and that without a clear future of sustained growth it will be more difficult for Japanese producers to maintain and build on their advantages. That is, it will be relatively easier than in 1980 for the Big Three to become more competitive. However, whether this probability becomes actuality depends on the ability of the Big Three to design quality cars and build them efficiently, in the face of foreign producers who have invested heavily in R & D and new facilities.

We began in Chapter 1 by discussing the role of government policy. What should the role be for North American governments in the 1990s?

Table 9.7. *Research and development expenditures in the motor vehicle industry, United States and Japan (billions)*

Year	U.S. ($)	Japan[a]	
		U.S.$	Yen
1980	4.30	1.66	373.45
1981	4.22	1.87	419.78
1982	4.32	2.11	523.00
1983	4.75	2.40	570.00
1984	5.38	2.55	606.00
1985	6.16	2.89	686.66
1986	7.19	3.34	797.20
1987	7.27	4.99	840.43
1988	7.80	6.36	814.77

[a] Fiscal-year basis.
Sources: U.S. National Science Foundation, personal communication. Bank of Japan, *Japan Statistical Year Book* (various issues).

It should not be one of protection. Protection has not produced tremendous benefits in the past. The VRA was enormously costly. In addition, protection in an industry dominated by a few producers can generate an increased possibility of collusion and the dissipation of protection in rent-seeking.

Any "industrial policy" must be carefully examined. First, the United States is not Japan; the United States is a complex, competitive society with its strengths in diversity. The Japanese model (if there is one) of MITI targeting winners is difficult to envision in the U.S. auto industry. American productivity lags behind Japan's, but R & D expenditures in the U.S. do not. Throwing more money at the North American auto industry will not solve its problems.

The last decade has seen substantial shifts in U.S. automotive market shares among U.S. producers and among all sellers. The major stories have been GM's loss of market share, the relative success of Ford, the relative failure of Chrysler, and the success of the Japanese – which is where we began.

To what, then, do we attribute the relative decline of U.S. producers? The econometric story told through 1984 suggested a substantial relative decline in U.S. country-specific efficiency, with part of this decline attributed to R & D. But we have seen that the dollars spent on R & D are greater in the United States than Japan. Therefore, the fall in CSE is not due to a lack of R & D expenditures in the United States, although our econometric results suggest that R & D dollars are more productive in Japan than in the United States (see Chapter 5).

One might invoke the "law of comparative advantage" to explain the Japanese rise in the auto industry, despite the suggestion by some that Japanese auto plants in the United States are nearly as efficient as those in Japan. The difference between "nearly" and "as efficient" could, however, be labeled a comparative advantage to Japan. The difference in efficiency between Japanese best practice in their North American auto plants and average practice in the plants of domestic producers is largely a difference in *management*. That difference involves organizational methods (*kanban*); human relations (quality control circles); means of production (few job classifications, little hierarchy, no gulf between line workers and engineers or managers); and psychology (no executive lunch rooms and offices).

As applied microtheorists, we can say no more about specific management techniques and instead refer the interested reader to the multitude of publications on the subject. This book, a rigorous econometrics application of a general cost function, yields results that – when analyzed with the data trends of the 1980s – are consistent with the following hypothesis: Differences in management techniques and effectiveness explain the superior performance of Japanese versus North American auto producers. No other hypothesis is consistent with the results and the data.

References

Abernathy, W. J. (1978). *The Productivity Dilemma*. Baltimore: Johns Hopkins University Press.

Abernathy, W. J., Clark, K. B., and Kantrow, A. M. (1983). *Industrial Renaissance*. New York: Basic Books.

Abernathy, W. J., Harbour, J. B., and Henn, J. M. (1981). *Productivity and Comparative Cost Advantages: Some Estimates for Major Automotive Producers*. Draft Report to the Department of Transportation. Washington, D.C.: Transportation Systems Center.

Aizcorbe, A. C., Winston, C., and Friedlaender, A. (1987). "Cost Competitiveness in the U.S. Automobile Industry." In C. Winston (ed.), *Blind Intersection? Policy and the Automobile Industry*. Washington, D.C.: Brookings Institute.

Alexander, W. E. (1974). *An Econometric Model of Canadian–U.S. Trade in Automotive Products, 1965–71*. Technical Report 3. Ottawa: Bank of Canada.

Anderson, M. L. (1981). "Strategic Organization of the Japanese Automotive Groups." Mimeo, MIT, Cambridge.

Bain, J. (1956). *Barriers to New Competition*. Cambridge, Mass.: Harvard University Press.

(1966). *International Differences in Industrial Structure*. Cambridge, Mass.: Harvard University Press.

Baldwin, J., and Gorecki, P. (1986). *The Role of Scale in Canada–U.S. Productivity Differences*. Background Study No. 5, Royal Commission on the Economic Union and Development Prospects for Canada. Toronto: University of Toronto Press.

Beigie, C. (1970), *The Canada–U.S. Automotive Agreement: An Evaluation*. Montreal: Canadian–American Committee.

Berndt, E., and Fuss, M. (1986), "Productivity Measurement with Adjustments for Variations in Capacity Utilization and Other Forms of Temporary Equilibrium." *Journal of Econometrics* 33: 7–29.

(1989). "Economic Capacity Utilization and Productivity Measurement for Multiproduct Firms with Multiple Quasi-Fixed Inputs." Working Paper No. 2932, National Bureau of Economic Research, Cambridge, Mass.

Berndt, E., and Morrison, C. J. (1981). "Capacity Utilization Measures: Underlying Economic Theory and an Alternative Approach." *American Economic Review* 71(2): 48–52.

Berndt, E., and Savin, N. (1975). "Estimation and Hypothesis Testing in Singular Equation Systems with Autoregressive Disturbances." *Econometrica* 43(5–6): 937–57.

Bladen, V. (1961). *Report of the Royal Commission on the Automotive Industry.* Ottawa: Queen's Printer.

Bresnahan, T. (1981). "Departures from Marginal Cost Pricing in the American Automobile Industry." *Journal of Econometrics* 17: 201–27.

Cline, W. R. (1983). "Reciprocity: A New Approach to World Trade Policy." In W. R. Cline (ed.), *Trade Policy in the 1980s.* Washington, D.C.: Institute for International Economics.

Conrad, K. (1987). "Productivity and Cost Gaps in Manufacturing Industries in U.S., Japan and Germany." Mimeo, University of Mannheim, Germany.

Conrad, K., and Jorgenson, D. (1985). "Sectoral Productivity Gaps Between United States, Japan and Germany, 1960–1979." In H. Giersch (ed.), *Probleme und Perspektiven der weltwirtschaflichen Entwicklung.* Berlin: Duncker and Humblot.

Cowing, T., Small, J., and Stevenson, R. (1981). "Comparative Measures of Total Factor Productivity in the Regulated Sector: The Electric Utility Industry." In T. Cowing and R. Stevenson (eds.), *Productivity Measurement in Regulated Industries.* New York: Academic Press.

Cox, D., and Harris, R. (1985). "Trade Liberalization and Industrial Organization: Some Estimates for Canada." *Journal of Political Economy* 93(1): 115–45.

Crandall, R. W. (1984). "Import Quotas and the Automobile Industry: The Costs of Protectionism." *The Brookings Review* 2: 8–16.

Denny, M., and Fuss, M. (1977). "The Use of Approximation Analysis to Test for Separability and the Existence of Consistent Aggregates." *American Economic Review* 67(3): 404–18.

(1980). "Intertemporal and Interspatial Comparisons of Cost Efficiency and Productivity." Working Paper No. 8018, Institute for Policy Analysis, University of Toronto.

(1983). "A General Approach to Intertemporal and Interspatial Productivity Comparisons." *Journal of Econometrics* 23(3): 315–30.

Denny, M., Fuss, M., and May, J. D. (1981). "Intertemporal Changes in Regional Productivity in Canadian Manufacturing." *Canadian Journal of Economics* 14(3): 390–408.

Denny, M., Fuss, M., and Waverman, L. (1981). "The Measurement and Interpretation of Total Factor Productivity in Regulated Industries, with an Application to Canadian Telecommunications." In T. Cowing and R. Stevenson (eds.), *Productivity Measurement in Regulated Industries.* New York: Academic Press.

Diewert, W. E. (1976). "Exact and Superlative Index Numbers." *Journal of Econometrics* 4: 115–45.

Eastman, H., and Stykolt, S. (1967). *The Tariff and Competition in Canada.* Toronto: Macmillan.

Emerson, D. L. (1975). *Production, Location and the Automotive Agreement.* Ottawa: Economic Council of Canada.

Federal Task Force (1983). *An Automotive Strategy for Canada.* Report of the Task Force on the Canadian Motor Vehicle and Automotive Parts Industries. Ottawa: Supply and Services Canada.

Federal Trade Commission (1984). "Report of the Bureaus of Competition and Economics Concerning the General Motors/Toyota Joint Venture," 3 vols. Mimeo, Washington, D.C.

Friedlaender, A., Winston, C., and Wang, K. (1983). "Costs, Technology and Productivity in the U.S. Automobile Industry." *Bell Journal of Economics* 14(1): 1–20.

Fuss, M. (1987). "Cost and Production Functions." In J. Eatwell, M. Milgate, and P. Newman (eds.), *The New Palgrave: A Dictionary of Economic Theory and Doctrine,* v. 3. London: Macmillan.

Fuss, M., and Gupta, V. (1981). "A Cost Function Approach to the Estimation of Minimum Efficient Scale, Returns to Scale and Suboptimal Capacity." *European Economic Review* 15(2): 123–35.

Fuss, M., and Waverman, L. (1990). "The Extent and Sources of Cost and Efficiency Differences Between U.S. and Japanese Motor Vehicle Producers." *Journal of the Japanese and International Economies* 4: 219–56.

The Globe & Mail (1985). "PM defends Hyundai plan as MPs told deal not final." November 20. Toronto, pp. 71, 72.

Gorecki, P. (1978). *Economies of Scale and Efficient Plant Size in Canadian Manufacturing Industries.* Ottawa: Bureau of Competition Policy, Consumer and Corporate Affairs.

Griliches, Z., and Mairesse, J. (1985). "R&D and Productivity Growth: Comparing Japanese and U.S. Manufacturing Firms." Working Paper No. 1778, National Bureau of Economic Research, Cambridge, Mass.

Harbour, J. E. (1980). "Comparison and Analysis of Manufacturing Productivity." Consultant Report. Dearborn Heights, Mich.: Harbour and Associates.

Helmers, H. O. (1967). "The United States–Canadian Automobile Agreement: A Study in Industry Adjustment." Mimeo, Graduate School of Business Administration, University of Michigan, Ann Arbor.

Hunker, J. E. (1983). *Structural Change in the U.S. Automobile Industry.* Lexington, Mass.: Lexington Books.

Japan Motor Industrial Federation (1989). *Future of the Japanese Automotive Industry.* Report of the Consultative Committee on the Automobile Industry. Tokyo: Japan Trade and Industry Publicity, Inc.

Johnson, H. G. (1963). "The Bladen Plan for Increased Protection of the Canadian Automobile Industry." *Canadian Journal of Economics and Political Science* 29(2): 212–38.

Jorgenson, D., Kuroda, M., and Nishimizu, M. (1987). "Japan-U.S. Industry-Level Productivity Comparisons, 1960–1979." *Journal of the Japanese and International Economies* 1: 1–30.

Jorgenson, D. W., and Nishimizu, M. (1978). "U.S. and Japanese Economic Growth, 1952–74: An International Comparison." *Economic Journal* 88: 707–26.

Kim, M. (1984). "The Beneficiaries of Trucking Regulation Revisited." *Journal of Law and Economics* 27(1): 227–41.

236   References

Kravis, I. B., Heston, A., and Summers, R. (1982). *World Product and Income. The Statistical Office of the United Nations and the World Bank.* London: Johns Hopkins University Press.

McFadden, D. (1978). "Cost, Revenue and Profit Functions." In M. Fuss and D. McFadden (eds.), *Production Economics: A Dual Approach to Theory and Applications.* Amsterdam: North Holland.

Miller, S., and Bereiter, S. (1985). "Modernizing to Computer-Integrated Production Technologies in a Vehicle Assembly Plant: Lessons for Analysts and Managers of Technological Change." Paper presented at the NBER U.S.–Japan Productivity Conference (Aug. 26–28), Cambridge, Mass.

Morrison, C. (1988). "Subequilibrium in the North American Steel Industries: A Study of Short Run Biases from Regulation and Utilization Fluctuations." *Economic Journal* 98: 390–411.

Norsworthy, J. R., and Malmquist, D. H. (1983). "Input Measurement and Productivity Growth in Japanese and U.S. Manufacturing." *American Economic Review* 73(5): 947–67.

Perry, R. (1982). *The Future of Canada's Auto Industry.* Canadian Institute for Economic Policy. Toronto: Lorimer.

Sharpe, A. (1983). "A Comparative Analysis of the Canadian and American Productivity Slowdowns." Paper presented at the annual meeting of the American Economics Association (Dec. 28), San Francisco.

Spady, R., and Friedlaender. A. (1978). "Hedonic Cost Functions for the Regulated Trucking Industry." *Bell Journal of Economics* 9: 159–79.

Toder, E. J., Cordell, N. S., and Burton, E. (1978). *Trade Policy and the U.S. Automobile Industry.* New York: Praeger.

Tsurumi, H., and Tsurumi, Y. (1983). "U.S.–Japan Automobile Trade." *Journal of Econometrics* 23(2): 193–210.

Viner, J. (1952). "Cost Curves and Supply Curves." In G. J. Stigler and K. E. Boulding (eds.), *A.E.A. Readings in Price Theory.* Homewood, Ill.: Irwin.

White, L. J. (1971). *The American Automobile Industry Since 1945.* Cambridge, Mass.: Harvard University Press.

Williamson, J. (1983, 1985). *The Exchange Rate System.* Institute for International Economics, Washington, D.C. Cambridge, Mass.: MIT Press.

Wilton, D. A. (1972). "An Econometric Model of the Canadian Automotive Manufacturing Industry and the 1965 Automotive Agreement." *Canadian Journal of Economics* 5(2): 157–81.

   (1976). *An Econometric Analysis of the Canada–U.S. Automobile Agreement: The First Seven Years.* Ottawa: Economic Council of Canada.

Womack, J. P. (1990). "Seeking Mutual Gain: North American Responses to Mexican Liberalization of Its Motor Vehicle Industry." Mimeo, International Motor Vehicle Program, MIT, Cambridge.

Wonnacott, R., and Wonnacott, P. (1967). *Free Trade Between the United States and Canada: The Potential Economic Effects.* Cambridge, Mass.: Harvard University Press.

Index

237